Sir Bobby Charlton

1966
My World Cup Story

With James Lawton

YELLOW JERSEY PRESS
LONDON

1 3 5 7 9 10 8 6 4 2

Yellow Jersey Press
20 Vauxhall Bridge Road,
London SW1V 2SA

Yellow Jersey Press is part of the Penguin Random House
group of companies whose addresses can be found
at global.penguinrandomhouse.com

Penguin
Random House
UK

First published in paperback by Yellow Jersey Press in 2017
First published in hardback by Yellow Jersey Press in 2016

penguin.co.uk/vintage

A CIP catalogue record for this book is available from the British Library

ISBN 9780224100519

Printed and bound by Clays Ltd, St Ives plc

Penguin Random House is committed to a sustainable future
for our business, our readers and our planet. This book is made
from Forest Stewardship Council® certified paper

MIX
Paper from
responsible sources
FSC
www.fsc.org   FSC® C018179

SIR BOBBY CHARLTON

Having survived the trauma of the Munich air disaster aged just 20, **Sir Bobby Charlton** played as if every game was for his fallen colleagues, recovering from his injuries to reach the pinnacle for both Manchester United and England. Playing as an attacking midfielder Sir Bobby is regarded as one of the greatest footballers the game has ever seen. During his playing career that spanned 20 years he won three League Championships, the FA Cup, the European Cup and the World Cup. With England he played in four World Cups scoring a then-record 49 goals. He is currently a director of Manchester United.

This is **James Lawton**'s third collaboration with Sir Bobby Charlton. Lawton, who was three time voted Sports Writer of the Year while Chief Sports Writer of the *Daily Express* and the *Independent*, also worked with World Cup winners Nobby Stiles and George Cohen on their memoirs. His *Forever Boys*, based on the Manchester City team of the late six   *Times* Sports
Bo

ALSO BY SIR BOBBY CHARLTON

My Manchester United Years
My England Years

For Sir Alf Ramsey, without whose courage and knowledge I would not have had this story to tell.

Contents

Prologue

When you have been very lucky, and to the degree that you frequently stop and look back at your life and wonder all over again how it was that so much came to you, it is not always so easy strolling back through the autumn leaves of memory. Certainly this is so as I contemplate the startling fact that it is now fifty years since I went out with my England team-mates to win the World Cup for the only time in our nation's history.

Where, I ask as I walk beneath the trees surrounding my home in Cheshire and scuff those fallen leaves, did all those years go? And where have they left me?

But if the questions can be taxing, and so often provoke the deepest yearnings to go back to when all was so fresh and inviting, invariably they also return me to one point of certainty, one bedrock of the deepest satisfaction.

The years, I tell myself each day, have bequeathed a pride that redeems some corner of every one of those occasions brushed by some of the sadness and regret which I suppose is inevitable in the process of growing old. And which in my case will, until my last day, always be touched by the tragedy – and unshakeable horror – of the Munich air crash that robbed me of dear team-mates and friends and, for a little while, made me question the basis of a life which until then had seemed to be such a gift of extraordinary and uncomplicated riches.

Now, in my seventy-ninth year, I know more surely than ever before the extent of the privilege that accumulated on the long and so often blessed journey away from that twenty-year-old's pain, confusion and despair.

I know, too, in this year of golden anniversary where to place the summer day of scudding clouds and rain and fleeting sunlight in 1966 when our young captain Bobby Moore wiped the sweat from his hands to receive the great trophy from the smiling and still youthful Queen of England.

It is on the highest ground of my experience. It is on that supreme plateau known only to the most fortunate of professional sportsmen. It is the place you find when you can tell yourself that you are part of a team of champions. This is a bond you know will last all your days.

Of course the years wage their attrition on us all. There is no immunity from that; a team of champions can seize the day but it cannot hold back the years and their consequences and we are depleted now.

Alf Ramsey, the man who made it all possible after telling us in his most formal style, 'Gentlemen, most certainly we will win the World Cup', Bobby Moore and Alan Ball, the majestic captain and the insatiably optimistic, ever-scuffling young hero, have gone, and in their huge absence some of us fret about each other's wellbeing as well as our own.

We go to our annual reunion, we re-conjure the past, and we wonder sometimes if perhaps it is time to put aside the ritual. But then one of the sturdiest among us, maybe George

Cohen or Geoff Hurst, says that we should go on, that we have something we should never willingly surrender: the still vivid memory of a day when all our hopes, and all our strivings, were fulfilled in a way that, even as it was happening, we knew we were never likely to surpass.

When I see my brother Jack, never far from the surface is that feeling we shared when we embraced on the field of celebration after he held out his arms and said, 'What about that, kidda?' and I agreed we had a moment that we could share for ever.

Like members of so many families we have known times of dislocation, and, yes, outright strife, and I will always regret that sometimes they became public, but the years do bring some healing and for us the sharing of that great moment has been an iron link of experience and achievement that we have always known can never be broken.

My dearest wish now, at this late hour, is that I could still easily rekindle such emotion with each of the comrades with whom I shared that day of triumph. With Ramsey, Moore and Ball it is no longer possible and with Nobby Stiles, the companion who became so close and precious to me it was as though we also shared the same blood, it has become difficult in the extreme. It means that now he resides, for me, solely at the core of my memories of some of the happiest and most tumultuous days of my life.

Nobby was inaccessible the last time I visited him in his home in Stretford, so close to Old Trafford, the great passion of our lives. He was present but it seemed only physically. He had never been so remote from me and I was shattered by the strong feeling that he no longer knew who I was. When his wife Kay came with me to the door I could not suppress my tears.

She said later that in fact Nobby, despite the effects of Alzheimer's, still recognised old friends and team-mates but suggests he does not out of embarrassment over his condition. His pride is still strong but when I left his home it did indeed feel as though I was leaving behind a great swathe of my life – and a part of it filled by fierce support and the warmest companionship.

If we were a team of champions, he was our competitive conscience. He was at the heart of all we did; he tackled for me and there were times when he seemed to be the guardian of us all, chivvying us along, reminding us that we could not let slip the chance of making our mark on the game of our lives.

I happened to score both the goals that took us to the final against West Germany, and some said it was the finest game I ever played in an England shirt, but nobody needed to tell me that all my efforts would have come to nothing if Nobby Stiles hadn't made himself the embodiment of our determination to finish our task.

Nobby policed the great Portuguese player Eusébio, who some called the Lion of Africa and predicted would one day rise above Pelé, with an unerring vigilance. He kept safe all our ambition and the hopes of all his countrymen.

I recall a thousand memories on my autumnal strolls. I play football as a boy back in the high winds of the North East, I run amid the sand dunes and the old wartime concrete bunkers on the coastline where my father collected the coal that spilled from the barges plying out of Blyth harbour.

I return to St James' Park in Newcastle with Jack at those times when we had saved up enough money from our grocery rounds to pay for the bus, a pie in the café near the ground and a place next to the flag where we were so close to Stanley

Matthews when he took the corners for Blackpool. Often a fan, noting that the great star was the first professional footballer in those days of maximum wage and one-way contracts to own a racehorse, would cry, 'Matthews, your horse has lost.'

We went behind the goal when a great goalkeeper was performing, someone like Bert Williams of Wolves and England or maybe my first great hero between the posts, Manchester City's former paratrooper of the Eastern Front and prisoner of war, Bert Trautmann.

In every game there was someone who captured our imagination and was at the centre of our conversation on the ride back home to Ashington: Len Shackleton, the outrageous Clown Prince of English football whose move from Newcastle to Sunderland caused such furore, Tom Finney, the rival to Matthews who saw the game quite differently (he was more concerned with practical effect than the creation of fantasy) and superb old-fashioned strikers like Tommy Lawton and Nat Lofthouse, the Lion of Vienna.

I remember the day my mother dressed me in a long green mackintosh she said I would grow into and sent me off to the great adventure that was Manchester United. I was fifteen then and the world lay at my feet when I stepped off the train in the big and sooty city that I have come to love so much and which a few years ago bestowed upon me, officially, the freedom and feeling of opportunity it had nourished in me since I was no more than a boy.

Before that I had played at Wembley as a schoolboy international and scored two goals against Wales after inspecting the manicured turf and the great sweep of the stadium with the sensation that I had arrived in paradise. It belonged in another universe to the wind-scoured field in the

North East where I played an important regional trial match in which a goalkeeper was cheered for brilliantly saving his own kick into the teeth of a gale.

There are teeming memories. They take me back across the world to places and scenes which I could not have imagined existed when Jimmy Murphy, Sir Matt Busby's assistant at United and my most ferocious and influential first mentor, collected me at the old Exchange Station and drove me to my digs as he talked, unceasingly and exultantly, about Duncan Edwards, the phenomenal man-child footballer under whose shadow I would have to pursue my professional career.

I go again to the bay in Rio de Janeiro beneath the statue of Christ the Redeemer where a giant stingray burst out of the ocean and seemed to symbolise all the colour and the excitement of the life that had come to me because it happened that I had a gift to play football.

I revisit the huge Lenin sports palace in Moscow as a twenty-year-old unversed in politics who could only be in wonder at the facilities provided for young people, but then of course I was in no position to evaluate the cost.

I return to the day in Guadalajara when, four years after we won the World Cup and just a week before our most crushing disappointment as the team Ramsey made, we played Brazil in perhaps the highest-quality game I ever experienced. We lost by one goal after playing Pelé and his team-mates to a standstill in the heat and the knowledge that maybe we were competing with the most sublime national team ever assembled, an assessment confirmed in the splendour and celebration that would soon surround their third World Cup triumph.

It was at the end of that game that we had the famous picture of Bobby Moore and Pelé exchanging their shirts and if you wanted an image of the respect that grows between great opponents at the highest level of sport you did not have to look any further.

Sometimes I find myself again in the old killing fields of Cambodia, where I have had the opportunity to help combat the scourge of landmines which still take a regular toll of lives and limbs. Or an African clearing designated as a football field and I see the excitement in the eyes of the young people preparing it. I range across the world, I meet again the old Japanese lady who told me I was the first European she had ever met and I talk with the widow of the great lithe goalkeeper Lev Yashin, who sent me the old Russian lamps which now hang in the kitchen of my home.

I'm thrilled, and moved all over again, by the fact that I found my success in a sport which touches every culture, and which still – in this time when the weight of money and commerce, and the smell of corruption, is so heavy – can provoke delight and ambition in the poorest corners of the earth.

It is because of this passion, this recurring love for the world's most popular game, that I have to believe that the wrong-doing by Fifa, the world's ruling body, which in recent years has been so relentlessly exposed, will one day be purged from the system through new levels of care and vigilance. There is, I know well enough, no easy way around the immensity of this task but I also have to believe that there is too much at stake for the challenge to be ignored.

Maybe football needs help in recognising its own importance in the hearts and lives of so many people of so many different backgrounds.

I still go to United, I still work as a director of the club and travel to Champions League games, but much of the travelling is done now along the lanes of memory.

There, I encounter the great players I have played with and against. Often the journey begins and ends with the uniquely strong, gifted and tragically unfulfilled Duncan Edwards, a friend and an idol, but there are so many who re-engage me and delight me with the sheer scale of their talent and their imagination: Pelé, Alfredo Di Stéfano, Johan Cruyff, Ferenc Puskás, Franz Beckenbauer and, not least, the extraordinary virtuosos George Best and Denis Law, who emblazoned themselves on the years which led to our European Cup triumph in 1968.

That victory may not have healed entirely the wounds of Munich but maybe it eased some of the ache which came when I thought of how that pursuit of the great prize had ended so cruelly. Certainly when in the first minutes after we had beaten Benfica in the Wembley final I shared an embrace with Sir Matt Busby, whose life had hung in the balance so precariously in the weeks after the crash and who would always feel a terrible responsibility in that he pushed so hard for our involvement in the competition in the face of opposition from the Football League, I believe we were as one in our emotion.

It flowed powerfully from the fact that we both felt that in some small but identifiable way we had in the end managed to honour the memory of the players who had been lost.

There is so much to remember as I walk beneath the trees, sometimes in the company of my grandchildren. So much to savour again and be grateful for. So many places which will never lose their charm or their excitement, so many people who touched my life in ways that I knew would always be with me.

But then sometimes I ask myself another question. If I could have one day back, if I could go to a football field and relive the most thrilling and satisfying time of my career, which one would it be?

Of course, it would be 30 July 1966. I have called it the diamond of my days, and so it was. Memory burnishes it still. More than anything I cherish the fact that all those who shared with me the day and the triumph – Gordon Banks, George Cohen, Ray Wilson, Nobby Stiles, Jack Charlton, Bobby Moore, Alan Ball, Roger Hunt, Geoff Hurst and Martin Peters – had the most overwhelming sense that the most wonderful opportunity had been put in our path.

When I think about this, suddenly it might have been yesterday when I boarded the bus at the Hendon Hall Hotel in north London and saw the people in the street, the boys on a football field who stopped their game and waved to us, and then, as we passed the fire station, the men lined up to salute us in their full dress uniform.

There wasn't much talk on that ride to Wembley because we had gone beyond the imperatives of tactics and the need for the greatest, most secure performances of our careers. If we hadn't grasped it before, the salute of the firemen was especially symbolic in that it told us we did indeed carry the hopes of our nation.

So mostly we were quiet. Even the irrepressible Alan Ball was subdued; he too seemed to be running back through the days that had brought us there and reflecting on what he had to do when the issue would finally be settled.

It was not necessary to spell out the question that faced us to a man more deeply than ever before, and in the years that followed no one was more eloquent than George Cohen when he returned us to the heart of the mood that gripped so tightly as the flags waved us towards Wembley.

He said, 'In some ways the spectacle in the streets, the excitement of the crowds, broke the tension that had been building inside us – but it didn't divert any of us from the biggest question of all. Could we deliver? Could we play our part?

'When the Union flags were not being waved, they hung limp in the still, heavy air and it was as if you could hear the beating of your own heart. You didn't need telling that for the next few hours you would be occupying a patch of terrain located squarely between heaven and hell. You bloody well knew that it was no time to unravel because, as never before, hell might just be around the corner. And if you didn't know before you set off for the stadium you knew it now.

'Lying around in some archive are newsreel shots of the England players in the dressing room an hour or so before the start of the game. I looked haunted. You get the impression that you could have come up to my face and peeled it. The sound of the five-minute buzzer went through me. The one-minute sound had the same effect.'

George says it for all of us. There was so much to catch our eyes on the road to Wembley, so many uplifting sights, as the sun flitted between the clouds. But none of them quite took you away from that conversation with yourself. However, I also have to say that no doubt was so great it undermined my belief that I shared the company of the players best able to justify and preserve the excitement and the hope we saw in the streets.

A huge controversy had swept the country in the days before we rode to Wembley. Jimmy Greaves, one of the greatest goalscorers in the history of the game, had been omitted and that had torn at his spirit in a way which, many years later, some who knew him well said he could never quite put behind him. But if I am very honest, and state the obvious when I say I felt sympathy for the disappointment of a brilliant fellow professional, I also have to declare that I felt not a single qualm about the men with whom I would take the field that day.

I knew in my heart then that this was indeed a team of prospective champions and that in charge of our destiny was a man who, like no other before or since, had understood so perfectly what it would take to beat the world. Alf Ramsey once gently chided my brother Jack who, in his wonder, asked him how it was he had come to be selected. The manager said that the mysteries of selection were his domain and that it was not simply a matter of which player had most talent. No, there were other factors and perhaps the most vital of them was the grasping of what it took to be truly a member of a team.

In his often laconic and sometimes ruthless way he never tired of stressing that the lifeblood of our quest was a willingness to subvert all pride in our individual ability, all our different vanities, and put everything we had at the disposal of the men around us.

It may have been quiet in the bus as we passed the crowds that grew so much thicker and more demonstrative as we neared the stadium, but that confident belief resided firmly in my heart. And the closer we got to the moment when we had to prove it was true, the more it carried the sound and the force of thunder.

1. Another Side of Alf

When I first saw the look on Alf's face in the half-light of the cabin I knew straightaway that something had gone from his life and those of the players he had led for so long with such apparently unbreakable conviction.

Looking back, I suppose what I was seeing more than anything was the unwelcome evidence that none of our certainties, however hard won, are free from the risk of ambush. Certainly that moment on the flight back from Mexico in 1970 provoked in me a broad reflection on the football life.

If a few seconds can change a game, a career and sometimes even make you reappraise everything you attempted to do, maybe it had been too much to imagine that we could hold the unconquerable mood we took into that summer's day in London, if not for ever, at least for another four years.

Some said it was an overreaching confidence – especially in Alf when he made the decision to take me off that was aimed at a semi-final place still to be confirmed on the field – that did for our ambition to retain on foreign soil the World Cup title we won before our own people.

Others decided more generously that we were caught in a

set of freakish circumstances. They agreed that the arrival of such accomplished and aggressively inclined players as Francis Lee, Alan Mullery and Terry Cooper had made the class of '70 in some ways stronger, and certainly more adventurous, than the one that graduated so triumphantly in 1966.

Whatever the cause of our downfall, there was no doubt that when Alf came down the aisle of the plane and sat in the empty seat next to mine there was something about him I had never seen before.

It was more than a hint of uncertainty, of self-questioning. Something very sure and strong and ultimately persuasive seemed to have ebbed away from him. It showed in the way he carried himself. For once, he didn't look ready to fight the world on the issue of how a football team should be prepared and the values it should be given.

Of course, I had known him under fierce pressure from time to time. Some of the sharpest of it had no doubt been created by the cussed streak in his nature. But always he had been implacable in his determination to separate in his own mind football right from wrong. If he could be unforgiving of others, those he believed had in some way let him down, he always made it clear that he was prepared to stand hard by his own actions and attitudes, however much angst and controversy they left in their wake.

He had, most enduringly, inflamed all of Latin America when he called the Argentinians of Antonio Rattín 'animals' after coming on to the pitch of the old Empire Stadium, his dark eyes blazing with anger, to prevent George Cohen exchanging his shirt with Alberto González, the winger he had been marking in that notoriously cynical and desperately fought quarter-final of 1966.

His remark put us under immense extra pressure when we attempted unsuccessfully to defend our crown in Mexico and another England team were still feeling some of the repercussions when they returned to compete in a second World Cup there sixteen years later. Diego Maradona's 'hand of God' ended that English challenge and all of Latin America seemed to believe that it was not so much a nefarious act as one of historic revenge.

Alf was always defiant when the flak flew about his head and it was only now, with the taste of failure, that he made little attempt to conceal a mood of vulnerability. Before, he might concede a degree of pressure with a rough phrase or a rueful, brooding expression. But this, clearly, went deeper.

In the past he could be angry, and ultimately unforgiving, over the details of a rare defeat, but it was never at the price of something that might be described as dogged resistance to any viewpoint that opposed his own.

His stance might signal the end of an individual's international career but it wasn't anything that couldn't be put right for the team by a new player or a new tactic.

The seed of Jimmy Armfield's failure to withstand George Cohen's challenge for his right-back position in the 1966 team lay in a mistake he made in one of Ramsey's first games as manager three years earlier. It was a reckless pass which led to the conceding of a goal, and it didn't help that the beneficiaries were Scotland and their brilliant, swaggering star Jim Baxter.

Armfield, of Blackpool, was a finely skilled, adventurous full-back, and would remain a wonderfully supportive member of the squad, but he could never quite repair the damage of that one critical error. It lingered too powerfully in Ramsey's mind, spoke to him a warning about an approach to the game which would always make him uneasy.

Ron Springett, the experienced and talented Sheffield Wednesday goalkeeper, made the same crippling mistake of an unconvincing early performance, conceding five goals in one of his poorest displays at the highest level. The manner in which he conceded each goal was an irreparable hammer blow to his international future.

When Alf spoke to his players – or maybe a sceptical sports writer posing potentially inflammatory questions – in his peculiarly clipped tone of voice, it was not an invitation to debate, it was a statement intended to be written down in stone.

I knew this better than most because, as the senior player, I was sometimes persuaded, against all my wiser instincts, to register with him some passing complaint of the team.

Invariably it was an exercise in futility. He gave what I had to say – which mostly concerned such relatively minor matters as pleas to wear lighter, more casual clothing on long plane journeys into hotter climates and make quicker trips to and from training grounds – the most cursory consideration, then, usually before I left the room, he said no. Each time I said to smirking team-mates, 'Never again am I going on that fool's errand.'

As for the world at large, it could take him or leave him and then wait for the results out on the field.

Now, suddenly, he was like the rest of us. He was carrying the weight of a beaten man. He had always insisted we would achieve our goals. We simply had to trust ourselves, our talent and determination, his judgement – and for the first time he had been proved wrong in international football's most important tournament.

We had believed strongly, or at least we had thought so, that the four years since that thunder had come to our game at Wembley was time enough to get used to the idea of being world champions.

Time enough to control the urge to feel too happy with ourselves, to understand our ability to compete with the best in the world. And that the only way we would lose this conviction that permeated everything we did was to compromise the values we had built together down the years.

The new problem, though, was that this state of mind, which we had come to wear like a well-cut, familiar uniform, had been ripped away in the most devastating circumstances.

Alf's expression seemed to me to be registering something more than sadness and regret, and the still raw disappointment of surrendering a World Cup quarter-final to West Germany – despite the fact that for much of the game we had produced football quite as biting and composed as any of that which had carried us to victory against them in the '66 final.

The look of him also suggested a certain resignation, a suspicion that the best of his times, and those of the players he had made into both his foot soldiers and his disciples, had passed twenty-four hours earlier on that sweltering field in the Mexican city of León.

Even in such a painful situation, though, it was strange, even shocking, to see for the first time an element of self-reproach, which up to then had always been concealed so effectively.

It was as though he was opening a door he had kept shut for so long.

I come to this so early in perhaps my last account of the greatest days of my football life because the conversation I had with Alf in the dim light of that plane cabin, it struck me then and still does today, went to the heart of the relationship which had transformed my career, lifted it into a place of fulfilment and confidence I had never known before and, indeed, for some years had seemed quite beyond my hopes.

It was a relationship which had never wavered, never prompted a flicker of serious doubt, since the moment he took charge of England on a snowy night in Paris seven years earlier.

The essence of our talk, as far as I was concerned, was not to do with the fine line between the success we had at Wembley and the sourness of failure under the Mexican sun. That, after all, is a high wire all professional sportsmen are required to walk.

No, it was about the force of trust, the impetus provided by good faith which comes when you know you have the best of leadership, and when that has been established there is a perspective which is always secure in the face of whatever fate might bring.

I tried to impress on Alf when he joined me on our retreat from Mexico that for me, at least, this was still the case. I said that I knew what he had done had come from the best of intentions. It was a call of judgement, one that could be argued about endlessly, not a breaking of trust.

Implicit in our talk, though left unstated, was that I had just played my last game for England. I would be thirty-five by the time of the next World Cup in Germany and though my great friend and rival Franz Beckenbauer once said that I had the lungs of a horse, it was clear to me that it was time to leave the international stage.

It was surely the end of the journey that had started twelve years earlier when, still reeling from the Munich tragedy, I joined England for my debut international against Scotland at Hampden Park.

So much of what had followed now played back in my mind as I listened, as I always did and always would, for the unbroken purr of healthy plane engines on the homeward flight.

It was all there, accompanying the rhythm of the engines. All the elation – and the pangs of regret – that came with 106 games and the World Cup finals of Sweden, Chile, England and Mexico.

One by one, all the way to this last disappointment which crowded into a match – and a tournament – that had promised so much, I ticked the games away. I retraced those endless summer days of Sweden, the colour and the passions and the frustrations of Chile, the great triumph of Wembley and, finally, the misadventure of Mexico.

First, I remembered that when I went up to Glasgow to wear the England shirt for the first time I was the most publicised survivor of Munich. I was supposed to conquer a world which for me had never seemed so harsh or confusing.

Some said I was the young hope for the future but if anyone had asked me in a way that would have made me comfortable responding to such a prophecy, I would have said I was still struggling to come to terms with what had happened at the snow-covered airfield. Somewhere, in all the pain, was the belief that I must play on, but at times it was buried deeply amid the new, and sometimes unfathomable, trials of daily life.

I recalled vividly being driven from the hospital in Munich, where I had seen the stricken Duncan Edwards for the last time, and he had said in one fleeting bout of consciousness, 'What kept you, pal?' Jimmy Murphy, fighting back his tears, accompanied me on the journey to the Hook of Holland, where I took the ferry to Harwich. There, my brother Jack and mother Cissie were waiting to take me home to the North East.

Home? Yes, it was home. I recognised easily enough the narrow cobbled streets, the colliery workings, and I saw many familiar faces who came to the house to try to offer some comfort. I even kicked a ball around the street with some young boys. But then everything, and not least these foundations of all my experience, were now touched by new realities that coloured in a most sombre way everything I did and saw and felt. Apart from the impact on some of my deepest personal life feelings, and the battle to find a little equilibrium and some of my old purpose, I was especially aware that whatever expectations had been placed on my shoulders, England's future prospects had been desperately, maybe irreparably, undermined by the loss of such as Duncan, Roger Byrne and Tommy Taylor.

In my heart I believed that with these men had gone England's most serious chance of making an impact in the World Cup later that year; that it had been reduced as profoundly as all those high hopes surrounding United's Busby Babes. I felt that a great opportunity had vanished along with a generation of the highest quality.

Still, for all those saddening thoughts I was thrilled and a little amazed when told I would be sharing a room with the captain of England, Billy Wright. He could not have been more sympathetic when he grasped how deeply the tragedy had torn into my confidence, even perhaps my enthusiasm for the football life that had previously been so all-consuming.

He said, in a gentle way not so common at the hardest edge

of the professional game, that I should not worry about performing in front of the Scottish crowd that on first sight resembled a vast flock of perching, noisy birds. I would be playing with some fine and talented professionals who knew my situation, understood the rawness of my feelings, and they would all look after me.

To room with the captain of England and Wolves, the team which, apart from the Real Madrid of Di Stéfano, had filled me with most awe as a young player, was indeed stunning. For a little while it brought me out of myself, away from the worst of my fears, and in retrospect I see clearly that it was a significant step along the road of recovery.

Wolves had opened up the wider world of football with their floodlit games against Spartak Moscow. They had big, tough defenders and quick, skilled forwards and Wright was one of the great figures of the English game.

Up in the room he helped me answer some of the mail that was still piling up in the wake of Munich. He was a kind and calming presence and what he said about the help I would receive out on the field proved true enough.

Tom Finney, no less a star and a boyhood idol, provided the cross for my first goal in international football, which I executed according to the fierce dogma of Jimmy Murphy, who had always told me, in the one-on-one sessions we had on Sunday mornings at the back of Old Trafford, that when a winger went to the line to cross, my duty was to run as hard as I could, however speculative I considered the attack, and that when I shot my first priority was to keep the ball on the target because then anything could happen, depending on the power and the accuracy that I produced.

There was, I knew very well from my days as a schoolboy

spectator, very little left to chance in the play of Tom Finney, only the most refined professionalism, and when he beat his full-back the resulting cross was perfectly tailored for my needs. I drove home the first of my forty-nine goals for England. I was then astonished, and moved, when the Scottish goalkeeper, Tommy Younger of Liverpool, came running into the centre circle before the restart.

He shook my hand and said, 'Congratulations on your first game for your country – and your first goal. There will be many more, laddie.'

It was a moment I would always treasure as an affirmation of all I hoped to find in the game which had always lured me so strongly. Here was the starting point of the re-awakened memories of the game I had played across the world that I carried home from Mexico, and as I persuaded myself that I was right to decide that my days of international football had come to an end.

Those memories, the great skein of them, were all in place, the highs and the lows, and shaping all of them was the most powerful sense that there had always been someone like Tommy Younger to remind me of the satisfaction that came when you could say that you had taken your chances as well as you could, that you never willingly compromised the belief that if you had a certain talent there was also a duty to develop it with everything in your power.

No, of course, this never proofed you against painful setbacks. I thought again of the deep disappointment I felt a few months after that day at Hampden when Alf's predecessor, Walter Winterbottom, left me on the sidelines throughout the 1958 World Cup in Sweden.

It was the price I paid for a poor performance when England

lost 5-0 to Yugoslavia and I couldn't clear from my head those horrific scenes in Munich airport the day after I'd played in the same Belgrade stadium for the last time with the team I believed was going to be the best in Europe. They were still so vivid in my nightmares when I returned there just a few months later.

Against the hard and talented Yugoslavs, I mourned afresh the loss of Duncan's power and brilliance, the cool authority of the captain Roger Byrne, the superbly sharp work of Tommy Taylor at the front and, not least, the snake-hipped inventions of Eddie Colman as he worked his way through midfield.

Back in his home street in Salford, where I had spent so many happy and carefree hours in my first years with Manchester United, for weeks Eddie's pet dog stood sentinel for the return of its master which would never come and, in Belgrade, I, too, felt that I had been abandoned.

While I sat on the sidelines in Sweden, however, the newspapers increasingly called for my selection and Jimmy Murphy, who on a leave of absence from United was in charge of the Welsh team which reached the quarter-finals before losing to Brazil by the only goal (scored in the seventy-third minute by Pelé), said he would have picked me for his team without a moment's hesitation.

It was an encouraging statement because the Welsh team was not exactly threadbare, not with such world-class assets as John Charles, Ivor Allchurch and Cliff Jones.

Murphy said he was staggered by my enforced idleness. But Winterbottom insisted I was too raw for the World Cup and I would have to learn my trade before I could consider myself a finished international product. I could only envy the trust Brazil placed in the seventeen-year-old Pelé.

I saw him from time to time with his team-mates strolling through the parks of Gothenburg, where we were based throughout the tournament. We shared their training ground and after their work was over they lingered in the city before being taken back to their headquarters deep in the countryside. Sometimes you saw one of the Brazilian players, still clad in his yellow training shirt, invariably with a beautiful Swedish girl on his arm.

For myself, I was content enough with the company of Don Howe, the West Bromwich full-back who was one of the closest to my age in the squad. He had also been on duty in Belgrade, which was England's heaviest defeat since the humiliations inflicted by the Hungarian wonder team half a decade earlier, and he encouraged me to believe that I would see some action before the tournament was over. But the call didn't come and I was hurting now because my appetite for football had been returning in the weeks since Belgrade.

I also had the unstated but nagging feeling that I had paid the heaviest price for a defeat in which few, if any, of my team-mates had distinguished themselves.

I respected Walter Winterbottom. He had a feeling for the game, he was tireless in advocating new standards of coaching in England after the indignities inflicted by the Hungarians, but his background and his style were academic. He had played briefly for Manchester United, certainly too infrequently to understand, I concluded, in the way that Ramsey did, the needs – and the fears – of the professional player.

Winterbottom talked the theories of football wonderfully well but he might have been conducting a university tutorial. He was much less acute in his perception of how to motivate a player unsure about his readiness, or his ability, to step up to the highest level.

While Winterbottom ran an endless seminar, Alf went to the heart of matters, hard and sure about his idea of the way a game would unfold, and what his players had to do to control it.

When Alf played against those brilliant Hungarians, his last experience of the international game as a creative full-back who, with much self-education, had flowered in the glory of Arthur Rowe's push-and-run Spurs, he was bruised deeply. Earlier he had a similar experience as a member of the England team beaten by the part-timers and amateurs of the United States in the mining town of Belo Horizonte, in the 1950 World Cup in Brazil.

Before that game Winterbottom had, as usual, been handed the team sheet by the Football Association committee of selectors, mostly club directors who often argued the case for players attached to their own sides, and despite the manager's pleadings there was no place for Stanley Matthews. For Ramsey it was another of many outrages inflicted by the 'amateurs' of the FA and for him correcting the weaknesses he had seen so vividly, and experienced so painfully, became nothing less than a personal crusade.

He had suffered wounds that only truly healed, I believed, on that day England won the World Cup.

Winterbottom's greatest interest, it seemed, lay in the administration of the game, and maybe that turn in the direction of his ambition became more entrenched after the World Cup in Chile in 1962. Soon after that he was disappointed when he lost his bid to succeed Stanley Rous as secretary of the Football

Association and he then settled for the job of directing the Central Council for Physical Recreation.

Clearly his long tenure with the England team had run its course. We had some good moments in Chile under the captaincy of the richly talented Johnny Haynes and had been strengthened by the arrival of Bobby Moore, who made his debut en route to the World Cup in a game against Peru in Lima. In that high altitude, the twenty-one-year-old from West Ham looked perfectly acclimatised to the demands of international football. His reading of the game, his timing despite a lack of genuine pace, was as breathtaking as the snow-capped Andes.

I couldn't imagine that there had ever been a more assured arrival on the international scene. He was so relaxed about all that was in front of him he might have been sitting back and puffing on one of the Havana cigars so pleasing to his Upton Park mentor and senior team-mate Malcolm Allison.

Though we reached a World Cup quarter-final for the first time, before being overwhelmed by the brilliance of the dynamic Garrincha, who performed for Brazil the improbable feat of compensating for the absence of Pelé, it was again still true that we lacked the force of real leadership that would have made us genuinely competitive in the great tournament.

The team never came together in that solid way which would mark our efforts under Ramsey four years later. Apart from the distance created by Winterbottom's manner, his remoteness from the day-to-day moods and concerns of his players, I had, unusually for me, some fiercely expressed problems with the captain, Haynes.

As a player I admired him immensely. Indeed, it was a privilege to play beside him. His passing was superb, his instinct to find a weak spot in an opposing defence was sometimes surreal. I would go to his funeral in Edinburgh in 2005 not only with respect for his personal achievements over many years but also to pay homage to one of the truly great English footballers, a player of rich gifts and intense commitment.

This, however, did not prevent an angry exchange – probably the most severe I was ever involved in through the whole course of my career – after we played a goalless draw with Bulgaria, who at that time were perhaps the least ambitious team on earth, to qualify for the quarter-final against Brazil.

Johnny was rubbing his hands as we came off the field. I was incensed at the nature of our performance, the absence of any willingness to attack such a negative and sharply inferior side, and I was particularly outraged by the fact that our captain, and most accomplished creative player, had been at the heart of our approach. When I complained, Haynes said, 'Bloody hell, we've made the quarter-finals for the first time, you should be happy.' I said I couldn't be further away from such a state. Rather, I felt ashamed to have been part of such a performance.

We had passed the ball about aimlessly with the sole intention of achieving a draw, which struck me as stupidly hazardous and, indeed, as I said to Haynes, we might well have paid a terrible price if the Bulgarians had not squandered a late opportunity.

Hungary, for whom beautiful performances from Flórián Albert and Lajos Tichy carried the promise of a significant renaissance in the football nation that had so recently stunned the world, had earlier beaten us deservedly, 2-1. We also touched on possible redemption in the next group game against Argentina. The young Rattín, not yet anything resembling the demon of Wembley four years later, displayed some fine skill, unlike the extravagantly overrated José Sanfilippo.

He was the toast of Buenos Aires and we heard, constantly, that his ability would overwhelm us. Instead, we won 3-1 and I was pleased with my performance on the left wing, creating one goal and scoring another.

That might have been the catalyst for more prolonged celebration in our mountain-top headquarters borrowed from an American mining company. But we were undermined by the Bulgarian game and Garrincha was too much for us in the quarter-final. His performance was so compelling; stunningly, he even managed enough thrust from his short, once-crippled legs, to head a goal, the most memorable counterpoint coming from us when Jimmy Greaves brought cheers by going on all fours to retrieve an invading dog.

Given Garrincha's luminous performance – perhaps only Diego Maradona's sixteen years later against England in Mexico City rivalled it as a quarter-final explosion of both pure talent and ferocious purpose – we did well to keep the score down to 3-1 and there was, however fanciful, a flicker of hope when Gerry Hitchens equalised near half-time.

The reality, though, was that in yet another World Cup we had been ultimately outclassed. There was also the problem of that lack of unity.

Some members of the squad were unashamedly waiting for the tournament to end and later I learned that the fine player Bryan Douglas had sat disconsolately on his suitcase when he saw our miners' retreat and announced that he felt homesick before he had unpacked his bags.

On the flight home from Chile I sat next to Alf's most serious rival for the Winterbottom succession. Jimmy Adamson, who had worked as the manager's assistant coach in Chile, had superb credentials and indeed he would have landed the job but for his passionate and, as it turned out, immovable attachment to Burnley Football Club.

While Ramsey was confounding the elite of English football with his title-winning feat in the backwater of Ipswich Town, Adamson was forming a superb creative axis with the brilliantly subtle Irishman Jimmy McIlroy as Burnley brought joy to their East Lancashire valley with their own title triumph.

Adamson would go on to manage Burnley, the only professional club he played for in a long and distinguished career, and he did so well initially that some predicted he would be in charge of 'the team of the seventies'.

Sometimes I've speculated on what might have happened if he had not ceded the England job to Alf. Certainly it would have been a different England, perhaps keener to play more expansive football and almost certainly not as preoccupied by defensive discipline. But there was no doubt in my mind, as Adamson spoke at length on the journey home, that he would have brought a strong sense of team and the responsibilities which came with international selection.

He spoke, in the familiar tones of our home town Ashington, of his disappointment in the attitude of some of our players in Chile. 'It is not enough just to arrive in an England shirt and believe you have done the hard part just by getting there,' he said. 'You have to embrace a new challenge, new demands, you have to produce more than you have ever done before.'

It was a stirring battle cry on another retreat from a field of English defeat and on this later one from Mexico, after Adamson's mission statement had been fulfilled in so many ways by the man who had just come to sit beside me, I could only be grateful that I had experienced all of it.

And what now? Maybe I could do a little more for my club, Manchester United, who were entering a difficult phase of descent from the 1968 European Cup win, the great manager Matt Busby admitting to me his weariness in the face of the challenges still before him and not least the growing indiscipline and disaffection of the astonishingly gifted George Best.

I would hold to that obligation for another three years, playing my last game for the club on a spring evening in Verona. Then, my team-mates presented me with a beautifully hand-carved clock that still sits on my mantelpiece. There were some kind speeches as we sipped the good wine of the Veneto in an old restaurant on the shore of Lake Garda, one of the wittiest inevitably coming from the new United manager, Tommy Docherty.

There were no such ceremonials in the passenger cabin of the airliner flying home from Mexico a team still numbed by the anti-climax of missed opportunity and a terrible sense of what had been lost.

I had intended to make a farewell speech a few hours after the game when we gathered for a consoling drink beside the swimming pool but the mood was not right and, after calling my wife Norma back home in England, I settled for an exchange of condolences with my team-mates and a bottle or two of Corona beer that did little for my spirits.

On the plane, though, there was a dialogue I will never forget. It was with a man who was dropping, just a little, the high guard he had presented so resolutely from the moment he took over England – a man whose passion for what he did I would never cease to respect, and one whose impending rejection by the establishment of English football to this day fills me with both anger and indignation.

First Alf, who at times could don a mask of coldness more quickly than anyone I had ever known, put his hand on my arm and said, 'I want to thank you for all you have done for England's football – and for me.'

Then he said how much he regretted the manner of my departure from the England team the previous day.

He apologised for his decision to withdraw me from the game in the sixty-ninth minute, a time when we appeared to have won control. He said that in the gruelling heat his instinct had been to save me from the worst of fatigue before the semi-final in a few days. He added that he had become confident that our performance had been so powerfully shaped we had made ourselves impregnable. He shook his head and said that taking me out of the game might well have been the biggest mistake of his career.

I told him that he should not be too hard on himself. It happened to be true that I had been surprised by his decision – and also that I had been distracted by the activity on the touchline when Beckenbauer, who by his standards had been quite subdued, stole away to score a relatively soft goal to reduce our lead to one goal.

Yes, when I got the call to leave the field and Colin Bell, a fine and marvellously strong player, came to replace me, I did still feel full of running despite the drenching heat. But I urged him to accept there were other realities not to be ignored.

The match, I felt, had unfolded perfectly for our needs. We were more confident, more aggressive than the Germans and the goals from Alan Mullery, who played with impressive force, and Martin Peters, did not overstate our superiority. However, who was to say I would not have later felt drained by a ninety-minute effort if we had made it through to the semi-final against the Italians?

That was one imponderable to set against Alf's sense of responsibility for defeat, the disconsolate figure he presented when sipping from a glass of post-game champagne in his hotel room in León.

Another and much more relevant one in my mind was the question about how different it might have been if Gordon Banks had not been struck down with sickness in the hours before the game and how, when that happened, when he left the pre-match meeting to vomit uncontrollably in a nearby bathroom, a look of dread touched every face in a room suddenly filled with unaccustomed tension.

It was unthinkable that we should lose the man who just a week earlier had made that amazing save from Pelé's header, one that I couldn't believe when I saw it on the field because it happened so quickly, so improbably, and which still stretched credibility on the television reruns.

His deputy, Peter Bonetti, was a talented goalkeeper who had recently performed brilliantly in Chelsea's Cup final defeat of Leeds United. He also had a superb England record, six appearances and six victories and just one goal conceded. But unfortunately all he could do as the Germans seized their chances, and rode their luck when the Argentinian referee mysteriously ruled out a Geoff Hurst goal, was confirm our belief that Banks was indeed irreplaceable.

Bonetti had been worried by the fact that his wife had joined those of Bobby Moore, Martin Peters and Geoff Hurst at the World Cup, and that there had been reports of their receiving a lot of unwelcome media attention in Mexico City. He had not, it seemed, come into the match with total concentration and when this emerged I could only say it was another vindication of Alf's instincts.

He had been against the idea of a cavalcade of loved ones journeying to a World Cup and there is no doubt he would have been appalled if he had known that by 2006 in Germany the wives and girlfriends of England players would be installed in their own official and media-besieged hotel.

I shook hands with Alf as he got up from the plane seat to leave me to my memories and return to his private thoughts, and no doubt self-recriminations. I told him nothing had happened in the last few weeks to make me question my huge debt to him.

He had changed my horizons, made me believe the greatest prize in football could be achieved. This was a gift which remained unsullied by the misadventures of León.

He had taken me to the mountain top and that enduring fact, along with the steady rhythm of the jet engines, I believed, would always carry me home.

2. Starting Cold in Paris

Had Alf sketched out a scenario for his first match as the officially appointed, if not yet fully instated, manager of England he might have given it the title, 'Notes on a game I can afford to lose'.

Win, and his effect, his professional weight, would be immediately apparent. He was – couldn't everyone see? – the strong arm which had been required so desperately through all those years of deeply entrenched failure. Lose, and, well, here was the evidence of all the work that he needed to do – and all the power he needed to be granted.

In shocking fact, the score on the night of 27 February 1963 on a field of frozen snow at the Parc des Princes Stadium in Paris was France 5 England 2.

For the Football Association here was still another international disaster, defeat in a qualifying round of the old Nations Cup, forerunner of today's European Championships. Yet if the loss was a final black eye for the time-expired England selection committee – they handed the new manager, who was still completing his contract with Ipswich Town, the team sheet shortly before the kick-off – the countenance of the man who had already pledged himself to winning the next World Cup was quite unblemished.

He may have regretted the woeful performance of his new charges but he did not show any serious signs of anger or frustration. In fact he made a small joke in the deadpan fashion with which we would soon become so familiar. When he asked the captain Jimmy Armfield if we always played as badly as that, and Jimmy answered with an emphatic no, he said, 'Well, that's the best news I've had tonight.'

But if Alf kept his reactions largely to himself, I could not. I had gone to Paris wrapped against the cold but also warmed by the idea that a bright new chapter was about to start.

We had been placed in the charge of a man steeped in the professional game, someone who had improved himself quite relentlessly through his own playing career and on his first managerial assignment had gone to obscure, Third Division, Ipswich Town and made them champions of England.

I considered how much knowledge and determination must have gone into that achievement and concluded that surely England would be put on an entirely new and competitive footing. Now, however prematurely, I felt that hope had been pushed somewhere over a very distant rainbow and after pulling off my frozen boots I threw them to the floor.

I was, to put it mildly, extremely cheesed off. Alf, however, remained serene enough after a few brusque comments on some of our inadequacies. And then, as we were driven back to our hotel through Paris streets emptied by the bite of winter, it occurred to me that it was not too hard to imagine that for him each French goal had been one more flurry of vindication. They underlined, he must have thought, everything he had believed about the running of the team since his own international playing career ended in that firestorm of Hungary's 6-3 victory ten years earlier.

Alf's greatest complaint was that England's lacerating experience that afternoon at Wembley was nothing so much as an ambush waiting to happen. The shattering nature of it could not have been better illustrated than in a recollection of Malcolm Allison, who would prove to be one of the most inventive coaches English football would ever know and was always acknowledged by Bobby Moore as the biggest single influence in his football life.

Malcolm recalled that before the game he and his West Ham team-mate, and future manager of Cardiff City, Jimmy Andrews, ran their eyes over the Hungarians as they warmed up on a patch of grass normally reserved, and appropriately as it turned out, for greyhounds.

Twenty years later Allison reported a still vivid memory. He said, 'I noted their light, modern gear and their streamlined boots and that registered with me vaguely. But Jimmy drew my attention to the "pot" bulging out of the red shirt of Ferenc Puskás and said, "God, we're going to murder this lot." I had to agree on the face of it even though you could see a neatness and an impressive level of skill as they did their limbering up.

'Then, out on the pitch, just before the kick-off, I saw the "fat guy" volleying shots into the arms of the goalkeeper Gyula Grosics from forty yards and I said to Jimmy, "They've got some skill, you know, this could more interesting than we think."'

Also in the stand that day was my future friend Geoffrey Green, the football correspondent of *The Times*, who would so often lighten the apprehension I felt on long plane journeys with his stories and his banjo-playing as he sipped a Scotch.

Geoffrey brilliantly conveyed the confusion that hit England's defence as the Hungarians deployed their withdrawn centre-forward strategy featuring Nándor Hidegkuti. He wrote a sentence which might have been, if anyone at the Football Association had been reading, the ultimately damning epitaph for all that had gone wrong since the day five years earlier when a superb English team featuring such players as Stanley Matthews and Tom Finney had strolled masterfully to a 4-0 victory over Italy in Turin.

Geoffrey wrote that England's centre-half, Harry Johnston of Blackpool, had responded to the brilliance of Puskás with the urgency of a fire engine but unfortunately one going in the wrong direction.

Even as a schoolboy I, too, felt that this was a significant moment, something more than another passing defeat, and that it demanded a major overhaul in the thinking of all those with a hand in running the national game. I remember declaring with much indignation, 'This just cannot go on. We have to stop believing our way is the only way. We can't keep kidding ourselves that we're the best in the world and that we have nothing to learn.'

My fellow schoolboy Bobby Robson, a future England manager, also had a telling recollection of England's second defeat to foreign opposition on home soil, the first one coming four years earlier against the Republic of Ireland. He said, 'We saw a style and a system of play we had never seen before. None of their players meant anything to us. We didn't know about Puskás – or any of those fantastic players. They might have been from Mars as far we were concerned. Their technical brilliance and new tactics completely kyboshed our old W-M formation in just ninety minutes.'

Ramsey paid the highest price that day at Wembley, losing not only his place in the England team but also a source of some of his deepest pride.

Many years later he would say that the circumstances surrounding the Paris defeat confirmed his belief that his predecessor Walter Winterbottom, who was just one shocked witness of the football equivalent of a car crash when the Hungarians were so effortlessly dominant, had been inhabiting a nightmare. It was something he remembered vividly when he was interviewed as a potential successor to Walter – and it stiffened his determination to win the powers that would enable him to do the job properly.

He thought the FA men in Paris, led by chairman Graham Doggart, who had a distinguished career as an amateur footballer, including international caps and a stint with Corinthian Casuals, were well-meaning in their way – but he also believed that there was nothing in their backgrounds to provide them with any real insights into the challenge he faced.

He couldn't see much chance of a meaningful dialogue with men speaking a football language different from his own. 'They were enthusiastic enough,' he confided to a friendly journalist, 'and the chairman seemed like a nice man. I liked him. But in all honesty I couldn't believe any of them were qualified to offer me a worthwhile opinion.'

England, Alf was more than ever convinced after those first few days on the job, had to be in the hands of a dyed-in-the-wool professional, someone who knew about international football, who understood its demands, its constantly changing trends represented by the emergence of superb teams like Italy and Austria in the thirties and then Hungary and Brazil after the interruption of the Second World War.

The Italian example, after all, had long been written into the history of the game. Vittorio Pozzo – known across all his country's football landscape as il Vecchio Maestro, the Old Master – was never the servant of committee men. He had learned the game at every level, played in England and Switzerland and returned home to Italy to serve as a player and coach of such great clubs as Torino and Milan. When he took control of the national team his authority was absolute. Pozzo was cast as part teacher, part messiah, and no one in Italy who looked for a moment at his background and record had the temerity to challenge his judgement.

It helped that he was reinforced by achievement every step of the way. The Old Master delivered World Cup triumphs in 1934 and 1938, and in 1936 won Olympic gold in Berlin, another success to underpin a tradition which has four times made Italy world champions, a record second only with Germany to Brazil's five. Such authority was only briefly interrupted that day in Turin when Matthews and Finney and their colleagues impressed themselves so strongly that one leading Italian sports newspaper said that England were a team of 'football gods'.

Now, a decade after the dire exposure by Hungary, England was finally being pushed towards some long-proven foundations of international success.

You just had to have, Alf insisted to the FA, someone who knew the game and was also free of any influence of committee men, who in many cases saw the worldwide game as a route to prestige, glamour even, not so readily available to mere leaders of local business and politics.

He made it abundantly clear that if the FA wanted him to take over, it had to be on his terms and, as he would prove on several critical occasions down the years, they would be broken only at the grave risk of his departure. It was a massive statement of self-confidence but it was implicit in everything he said and did.

As I've never been slow to declare, I was a believer right from the start. I travelled down with Roger Hunt for our first meeting with him at the Hendon Hall Hotel en route to the Paris game. The hotel in north London would become both the principal home and the laboratory of all our hopes over the next few years.

Its walls could tell so many stories of how it is when a group of men, who in this case happened to be professional footballers, come together in a common purpose which demands both heightened ambition and an understanding that they have to work together in every situation – and that if they cannot do this, if the discipline or the pressure is too great, the only option they have is to walk through the lobby and out of the swing doors as they settle for something less.

Even today when driving to some appointment in London I try to go by way of the hotel; it remains so much part of the furniture of my life it seems wrong to go about my business without giving it a nod of the most affectionate recognition.

When I do this so many old scenes and sounds come back to most vivid life.

I see the troubled, often angry look on the face of Jimmy Greaves when it became obvious to him that his chances of making a mark on the football history of his country were fading away under the muscular challenge of Geoff Hurst.

I see the thrill and anticipation on the face of my brother Jack and remember the joy and astonishment in his eyes when he burst into the United dressing room – after his Leeds United had beaten us in an FA Cup semi-final – to tell me that he had just heard he had been picked to play for England for the first time.

I see the unchanging, resolute expressions of our great goalkeeper Gordon Banks and his fellow Yorkshireman Ray Wilson, who would sometimes tell me that he had never imagined, while learning his trade with Huddersfield Town, that he would get such an opportunity. I see the cool demeanour of Bobby Moore, never rattled in any circumstances, including the attempt to remove him from the 1970 World Cup with the fabricated charge that he had stolen a diamond bracelet in Bogotá.

I hear the eager chatter of Alan Ball, which for a little while became subdued when Alf left him on the bench until recalling him before the action became most serious. I hear the encouragement of George Cohen – and the mystification he expressed over the northern sense of humour which had Nobby Stiles falling out of his seat when we went to see the Liverpool comedian Ken Dodd in the West End.

I hear, too, the laughter when Nobby knocked something over in the fashion of Inspector Clouseau – and the groans when Alf announced after training that he was taking us to see still another western starring John Wayne.

For Roger and me, back on that February Saturday in 1963, Hendon Hall was the place where we hoped to confirm the suspicion that our international careers might just be moving on to another and much more soundly based level of expectation.

Like me, Roger had suffered frustration in that huge gap between the intensity – and success – of our club football and the drift we encountered on international duty. The previous year he had lived through his version of my Swedish experience when he was called to the World Cup squad in Chile.

He was first selected as a Second Division player marching forward with Bill Shankly's Liverpool, then in South America spent the entire World Cup tournament on the bench while sharing with me a resentful disappointment that the squad contained too many players of something less than full commitment.

The weekend we travelled down to Alf's first gathering we had played against each other in a ferocious match at Anfield between a reviving United and a Liverpool filled with that storm of passion brought by the extraordinary Shankly. There was plenty to reflect upon from that day's action, not least the sharply different styles of our Scottish managers, the unswervingly diplomatic Busby, the inflamed activist Shankly with his stories of youth among the miners of a village which was fast disappearing. But then our thoughts and conversation turned quickly enough to what we might find in London.

We agreed that England's new manager could not have performed his wonders at Ipswich without formidable strength of character and authority and an outstanding feel for effective tactics. He had produced a stunning body of work, catching the elite of English football with a series of surprise punches which were all the more devastating for that.

A team as sophisticated and talented and poised as the Double-winning Tottenham of Danny Blanchflower, Dave Mackay, John White and Cliff Jones were among their victims.

Alf made a previously lightly considered Scottish winger Jimmy Leadbetter the most influential player in the First Division as he became the tactical hub of a stunning title triumph. Leadbetter was a withdrawn winger. He played finely delivered passes into the path of Ipswich's striking pair Ray Crawford and Ted Phillips, and many years later Brian Clough, a fierce critic of

Alf in his time, would pay him the compliment of handing a similar role to another Scottish winger, John Robertson.

That was crucial to Clough's extraordinary achievement in winning two European Cup titles for Nottingham Forest. It was also a reminder that when Alf claimed that Martin Peters, the player he brought into the World Cup squad with Alan Ball at the expense of England's top echelon of wingers represented by John Connelly, Ian Callaghan, Terry Paine and Peter Thompson, was 'ten years ahead of his time', he might also have been referring to himself.

I met Jimmy Leadbetter again while walking down an Edinburgh street. It wasn't long before he died in 2005. He looked even less like a footballer. I said how good it was to meet him again. We were two men who owed so much to one man who could see in us the potential to do some of his most vital work. Alf was a man of great judgement and force and, no, we agreed, it couldn't be denied by anyone, and least of all those who knew him as such a strongly opinionated and effective player at Southampton and Spurs.

I recalled our first game against each other in the season Ipswich consigned those superb reigning champions Spurs to second place. I told Leadbetter the mood of United when we faced the upstarts Ipswich. We did it with great confidence. We would put them in their place, sweep them aside with a bigger game and more gifted players. We had the players and a much stronger background. And then I told him how rueful we felt about those opinions when we looked back on our 4-1 defeat. Jimmy smiled and said, 'Aye, there was no doubt about it, Alf could be a strange character at times, you didn't always know what was going on his mind, but he knew a thing or two about "fitba".'

In the end, no one could argue with that assessment. Alf Ramsey knew football all right. He knew how to play to strengths – and to obscure weaknesses. His whole late-starting playing career was a testament to that. He had improved himself relentlessly, learned from whomever he could find a hint of guidance. But then the question for Roger Hunt and me as we travelled south concerned whether Alf could be truly his own man in the new environment of international football; could he break the shackles imposed on a Winterbottom also handicapped by a lack of anything resembling the new man's professional background?

We didn't have to wait long to put away our concerns. If nothing else, Alf Ramsey was certainly his own man – and he was quick to display to us the firmest set of priorities.

Chief among them was the understanding of his players that he would have the last, decisive opinion.

He was waiting, immaculately dressed and composed, in the hotel lounge when we arrived, welcoming his troops and giving a first strong indication of his style of command. Clearly it had little to do with the politics of consensus.

His first move was to separate the more experienced players from the rest. It meant that I found myself in a room with Jimmy Armfield, the captain who had taken over from Johnny Haynes when a car accident ended his international career, Ron Flowers and Ray Wilson.

Alf didn't waste too much time on pleasantries. He said he wanted some candid opinions about what had been wrong with the old regime. How might we improve, how might players feel better about their call-ups to England? He said he wanted us to speak freely, and confidently, because that would be the quickest way of telling ourselves that we were part of something new that would swiftly and naturally clear away so many of the old problems.

I was the first to break an uncomfortable silence. I was anxious, perhaps too anxious, not to give the impression that I didn't have a mind of my own – or that I had made no attempt to analyse any of our problems. I was, after all, the most senior player with the departure of Haynes and if I didn't have anything to say, who did? Even so, I was reluctant to go to the heart of the matter, which was Walter's failure to carry the players with him. Instead I settled on the familiar complaint about the time it took us to negotiate the North Circular Road on the way to our training headquarters at the Bank of England complex in Roehampton. Would it not be easier to either find a place to work in north London – or change hotels?

Alf's face was sphinx-like as he listened to my logistical input. Then he said, 'Thank you, Bobby, but I think we will keep the arrangements as they are.'

Looking back, I suppose it was a simple enough device. He was inviting suggestions, then shooting them down as though they were clay pigeons. The message could hardly have been clearer: we could propose but, most certainly, he would dispose of all that didn't originate in his own carefully prepared thoughts.

However, by way of compensation he said we should believe we were going to win the World Cup before the gaze of our own people. We had enough talent, enough competitive character. Now we merely had to do the work.

Quite how much this involved became clear enough in Paris a few days later.

The casualty rate wrought by Alf's regime, his reluctance to proceed with players who hadn't earned his complete

45

confidence, is clear enough from the briefest glance at the team presented to him by the FA selectors before we went out in the Siberian setting of Parc des Princes.

Only two of the names would appear on the sheet Alf handed to a Fifa official before the Wembley final two and a half years later. They were Bobby Moore's and mine. The Paris team read: Ron Springett, Jimmy Armfield, Ron Henry, Moore, Brian Labone, Ron Flowers, Charlton, John Connelly, Bobby Tambling, Bobby Smith, Jimmy Greaves.

Springett's nightmare of indecision and faulty positioning stripped away any belief Ramsey might have had in him, for all his impressive progress in the game to that point. Armfield, who complained strenuously that the Paris game should never have been played, so difficult were the conditions, survived the Parc des Princes but for him there was a trapdoor waiting in the next game, and Alf's second straight defeat, against Scotland at Wembley.

In Paris I felt particularly sorry for Henry, a fine left-back for Spurs who arrived at White Hart Lane towards the end of Alf's time there. He had to wait several years to replace the Welsh defender Mel Hopkins in the beautifully pitched Spurs team but when he did, he performed so impressively he made himself part of the great Double triumph, playing behind such stars as Mackay and Jones.

Yet his one game for England was in Paris. Like the rest of us, he came into the debacle after being been made inactive for two months by a harsh, record-breaking English winter.

It was the worst kind of preparation for his one chance to make an impact at the highest level and later my sympathy was renewed when I read his low-key and philosophical reflections on the night which put a brisk end to his international hopes.

Ron recalled, 'Before the game Alf just said, "If you behave yourself and work hard you'll get on all right with me." He didn't talk tactics much that night. He just said, "Go on, you know what you have to do."

'It was such a terrible night. We hadn't played for so long because the winter had been so bad at home. The pitch had a covering of snow, Ron Springett was in goal but he might not have been there because he was frozen and didn't move. It was so cold that when we finished we had to sit around the edge of a big square bath and dangle our boots in the hot water because our laces had frozen solid. Alf could not really say much afterwards but he came round and shook all our hands.'

As it happened the odds were always against the admirable Henry. His greatest problem was not the extreme conditions of the Paris night but the inevitability of Ray Wilson, my regular room-mate on England trips, reclaiming the left-back position. Ray didn't have a lot to say for himself but when he spoke his words always carried weight. They were underpinned by his superb consistency in understanding his role as a full-back, one who was able to go forward with sharpness and conviction but never at the cost of his defensive responsibilities.

When he first came into the team in 1960 it was at that time when I was operating, not with total enthusiasm, as a left-winger and I valued his presence from our first game together. We developed a clear understanding of our roles when the other team had the ball; I would go with a runner while Ray would attend to the man in possession. His tackling was as sharp and hard as anything I have ever seen in the game and always he showed that willingness, and capacity, to take the action to our opponents.

Shankly, making his name at Huddersfield, had first seen

Ray's potential as a youngster splitting his time between working on the railway lines by night and in the day attempting to establish himself as a professional footballer.

Ray could be quite a solitary figure and talked often of his passion for walking on the moors, once giving me a long and fascinating account of a trek he made along the spine of northern England, from the Peak District to the border hills of Scotland. He said he loved the freedom that came to him in such terrain – and certainly when he played there was always the sense of someone who was perfectly self-contained in his knowledge of what he could do to help in any situation on the field.

We got on extremely well, right from the start. We were comfortable in each other's company on and off the field and very soon we agreed that we had enough in common – we were both very happy in our club football in the north, him in Yorkshire, me in Manchester – that it would make sense if we stuck together.

He was better on the ball than his World Cup full-back partner George Cohen but he also had the ability to compete physically with anyone he marked. If you wanted to discourage a potentially dangerous right-winger he would do the job, starting at the very first opportunity.

Most remarkable was his ability to recover from a mistake, something he proved for all time in the most important match any of us would ever have to play, the World Cup final. Everyone makes mistakes but Ray was one of the few players who could expel one from his mind in the course of a few strides.

He was indeed a rock, as formidable as any outcrop of it on the moors he loved so much, and if Ron Henry had some legitimate regrets about the difficulties presented by the challenge that came to him at the Parc des Princes, an even greater one, no doubt, was that he was in competition with a man of Wilson's ability and extraordinary competitive character.

Alf quickly made it clear that as an old full-back he adored Ray's all-round qualities. They might have been custom-made for the requirements of a team that might just beat the world.

So, too, was another man who became so quickly strong, and irreplaceable, in the wake of the Paris shambles.

Occasionally Alf would take me to one side and ask for my opinion on certain players and invariably I felt they were the ones he had already decided would provide the strong foundations of everything he hoped to achieve.

When he came to the issue of goalkeeping – one of the most fundamental aspects of any team's success – we reached instant agreement. Yes, I also felt that not only was Gordon Banks the outstanding candidate but that also there was every reason to believe that very soon he would announce himself as the best in the world. If I ever had a morsel of doubt about this it disappeared very early in his run of seventy-three England caps.

His brilliance, and his resolution, created so much confidence that I remember thinking, after the great prize had been won, how much harder it would have been to believe in our chances had he not been there to retrieve our mistakes, to make us believe that with him around everything was indeed possible.

Once while reflecting on this I watched him closely as he worked on a training pitch in Mexico City which had the yielding capacity of solid concrete. Time after time he would throw himself down on that cruelly unforgiving surface. His commitment, and durability, was staggering and when we came off the field I asked him a question to which he provided an answer I've never forgotten.

I wondered why he put himself so constantly in danger of injury while training. Did he never feel inclined to save at least some of himself for match action? A small smile flickered across his face and he said, 'Bobby, without doing what I did today, with all the risks, I simply couldn't do my job.'

The pain, and the possibility of injury, was the price he had to pay. It was a simple equation. So many times before a car accident and the loss of an eye ended one of the great football careers, I had reason to recall his matter-of-fact statement of professional dedication.

It was the recurring reminder that when Alf Ramsey came to the great challenge of his professional life, his most vital task was to decide not on whose talent was the most arresting but on those in whom he could invest all his trust.

Not so long before he lapsed into the half-world of dementia that brought such sorrow to his beloved and wonderfully protective wife Vicky and all those who would always be indebted to the strength and the precision of his judgement, Alf said to me, 'To have a chance we had to identify the players who were capable of producing all that was asked of them. My job was to make sure that was always the first – and last – consideration.'

It was a task that I suspect brought him agonies of private analysis – and one fierce national controversy – but there was no doubt that he was least taxed when it came to deciding who would stand in our goal, who would make saves to rival any in the history of the game; someone who would never forget that if the training for the job didn't hurt, if it didn't demand every ounce of your commitment and physical resilience, you would, sooner or later, fail.

The key to so much of what a goalkeeper can achieve lies in his ability to handle the pressure of living with the knowledge that on so many occasions he is going to be the difference between the joy of winning and the irreparable regret of losing the most important matches. You need a special turn of mind and character for that and the more I got to know Gordon, the more I saw that he had it. I would never call him arrogant but nor would I say that he was ever going to be in danger of underestimating himself. Long before the end of his career he didn't need telling that he was the best in the world. 'I just do what I have to do, Bobby,' he always said whenever I told him how much I admired his work.

Those occasions included the time when I said how much I wished he could do some of it on behalf of my club United. That was a hope that didn't survive the mysteries and the intrigues of the transfer market so I had to settle for all the reassurance he brought to me and the rest of his team-mates in the national team.

Banks of England elected himself to do the job. More than fifty years on, it is still so easy to say with certainty that without him we couldn't have so truly believed that we had the means to do all that we set ourselves. Banks made a fortress of his goal. It was a place which never ceased to make us feel both safe and inspired.

3. Ice Man Moore

For most of my team-mates it was just one of the less spectacular examples of Bobby Moore's ability to remain uncannily calm under even the most intense pressure. If I ever mentioned it to them, suggested that I found it, well, sometimes a little disconcerting, they would laugh and say, 'You should know by now, that's Moore.'

They would go on to point out something about which in almost every other context I was perfectly aware. He did, after all, operate in another dimension from the rest of us once he put on an England shirt. This was why when he was made captain it seemed no more than the most inevitable and natural extension of his personality.

What I was talking about, they said, was as much a part of his nature as his extraordinary capacity to read the flow of a game, to make, for a classic example, the kind of tackle which robbed the explosive Jairzinho in our great World Cup game in Guadalajara in 1970 when one false half-step could so easily have yielded a penalty. Instead, Bobby moved forward quite imperiously, the ball at his feet, the huge yellow-clad Brazilian throng hushed by a sublime example of skill and authority.

For me, this particular habit was, though for no more than a second or two, as startling as a visitor from another planet, which I knew was certainly not the intended effect.

Maybe we were defending against a potentially dangerous free-kick, perhaps we were deep into a battle to survive and Nobby was shouting at Jack, or vice versa, but it didn't matter, Bobby would still stroll beside me apparently without a care in the world and say, 'All right, Bobby, mate, how's Norma and the kids? Everything okay?'

Sometimes I would respond a little tetchily, even by my occasionally grumpy standards, with something like, 'Do you realise we've got an important football match going on here?' Invariably he would reply, 'Oh yeah, no worries, Bob.'

In another man you might have suspected a bit of play-acting, the self-conscious building of a little personal mythology. However, for Bobby, England's youngest skipper, there was never a requirement to create an impression of elevated calm or superior nerve. He didn't have to strike poses and that perhaps more than anything spoke of his awareness that when it came to the international game, he was born to handle anything that came his way. He didn't role-play. He just played.

The moment he stepped on to the field he was perfectly attuned to his environment. He seemed to grow taller, become that little bit more composed. He had a corner of himself that was quite untouchable and anyone could see it. Alf saw it at once and great players like Pelé and Franz Beckenbauer came to put a higher value on it each time they played against him.

When he died so prematurely at the age of fifty-one in 1993, and we went to Westminster Abbey, a place normally reserved for the honouring of great statesmen and warriors and poets, to pay our respects to one of the nation's finest sportsmen, the words of such titans of football were inevitably bound up with the reflections of all those team-mates who would never forget the value of his leadership and the uplift brought by his presence.

The tributes swelled as stirringly as the choral music that filled the building so woven into the history of the nation.

Alf was not so well on the day of the service but already he was on the record, his words as thunderous as any of those of some hymn of praise. He said, 'My captain, my leader, my right-hand man. He was the spirit and the heart-beat of the team. He was a cool, calculating footballer I could trust with my life. He was the supreme professional, the best I ever worked with. Without him, England would never have won the World Cup.'

Pelé and Beckenbauer pitched their tributes just as high. Pelé said, 'He was my friend as well as the greatest defender I ever played against. The world has lost one of its greatest football players – and an honourable gentleman.' Beckenbauer echoed Pelé's assessment, saying, 'Bobby was the best defender in the history of the game, a gentleman and a true friend.'

When Alf outlined his earliest vision of his England's future, and his need to identify swiftly the players who would be the cornerstones of his hopes, he was quick to say, 'Bobby Moore must be one of them, he's going to form a key part of what we're trying to do.'

Of course, I agreed. I was beginning to look at England's prospects more confidently than ever before. I was comfortable playing for this manager and his selection of Bobby as our leader, despite the fact that he was not as experienced as myself, seemed entirely logical. I liked to think I had a good and still developing sense of what to do to best influence an important football match but it did not include the shepherding of my team-mates. For one thing, I didn't tackle, at least not in any way that did not inspire derision in expert practitioners like Nobby or Ray Wilson, Jack or George Cohen.

Bobby did it so well, with such extraordinary timing, that it became almost the fulcrum of our game, our belief that we could compete with anyone.

It was inevitable that sooner or late Alf would make him captain and when he did so in Bratislava against Czechoslovakia for our third match after that bad night in Paris, Bobby's performance, the easy way he carried himself, the certainty of his play, made the fact that he was a mere twenty-two years and forty-seven days old seem like some trick of the calendar.

Just a year had passed since he made his faultless debut in the thin air of Lima en route to the Chile World Cup, and almost every step he had made for England since then had carried the weight of an extremely convincing job application. Every intervention, every easily stroked pass, seemed to be saying, 'Look, this is what I do, this is who I am.'

Jimmy Armfield's misadventure in Alf's second game, the loss to Scotland at Wembley, was almost certainly the manager's first invitation to consider the question of the team's leadership, and then when Jimmy was injured for the Bratislava game the door opened a little wider. In one way Jimmy was extremely unlucky because I don't think his mistake could ever, however well he performed, be detached in Alf's mind from the image of Jim Baxter, who dominated the match with his extraordinary combination of skill and the most refined arrogance, exploiting it with such triumphant glee.

With Johnny Haynes no longer around, I had become the

most experienced player with the greatest number of caps (forty-two) and it was perhaps because of this that Alf made a point of mentioning to me that he was considering giving the job to Bobby. Without offering the slightest impression that my verdict would ultimately do anything to shape his decision, he said he was interested to know my reaction.

What did I think of this most composed young east Londoner? I said that there was something quite remarkable about him and it was reflected most in the way he seemed to just get better and better with each new performance for England. It was as if he was born to inhale the atmosphere of international football, that if for others it could be an examination in which they would never be able to feel completely at ease and in charge of everything they did, for him it was a source of oxygen.

Bobby was, despite his lack of cutting pace, an impressive player in the First Division but at Manchester United we didn't attach huge weight to his club West Ham's reputation for sophisticated football. Yes, they had had some considerable success in knock-out competitions, beating Preston North End in the 1964 FA Cup final and going on to win the old Cup Winners' Cup, and Moore had displayed good leadership and some fine skill and sound defence, enough to make him at that point England's youngest Footballer of the Year.

But it was only when he played for the national team that you got the full measure of his quality. He simply grew before your eyes.

I said all this to Alf – and also made it clear that I had no ambition for the job. I had my game to play and often I found that enough of a responsibility. I was thrilled to be part of this reshaping of England and with such a strong sense that, finally, we were being given the right foundations. I liked the feeling of optimism in the dressing room, one that was already plainly building from game to game, and I believed the elevation of Bobby could only reinforce the development of such a mood.

If Paris and Wembley had brought defeats, the significance of these setbacks had already dwindled in my mind. They were fast retreating into the past, along with all the other disappointments. Not least among them was that time when I found myself lost on the field in Belgrade and had to pay for it on the World Cup bench in Sweden. Now I felt an increasing conviction that my international career had a new edge, a new purpose.

The appointment of such a youthful captain may have raised a few eyebrows at the time of the announcement but Alf could not have been more convinced that he had found a most powerful catalyst in the effort to win the World Cup.

He said to me, 'You know this Bobby Moore is quite something. He has set a mark for himself, he is so very confident and I believe the leadership of the team will be in very good hands. No, he is not fast but he thinks so quickly it doesn't matter. It is always so clear, and reassuring, that he knows what he is doing.'

It was the same level of confidence he had expressed when discussing Gordon Banks, saying, 'I want you players to know that every match is important because it is telling me new things about your ability and your willingness to do things that are so important for the team.'

One of the most remarkable aspects of Alf's leadership, and personality, was his ability to separate any personal reservations, even resentments, about the style and attitudes of someone, from their ability to do the job that was needed.

This was very relevant to the rise of Bobby because, it has to be said, he and the boss were not always the most natural of bedfellows.

They certainly didn't, for example, share the kind of empathy I enjoyed with Ray Wilson as we returned to our hotel room, to drink tea and reflect on the day. Nor the noisy amiability shared by Nobby Stiles and Alan Ball down the corridor. Alf and Bobby were of different generations – and different worlds.

Bobby could be less than respectful in his response to some of Alf's foibles. At times he mocked the manager's clipped tone of voice and occasional faulty pronunciation, and never more so than on that famous occasion when Alf thanked 'Seen' Connery for his warm welcome when we visited the Pinewood Studios at a critical point in the World Cup finals. Bobby and Jimmy Greaves made little attempt to conceal their amusement.

Once Alf angrily sent the trainer Harold Shepherdson to summon Bobby to the waiting bus after he had lingered in the hotel lobby with Jimmy. Bobby eventually arrived with a shrug of indifference over the impatience and irritation of the manager.

Nor was Alf enamoured by what he considered Bobby's sometimes flighty approach to the important, and indeed in his opinion fundamentally vital, aspects of team discipline, especially in the matter of curfew times.

There was the notorious occasion early in Alf's reign when Bobby and Jimmy were the inspiration for a foray by some of the players into the West End on the eve of a flight to Europe. It was one which I joined innocently enough. However, the drinks went down pleasantly in one of Jimmy's favourite bars and we didn't leave until well after Alf's curfew of 10.30 p.m.

We were relieved not to see Shepherdson and his fellow trainer Les Cocker standing sentinel in the hotel lobby but our relief was only passing. Alf had ordered a room check at the time of curfew and we were shocked to see our passports, normally left in the charge of a team official, resting on our pillows. The implication was huge and dark.

We were in danger of being sent home, perhaps in national disgrace. This made for a night of considerable tension and the following day Alf didn't hold back his anger. He said that if there had been time to call up replacements he would have done so. He had to be able to trust his players. This should be seen as a last warning.

Yet if Bobby was disinclined to doff his cap to authority, he never pushed his rebellions too far. Above all, he respected Alf's professional judgement, his reading of tactics, and he was not likely to jeopardise his place in the success that, in his well-considered estimation, they foretold.

This was evident enough in the shadow of that first defeat in Paris, when Bobby was quick to say that he was impressed by Alf's low-key reaction. 'It was good that we didn't get any of the ranting and raving you would have expected from some managers,' said Bobby. 'He seems like a man you can work with, someone who isn't going to insult your intelligence on a regular basis.'

This vital matter of mutual respect had developed very quickly and was perfectly expressed by the sight of Bobby leading us out against one of Europe's strongest football nations in Bratislava. Bobby might not have been the most dutiful lieutenant in all aspects of the team operation but when it mattered most, when it was time to perform, there was not so much as a flicker of worry that he wouldn't be at the evenly beating heart of our effort.

Alf had been encouraged by a much improved performance against Brazil at Wembley, a 1-1 draw earned when Bryan Douglas scored a late equaliser against the reigning world champions – a good, steadying result after the defeats by France and Scotland, despite the fact that both Pelé and Garrincha were absent.

George Eastham had been awarded his first cap – and invited to make his considerable claims, as a highly skilled inside-forward, on a place on the road to the World Cup. Eastham, apart from his impressive creative touch, was a man of great strength of mind who had struck a huge blow for players' rights when he successfully sued his club Newcastle United for their refusal to grant him a transfer to Arsenal.

It was that time when so many players, including me, waited for their clubs to hand down their rewards, the most pressing one being inclusion in the end-of-season retained list; for us it was hard not to believe that we were lucky to play football for a living and that any improved terms that came trickling down had to be seen as a bonus. George, though, had a different cast of mind. He said that a player's terms should be negotiable, along with his right to choose his employer. As it was, footballers had fewer rights than many of the people who filled the stadiums to watch them play.

His mission statement was very impressive. He declared, 'Our contract could bind us to a club for life. Most people called it the "slavery contract". We had no rights at all. It was often the case that the guy on the terrace not only earned more than us – though there is nothing wrong with that – he had more freedom of movement than us. People in business or teaching were able to hand in their notice and move on. We couldn't. And that was wrong.'

When I heard these measured, dignified words it did make me reflect a little on my own willingness to leave my fate, financial and otherwise, largely to the instincts of fairness of my employers. Of course, I was happy at Manchester United, I loved the club and I was bound to it by some very strong emotional ties, but there were maybe times when I might have been a little more assertive. Certainly I remember going to a meeting of the players' union, which was brilliantly led by the chairman Jimmy Hill and the astute, full-time secretary Cliff Lloyd, and being impressed and amused by a comment of Tommy Banks, the rock-like full-back of Bolton Wanderers.

Someone told the meeting that they should remember they didn't have to go down a mine to earn their living and Tommy shot back, 'Yes, all right, but a miner doesn't have to mark Stanley Matthews on a Saturday afternoon.' That raised a smile even in someone like me who had spent his childhood under the shadow of the colliery and whose brother Jack had fled, so gratefully, the prospect of a working life underground when he was signed by Leeds United.

When my primary school team was issued with a new team kit, the headmaster had me put on one of the bright crimson shirts and run into a classroom while he hummed the signature tune of BBC Radio's *Sports Report*. I remembered the occasion warmly. When I jogged down the corridor I passed a cabinet containing some of the artefacts of the mining industry in which my father Robert worked all his life and, maybe, even at that early age I had a sense of running away from an unwelcome fate.

So maybe at times I was a little too content as I proudly wore my United blazer and waited for a word or a nod from Matt Busby or Jimmy Murphy that perhaps the time was right for me to seek a raise in my wages. I didn't know then that my success as a player down the years, and the celebrity it brought, would bring for me and my family so much security when I got involved in business after I stopped playing and decided, soon enough, that my future didn't lie in a football manager's office.

That, I know, was one of my good fortunes, one that wouldn't be shared by so many of my contemporaries in those days when we filled the big stadiums of England. I was bound to reflect on all of this with the news of Jimmy Hill's death at the end of 2015 – and put a fresh value on his vision for the future, which included pushing for the psychologically huge addition of an extra point to the value of a win in league football, and respect for all his determination to improve both the game and players' terms.

George Eastham had a similarly sharp view of some of the injustices inherent in professional football life, certainly stronger than mine, despite the fact that my own family had strong connections with the professional game through my mother's cousins, the Milburn clan led by the great Jackie. Maybe the difference was that George grew up as the son of a footballer, a distinguished one, too, his father, George, playing for Bolton Wanderers and England.

A sense of injustice flared in young George and his determination to make his fight in the most significant way was mirrored in the fine work he produced on the field. He was a quick and clever player and did well against Brazil and in

Bratislava. In all he played nineteen times, all the way to the World Cup finals.

He had a talent that was both delicate and biting and if in the end he gave way to the more muscular presence of those such as Geoff Hurst and Roger Hunt, he never lost the respect of Alf. Also, after impressive stints at Newcastle and Arsenal he received a call that back in the sixties represented membership of a working roll of honour, Tony Waddington's vintage collection of some of the finest players to grace the First Division at Stoke City, men like Gordon Banks, my old United team-mate Dennis Viollet, Jimmy McIroy, Jackie Mudie and, for a little romantic while, Stanley Matthews no less.

Another who was involved in that Bratislava dawn of an England team with new and exciting horizons was Chelsea's right-back Ken Shellito, who had emerged impressively in Tommy Docherty's young Chelsea team. Shellito was a beautifully balanced defender, good going forward and sound in both the tackle and his positional sense, and while Armfield's injury had given the captaincy to Moore it was also a great opportunity for the debutant Shellito.

He played well, showing the composure which had become one of this trademarks, but all his efforts and his ambitions were destroyed soon afterwards when he suffered a sickening knee injury while marking Sheffield Wednesday winger Edwin Holliday. He never recovered. Tommy Docherty did bring him back into the team, and with a little time left for him to restate his claim for a place in the World Cup squad, but good fortune, as well as his old fitness, had plainly deserted him. He faced my United team-mate George Best in his most withering form and the result was hard on all those who had come to respect his talent so much.

George Cohen, who won his first cap for England a year later, when Alf had finally decided that Jimmy Armfield, for all his skill and vision going forward, was not the answer to his needs defensively, later reflected powerfully, and movingly, on the fickleness of fate that can sometimes shape a professional career – and a life.

He said, 'In football it is the oldest truth that one player's mishap is another's opportunity and my good fortune in the unravelling of Jimmy Armfield's distinguished international career was compounded by another stroke of fate. It was the career-shattering injury of Ken Shellito. He was considered the heir apparent to Armfield, and for some very good reasons. He was strong and skilled and had a very good defensive technique, and he got his one chance a year before Alf brought me into the team.

'That game against Czechoslovakia was a perfect opportunity for Ken to make his mark – and to confirm Alf's doubts about Armfield's candidacy for another World Cup. Sadly for him, the Bratislava launching pad, which he trod impressively, fell apart when he was injured, and not only his international prospects but his professional career. Such are the sudden twists of football.

'One man falls, another slips back, and the race that seemed to be over is suddenly wide open. Being brilliant is good. Working hard is important. But without the breaks you can disappear in one moment of bad luck.

'There was no doubt I was trailing Ken Shellito, but then suddenly his name was scratched from the contest.'

When I read those words from George many years after our

playing careers were over – and his was ended so soon after the 1966 World Cup when he watched his torn knee swell up alarmingly after a freakish bounce of the ball while he was marking Liverpool's Peter Thompson – I had another reason to feel a sense of wonder over my own good luck.

It strikes me still with great force as I walk without any of the discomfort suffered by so many of my contemporaries. While they have faced surgery and months of painful rehabilitation, I have marvelled that I carry just one small piece of evidence of spending so many years risking injury while playing professional football at the highest level – a small scar above my ankle. It came to me in a reserve game at Old Trafford – and kept me out of football for less than a couple of weeks. And this, of course, has always been dwarfed by the fact that I was able to walk away from the Munich tragedy with no more than a small graze on my head.

George lost his one-club career with Fulham in that disastrous flashpoint and when the football was over he was required to overcome cancer with great courage. He also had some setbacks in business but always he was the same character who did so much to justify Alf's faith in him by calling him to the squad and then, nine months later, giving him his first cap against Uruguay two years before the unveiling of the World Cup at Wembley.

Alf had given him the traditional welcome when he joined us at Hendon Hall, saying, 'Welcome, George, I'm sure you know a lot of the players, just settle in and enjoy the experience. I'm sure you will do well. Just keep working hard as you have been doing for so long.'

So here in the strong, amiable man from west London was a classic representation of the qualities that Alf considered so central to all his ambitions with England. Jimmy Armfield had so many assets to commend him as an international player and a captain with a fine understanding of the game and the people who shaped it. He had been touched by the genius, and the demands, of playing in the same Blackpool team as Stanley Matthews. He had loved the excitement of the international scene, the chance to compete with and against the great players and all the colour and rewards of worldwide travel.

When, so long after the action was over, I was asked to name my all-time England, I did not hesitate to include Armfield, no more than I did when choosing his fellow casualty on the road to the '66 World Cup, Jimmy Greaves.

I tried to separate individual talent from the special requirements of Alf, to say that the men in my imaginary team would have perhaps offered the best balance and options in the competing demands that face every football manager in all their different situations. And so when I chose Jimmy at the expense of George, I was careful to make clear that I didn't believe he could have performed any better than my World Cup team-mate but simply that he was a superbly rounded player of skill and one of the first, and best, overlapping full-backs football had ever seen.

For Alf, of course, the overwhelming imperative was to have players who understood most completely his needs – and his priorities. George did this quite perfectly and when he made some great charge down the field, and capped it not with some delicate chip into the box but a blast that endangered the press photographers more than the opposing goal, Alf didn't share the exasperation, at least not entirely, of some of his team-mates. He thought more of the absolute reliability of his defensive instincts, the certainty that no winger, however tricky or brave, would deflect George from his overriding purpose of shutting him down as a source of danger.

So, as we moved surely from the cold and the bankruptcy of that night in Paris, many crucial pieces seemed to be fitting into place.

We had the strongroom of our goal in the safekeeping of Banks, who would so quickly placate the irritation of Alf that came when he surrendered a couple of soft goals in otherwise impressive early performances and, most seriously, seemed not to have absorbed totally the manager's warning about the full range of danger that came with a Brazilian free-kick.

We had the leadership of Bobby Moore, who was installed as the unchallenged captain when George came in for his first cap in the 2-1 victory over Uruguay in May 1964 – a win that eased Alf's angst over the fact that a solitary defeat in a run of increasingly surefooted performances had been administered, for a second straight time in his brief reign, a few weeks earlier by Scotland at Hampden Park.

Though Alf was always terribly intent on winning the tribal battles with Scotland – 'You must be joking,' he snapped to a local reporter who had been bold enough to say to him, 'Welcome to Scotland' when he got off a train in Glasgow – he also knew that his broader ambition, if not all the details of it, were already beginning to show the first signs of taking shape.

If the draw with Brazil represented a distinct improvement, the triumph over the World Cup finalists Czechoslovakia had to be seen as something of a breakthrough, an early announcement of serious intent. They were a skilled team and they played with a flourish that was not so evident on the streets of a beautiful city subdued and brooding, it seemed to me, under the weight and the harshness of life in a hard-line

Communist state, but we always felt that we had a strong edge in the 4-2 win.

A few days later we beat East Germany 2-1 after recovering from one of those rare slips from grace by Banks, with the help of a spectacular goal by Roger Hunt, who was replacing a sick Jimmy Greaves, but if we expected even a hint of euphoria over this defeat of the always combative East Germans we were quickly disabused. Alf told a cluster of surprised reporters, 'No, I'm certainly not entirely satisfied with our performance. There were some serious problems. Our passing was erratic and careless – and lacking in imagination. We can, and will, do much, much better.'

Our response a week later in Basle was an 8-1 defeat of Switzerland. I scored a hat-trick and drew level with the thirty-goal England mark of two of my heroes, Tom Finney and Nat Lofthouse, and even Alf was bound to say, 'Yes, I was happier today, this was a better, more convincing performance.'

As we flew back to England to much improved critical notices, I got the chance to tell him that playing for England was becoming an experience of growing satisfaction. Of course, I didn't make too much of it, I didn't want to suggest that I was beginning to feel at home. That was the last thing he wanted. True professional contentment, everything he said cried out, could only come much further down an extremely hard road.

4. A Price for Glory

No, Alf never said the way ahead would be either easy or secure against the deepest of personal doubts and he could remind you of this on the most unlikely occasions. Sometimes, he did it with a quite shocking abruptness.

It was as though he had weighed up the potential for maximum effect, sniffed out the moment when maybe you had let down your guard, perhaps with a casual remark, and then he would pounce. At times he might have been a sergeant-major measuring out a parade ground with his yardstick.

That, maybe, was his most enduring weapon, this capacity to plunge you into an examination of yourself and the degree of your ambition and determination without a hint of warning. You could be in the most serene of moods, smelling the roses that seemed to be blooming wherever you turned, strolling through an airport lounge or sitting in a coffee shop chatting with team-mates, and then Alf might hit a note that went far beyond a breath of steadying caution.

He would bring you back to the starting point – and all those questions which he never stopped asking, in one way or another. How much did you want this? How much were you prepared to sacrifice, how many comforts of the body and the mind were you prepared to forgo?

Once he noticed that one of his new boys, Allan 'Sniffer' Clarke, the usually cold-eyed striker of Leeds United, seemed to be in a particularly cheerful frame of mind during a flight. 'Enjoying yourself, Allan?' Alf asked curtly. 'Yes, thanks, boss,' Clarke replied. 'Well, you know, that's not the purpose of your presence,' said Alf.

It was the old, mostly unstated imperative. Had you thought it all through? Were you ready to go all the way on this long and difficult journey? A mistake in Bratislava could be redeemed in Leipzig but the detail of it would never obscure the broader vision.

Sometimes it could be a cutting remark from Alf that went straight into your bones. Or maybe it was a brief but hard analysis of his view of certain deficiencies in your game. In my case almost invariably it was to do with a tendency to put attacking possibilities too far ahead of defensive security. I knew he valued my ability to attack, to be creative, but I was also aware it would never be an open licence.

Occasionally it could be a withering look or a gesture of resignation as to the limits of your ability to respond to the challenges he was laying down before you, one by one.

Famously, he was particularly irritated when one of his players, assuming that he had become integral to the manager's plans, spoke jauntily about seeing him on the team's next assignment. Geoff Hurst and Gordon Banks and our Jack, in their brisk and open manner, could be a little prone to this.

'If you are picked,' he would growl and send home the guilty player with previously unsuspected demons suddenly released. It was the presumption of permanence surrounding a casual phrase like 'see you next game' that offended Alf to his core and when he rejected the first sign of it so forcibly, his hope, no doubt, was that he had put up still another barrier against the worst effects of complacency.

At the very least, he had let some of the air out of a balloon that perhaps someone had allowed to fly a little too high.

Looking back it is clear enough that he was in the grip of an obsession, one that he was intent on spreading into every corner of the squad.

The verdict of history had to be that it was a magnificent and ultimately rewarded preoccupation. He had created a single, self-justifying goal. He had waged war on all our illusions, on any shortfall in understanding of all that was involved when he picked you out for a role in his grand plan. Yes, it was a magnificent, sometimes brooding obsession. But in all honesty, all the years that have gone by have never softened the fact that it wasn't always so comfortable to be around.

My most striking experience of this came in Rio a year after that hugely encouraging victory in Bratislava. By this time my feeling of wellbeing within the England fold, I would soon be reflecting, had maybe struck Alf as being on the point of overflowing to a dangerous degree.

We were at the end of a summer tour which had been extremely demanding physically, following the routine hard labour of a domestic season played on pitches which sometimes seemed designed to drain the last of our energy, but still the mood was good despite the fact that we had lost 5-1 to Brazil in a 'Little World Cup' tournament.

The circumstances of the match had been extremely difficult and played at a level at which Alf was entitled to feel none of the gloom suffered by Walter Winterbottom in Belgrade eight year earlier, when England had suffered their previously heaviest defeat.

In Rio we were going down to only our second loss in the eleven games since the draw with Brazil at Wembley and we had gone on to the Maracanã pitch just thirty-six hours after boarding a plane in New York, where we had thrashed the United States 10-0. Before that we had beaten Uruguay at Wembley, with George Cohen winning his first cap in such a forceful fashion it could only increase the concern of the injured Armfield, the Republic of Ireland in Dublin and Portugal in Lisbon.

The sense of progress was so strongly underpinned that after the defeat by Brazil, and a particularly impressive performance by Pelé, Alf was completely unruffled.

He had noted that despite the weariness of everyone – and severe discomfort for Cohen, who had rejected the advice given to him by the team doctor Alan Bass that he should leave the game at half-time – we had done well for most of the ninety minutes. Indeed, Peter Thompson played so well, so bitingly, that no one that day could have imagined that in the last days before the World Cup finals he would be the victim of tactical opportunities offered to Alf by the late but compelling contenders Alan Ball and Martin Peters.

It was only in the last twenty minutes that the Brazilians fully exploited our exhaustion, scoring the four goals that gave the scoreline more than a hint of disaster. Alf told us, 'Don't worry about this result, it has come out of the worst possible circumstances for us – and I'll tell you something else, Brazil have no chance of winning the World Cup when they come to England in two years.'

Alf's lack of deep concern was somewhat justified when we

played a much stronger Argentine team than the one we had defeated in Chile two years earlier and lost a close match by the only goal. We then went to Maracanã to see Brazil outplayed by Argentina.

With the usual vast crowd baying for the blood of a referee whose judgement had been excessively lenient towards Argentine tackling that seemed expressly intent on leaving Pelé a casualty, Alf got up from his seat and announced, 'Gentlemen, I think we have seen enough. We can go now.'

On the way back to the hotel he insisted that Brazil, despite their triumphs in Sweden and Chile, would not represent a serious threat in England. Yes, they had in Pelé indisputably the world's most accomplished player and perhaps they would also have Garrincha revived and ready to augment still more the legend of the Little Bird. But in his opinion they had not properly reseeded their team; too many of their players were living on what they had done yesterday rather than what they might do tomorrow.

'Most certainly,' said Alf, 'this is a team going backwards, and if we had been in fresher condition against them I think we would know this more clearly.'

Against this background, and filled again with the pleasure of having enjoyed one of the world's most exciting cities, I was perhaps understandably emboldened and relaxed enough to pass on some of my feelings when I sat next to Alf at the gathering in a Rio bar arranged by the press corps.

The evening was casual and pleasant, with such journalistic stars as Geoffrey Green and Frank McGhee in their most exuberant form, and there had been much chatter between the players and the reporters by the time Alf turned to me and said, 'Well, Bobby, what did you think of the tour?'

I said that after six years and fifty-five caps with England I could say, despite the results – the best of which in South America was a draw with Portugal – it was the most enjoyable and satisfying I had experienced. I told him I loved the way we were developing as a team, how Bobby Moore was growing so easily into the captaincy, how George Cohen and Ray Wilson were striking up such great understanding as the new full-back pairing and how much security Gordon Banks had injected into our defence.

We had the superb goalscoring instinct of Jimmy Greaves, Johnny 'Budgie' Byrne had also displayed a wonderful touch recently with his hat-trick in Lisbon and George Eastham continued to make his claims with much guile and skill. As each day passed I felt more confident that we were on course for a good performance in the World Cup.

We were developing a system perfectly geared to our strengths and on the training field the work had never seemed less like a chore to be endured rather than benefited from.

And then, in what I meant to be an aside, I added, 'But of course, Alf, it has been a very long, tough tour and I've really missed my wife and daughter. I will be very glad to see them.'

I was shocked by his response. A very hard expression came to his face as he said, 'If I'd thought that was your attitude I wouldn't have brought you on the trip.'

There, in a moment, was the driven Alf, the man whose inner feelings had for long been so elusive to all but his wife Vicky. Beside me, suddenly, was not the guardian of all my hopes for success with England but the man who could just as suddenly become a stranger, someone who kept a distance from all those who wanted to know more about his progress from humble beginnings in Dagenham, how it was that he had become so single-minded in his thinking and his attitudes towards both life and the game of football. So much of the former he had always kept hidden but never before had his ability to draw a line between them been expressed so starkly.

However long I worked with Alf, and saw him on the social occasions that accumulated when our direct involvement with England was over, there would always be some of him residing in another and quite inaccessible place.

At times he could be engaging and funny, sometimes away from the public gaze he would relax quite thoroughly, have a drink and show that he could celebrate his victories as heartily as anyone. In the right setting, and in the right mood, he was happy enough to do his version of the Lambeth Walk. But always there was this other Alf, watchful for a perceived slight, some evidence that he hadn't carried with him all his listeners and, most crucially, all his players.

This, as I learned in Rio, could be troubling but then I also have to say that over the next two years it became progressively easier to understand the apparent contradiction between the devotion he had for his wife and their daughter, and how he so obviously cherished his time with them, and what had seemed to me the mad assertion he made on a night intended for some welcome relaxation.

Was he really saying that however dedicated a player, however intense his commitment to the future of the team, he was wrong to be distracted by even a passing thought of his personal life? Was he really relegating the importance of those feelings which could never in the end really be governed by the result of a single football match – or even a whole series of them?

Time would tell me that he really wasn't doing that.

Time – and his absolute refusal to milk any of the personal glory that came when his methods and, if you like, those obsessions brought ultimate success.

Then, he retreated to the rewards of his own private life and he seemed to be saying, 'Look, all I asked you to do, all the sacrifices you had to make, were for your benefit – so that one day you could tell yourself, and your families, that you had done something that required tremendous concentration, a single, uncluttered vision of what was in front of you for a few years. And then it could be enjoyed by both you and your families for the rest of your lives. You would never have to look back with the terrible regret that you might have done more. And, if I have learned anything in life and football, there is none greater than that.'

That, though, I have to admit, was not quite the philosophical understanding I took back to the hotel room before packing for home – and those pleasures which my yearning for had been so brusquely and roughly chastised.

Yet again, though, the more I thought about it – and once again there was plenty of time for reflection on another of those marathon flights which always seemed, at one stage or another, to lead me to some new assessment of where I was and what the future might hold out for me – the more I concluded that with Alf you had to work out a very important equation.

Mine, maybe inevitably given all my long-held ambitions to succeed in the England shirt, was that it was important to take the very best of him and live, and work, with the rest as comfortably as it was possible.

Certainly there was no shortage of examples of the best of him on that homeward flight.

High among them was Alf's wonderfully clear and practical

preparation for that watershed victory over Czechoslovakia a year earlier. It still shone in my mind as a masterpiece of clarity, a simple but persuasive statement of how we should proceed, and how we did that was not only to beat one of the world's most respected teams on their own soil but set a pattern for ourselves we now could see might well bring the highest rewards.

We had been given an example of hard but easily absorbed professionalism that had never been available to England in the days of Walter Winterbottom's theory. This wasn't because Walter was without knowledge, and certainly not because he lacked intelligence, but the fact that none of it was touched by the fears and the insecurities that sooner or later come to someone who plays the game for a living, who will always be in some corner of his mind only as strong as his last performance.

By comparison, Alf seemed to be saying, 'Look, I've been here, I've been in your place – I know what you need to know about operating at this level. It is never going to be easy, there are always going to be questions in your mind. We have to answer as many as we can before it is too late.'

As we went into the training session, Alf said, 'I want you all to go to the positions that you would take up naturally before the start of the game.' After we did this, he said, 'Right, now I'll tell you where I want you to be.'

Position by position, he worked through the team. No one was left in any doubt about what was expected of them. Banks had to be aware of every possibility provoked by a Brazilian free-kick. Every defender could never for a second be unaware of his position and his immediate duties. Before a match I had to familiarise myself with the sweep of the pitch, make myself feel at home.

But then there was nothing of the schoolmaster about the style and delivery of the instructions. The practicalities, the good of sense of them, were in their way not a burden but a kind of liberation.

He was always at pains to say that each player he had called up had already proved to him his capabilities. Each had gone beyond the need for any refreshment from him on the basic demands of his job. What was happening now was a honing of individual responsibilities and how they could best benefit the team.

What we were all working on now, he never stopped stressing, was a swift understanding of the needs, and the nuances, of a newly assembled team – and one that because of the demands of club football could never work together frequently enough for his liking.

Some old habits had to be dropped, some new ones had to be installed. It was a development, in calmer circumstances, of the point he had made so angrily to Gordon Banks, a player who had already convinced him of his value, when Brazil scored their goal from the free-kick at Wembley. The attitudes that created the climate for error, for needless mistakes, had to be eliminated, one by one.

Many years later he made an assessment of George Cohen, which threw considerable light on the way he judged the potential of all candidates for a place in his team. George had just suffered his career-wrecking injury at Craven Cottage and Alf reflected on what proved to be one of the most valuable contributions to his winning campaign.

He said, 'I was told that when George came back from an Under-23 tour in 1960 he said, "That's me, finished." He knew that by the time the next match came along he would be overage and the conclusion was that he was not considered good enough for the senior team. How wrong he was.

'He had all the qualities required of an international player, particularly in defence. When he went forward his finishing was perhaps not all that could be desired. However, this was not how he should have been judged. He was a serious-minded young man, dedicated to his task. Playing against him must have been a very frustrating experience. I was always grateful to him for the job he did for me. His injury cost the game an outstanding player while he was still at his peak.'

By the time we reached Rio, Alf had already resolved some important challenges to the power of his assessment of individual players and they were embodied in that tribute. George had made his mark with some impressive performances and, not least, in the determination he showed when he refused to follow the doctor's advice and strode out with his team-mates for the second half against Brazil. It was an unforgettable example of one player's absolute resolve to get to the end of the road.

George had a few odd ways; he was the warmest of team-mates but often he could be, well, just a little unfathomable. One of his most unshakeable habits was to take his clothes off and have a shower as soon as he walked into the dressing room before every international game. At first I would say, 'George, what on earth are you doing? Surely you shower after the game. You are doing something none of us understand.'

He would frown and say, 'Bobby, this is what I do, it is part of what I am and it has worked very well for me so far.' He would then go off for his shower and when he returned he would immediately launch himself into a private ritual of preparation. He would do a series of push-ups and when they were over he ran on the spot, very vigorously and for quite some time. With each new contact I grew increasingly fond of him. It is an affection which survives strongly to this day and whenever I'm in London I try to see him and his wife Daphne.

He is an unchanging presence in my life and when you reach a certain age this becomes the most precious of contacts. It reminds you of some of the best of your experience – and that which was so vital to any success you might enjoy.

I still see him about his rituals, disappearing into the shower oblivious to the cries of 'bloody hell, George, what are you up to now?' As he would be in later life, when he had to fight so hard for his health and his business life, George was unswerving. He ran so hard and if his finishing skill was not the greatest he was never discouraged – even when a team-mate said something like, 'George, I never had an idea you were going to do that' and quite often it wasn't something anyone would have been proud of. Nor when his Fulham team-mate said that when he crossed the ball he hit more photographers than Frank Sinatra. But then no one doubted that George would march triumphantly through such ribbing.

He was simply locked into a commitment which became one of the staples of our effort. You could no more shake it out of him that you could get him to alter his pre-match formula or intrude into his self-absorption in that vital mental preparation before the kick-off. No one could have been more part of the team but, first, he had to be himself.

He still represents to me the very essence of what Alf was striving to achieve. It was a total immersion in the idea that we all had to push ourselves harder than we had ever done before and he would do it his way. He knew that if Alf was emphatic about how a player should perform on the field, he wouldn't dream of interfering with a rhythm of personal preparation which so plainly worked.

And so George pounded his way to the greatest day of our football lives. He had his shower, he did his push-ups, he ran on the spot, and then in the moments before we were called to the field he would take off his vest, put it back on again, and then slip on his shirt and shorts. Sometimes he would say, with a small smile, 'I'm ready now.'

George's assessment of Alf, his understanding of what made him so effective, has always chimed perfectly with mine. This was never more so than when he said, 'What was so impressive about Alf when he took charge of the England squad was that there was no player bigger than him, unlike Haynes with Winterbottom or Keegan with Revie and Greenwood. He was strong on discipline – but it was subtle. He advised you to go to bed early but he never demanded. But when he said, "I'd like you to be in by such and such a time" it was like paying the rates. You couldn't avoid it. He could be a very kind person and thoughtful and he displayed a dry wit. Most of the time it was easy to like him. He was very fond of his jellied eels and brown ale.'

Much later my United team-mate John Connelly, who for all his ability and competitive character would never make himself as integral to Alf's plans as the late-challenging George, delivered a similar verdict. He said, 'You could never truly weigh him up, never reckon him. Yet I always wished I could have played under him at a club. He brought the best out of you. He had different ways of getting to you – and sometimes they could be quite gentle. Other times, less so.

'Once when the ball ran out when we were playing at Hampden I went and fetched it and threw it to a Scot. They took a quick throw, went down the line and damn near scored. Watching the video afterwards Alf said to the rest of the lads. "Just watch this pillock. What do you think of that, running after the ball for an effing Scotsman."'

That lingered powerfully in John's mind, plainly, and for me it was another reminder of the difference between Alf and Walter Winterbottom. The language was not the same – and nor were the competitive instincts.

That was the most fundamental difference between the two men. Alf talked about the game always with a hard edge – like a real club pro. Alf had been one, he had immersed himself in all the nuances of being a pro, of thinking a little harder than the man he faced. He honed his own strengths, the greatest in his case being an ability to open the play for some very creative teammates with passes of the highest quality, and he worked slavishly to obscure his greatest weakness, which was a lack of true pace.

He never said an opponent was good unless he had proved that to him completely. He put so much thought into his verdicts and this sometimes made him very difficult to approach with opinions. But this was almost certainly right. It is so often true that the players don't know best. Their ideas are so often shaped by a single perspective – their own.

It meant that I never saw him influenced by the view or the pleadings of an individual player. The growth of individuals was never his priority. He always assumed that would be the inevitable result of the growth of the team. He was always after what made a team rather than individuals and as the weeks slipped into months and then the years which separated him from the dawn of his challenge to its possible completion, this was always the growing pressure even such a great player as Jimmy Greaves had to deal with.

For myself I just could not imagine being outside of Alf's chosen ones. If the possibility arose even in a corner of my mind it would bring the fearful chill of a great, impending loss.

One certainty was that if Alf was going to be hanged, it would be as the result of his own decisions. I have seen managers influenced by players and I've never thought of it as healthy.

He made you feel that you had been picked because you were a good player and he always talked more about what you needed to be successful. In Bratislava he insisted on my training on that part of the pitch on which I would be playing. I should get in some corner kicks to get the feel of the run-up. He was meticulous. Yet although I respected him, and liked him, I've never really known anyone, apart from perhaps his wife, who really knew him. He could be so obstinate you knew right away that you had no chance of shifting him.

Once he got over his exhilaration at being called to the squad, and playing his first few matches, my brother Jack was most impressed by Alf's ability to shape a group of players into such a strong sense of a common effort – and mutual respect. He contrasted Alf's style with that of Don Revie, his boss at Leeds United and the other most influential manager in his life.

Revie was famous, or notorious, according to your turn of mind, for his elaborate pre-match dossiers and intense indoctrination of his players, one notable example being the time he told the great Scottish midfielder Billy Bremner to get down on his knees and thank God for all the blessings that had come his way. By comparison, Alf was much more economic with his words and his emotions.

Recalling the time he asked Alf why he had picked him out, Jack said, 'He told me it was because I was tall and good in the air and was mobile and could tackle. He knew how he wanted to play and he went out to get the right players for his needs – not necessarily the most gifted ones but those most right for his plans.

'There was enormous pressure on him from the media, especially the London press. It's easy to see how a manager's mind can be inundated with the names of players he has not seen, or not had a chance to properly assess. But Alf's reaction to this situation was always the same. "Don't tell me, I'll tell you," he said.

'He had a feel for players. In a real team you can't have stirrers around. If there's someone you don't trust, you get rid of him. They were just about totally absent from his squad. I never ever heard one player questioning the merits of another, whether he should or shouldn't be in. Alf was totally different to Don Revie, he achieved what he did with just a few words.'

That, certainly, but also an increasingly ruthless willingness to make the hardest decisions. Now that Gordon Banks had surpassed Ron Springett in Alf's mind, George Cohen had won his battle with the extremely talented Armfield and formed such a promising partnership with my pal Ray Wilson, the task was clear enough. Alf had to put in place the final pillars of defence – and then deal with the great dilemma of his reign, getting right the balance between players of creativity and those more mindful of other, less thrilling duties. Soon enough this would carry him into the agonies of Jimmy Greaves's career crisis and the kind of controversial debate which might have unnerved, even broken, a less self-confident man.

In the meantime, however, there was the accumulation of certainties which had names like Moore and Banks, Cohen and Wilson and Stiles and Charlton, J.

As to Charlton, R., there was a never a moment right up to the last pages of the story when I was able to tell myself that I was guaranteed a place. I never had that assurance from Alf and I never expected it but then I could see clearly the value of the commitment the manager was asking of all his players. I didn't want to imagine the devastation I would have felt if Alf had taken me to one side, perhaps in a corner of Hendon Hall or in the cabin of an aircraft, and said that I had failed my test.

It would have been – I can see as clearly now as I did more than fifty years ago – the disaster of my football life. It would have thrust me into a very cold place indeed, one stripped of that which deep down we all most need from life.

I didn't want to contemplate the loss of that wonderful sense of expectation which comes when you feel part of something that may well have laid a claim on the future. I didn't want to surrender the chance of being part of an achievement that would last for ever.

That didn't lessen my joy when I embraced my wife and daughter after that long haul through Europe and the United States and South America. But then maybe I also had to concede that Alf had been right to point out quite what it takes when you seek to elect yourself to a team of champions.

5. Jack and Nobby

When Jack and Nobby joined us so exuberantly in the April of 1965 – their eyes shining like those of boys out on their first adventure – England's march to the World Cup had, we would know soon enough, reached one of its most significant milestones.

The foundation of the proposed team of champions had been laid down and now it could be examined, shaken and pounded in its entirety. However many times Alf did this he made no attempt to disguise his confidence that it would hold.

The first six names on the team sheet for the World Cup final fourteen months later would be the same as those for Scotland's visit to Wembley, a challenge which would always occupy a special place in our manager's competitive vision. It was a 2-2 draw despite the fact that we finished with just nine fit players and I was required to move to left-back, which was a brief development that Alf was quick to point out, and as dryly as I expected, would play no part in his master plan.

Here, despite his well-earned reputation as a full-back of great craft and creative instinct, was the unveiling of our manager's first principle: before anything else, a winning team must be able to defend.

Here too was the first solid and, as it would turn out, immutable raft of the Ramsey calculations: Banks, Cohen, Wilson, J. Charlton, Moore and Stiles. There were other questions to be resolved, finely balanced choices to be made, but none of them would concern defensive deployment. That matter, most certainly, had been resolved

A vital, and he would say fundamental, stage of his work was, barring accident, complete. He believed that after two years of trial and error and an increasingly encouraging trend of performance he had gained the first strong foothold on success: he had a set of defenders he would continue to hone to his needs but now he could proceed with this crucial task in an atmosphere of mutual trust.

In the time between a 1-1 draw against Holland in Amsterdam and the Scotland game four months later, Alf had settled on his new defensive order. He had done it against the knowledge that the completed unit needed time to knit together. In the attacking aspects of midfield and at the front, he decided, there were still opportunities for considerable experimentation. But at the back certainties had to be imposed without any further delay.

Banks, inevitably, was returned to goal in place of Tony Waiters of Blackpool, and Bobby Moore also automatically reappeared as captain and central defender along with Ray Wilson at left-back. This meant that George Cohen was the only defensive survivor of the Dutch game. For Bobby Thompson, the strong Wolves full-back, and such notable performers as Alan Mullery, Maurice Norman and Ron Flowers, it was the discouraging hint they were no longer prime contenders.

There would, still, be time for a few missteps. The following autumn we lost 3-2 to Austria, which was only England's third defeat on home soil, and a rare mistake by Nobby contributed to one of the Austrian goals.

After the game Alf was besieged by reporters wanting to know quite what had happened to the World Cup strategy. However, they were infuriated by his refusal to concede that the result constituted anything approaching a crisis less than a year before the opening of the World Cup.

'I'm disappointed by the result,' he said, 'but I'm not very disappointed. Overall, I'm happy with our progress. We have a lot of good things in place.'

One of them, much to my encouragement, was that he was particularly happy with my performance as an attacking midfielder. Such assurances, coming from Alf, always carried a considerable measure of extra weight. However well you liked to think you had played, and however much encouragement you received from your team-mates and the media, it was always his approval which you valued most highly.

Looking back, it is hard not to see that a touch of hysteria had become part of the intense monitoring of our campaign. Jimmy Hill, who had become the doyen of TV football criticism, went as far as declaring, 'We will not win anything with this lot.'

Against this sceptical background, Alf could hardly have been blamed for retreating into an ivory tower. Had he cared to, he could have pointed out that before the mishap against Austria we had gone ten games without defeat since losing to an extremely impressive Argentina by one goal in Rio the summer before last.

Jack and me signing autographs after a training session.

Front row (left to right): Jack Charlton, Keith Newton, Alan Ball, Geoff Hurst, Bobby Charlton, Bobby Moore; back row: George Cohen, Nobby Stiles, Joe Baker, Peter Thompson, Gordon Banks, George Eastham, Ron Springett, Gordon Milne, Ron Flowers, Ray Wilson, Paul Reaney, Jimmy Greaves, Gordon Harris, Norman Hunter, Roger Hunt, assistant coach Harold Shepherdson.

Top: The 1966 World Cup squad getting ready for our team photo.

Bottom left: Being put through our paces at Lilleshall training camp.

Bottom right: We had a few laughs too, here Nobby Stiles and Alan Ball relieve the pressure with some tomfoolery.

Top: At last, our (and my) first goal at the World Cup. We went on to beat Mexico 2–0.

Bottom left: England v Mexico on 16 July. Mexico's goalkeeper Ignacio Calderón punches the ball away from Jack.

Bottom right: On our way out to face France on 20 July in our final group game.

Top: An unforgettably-scarred game against Argentina on 23 July.
Captain Antonio Rattín refuses to leave the pitch after his red card.

Bottom: Jubilation as Geoff Hurst's goal puts us through to the semi-finals after we win 1–0.

Top: We faced Portugal on 26 July and here Alan Ball (second left), me (third left) and Roger Hunt (second right) celebrate my opening goal, to the disappointment of José Pereira (third right), Mário Coluna (right) and Hilário (left).

Bottom: The great Eusébio and my friend Nobby Stiles duel for the ball.

Top: Our second goal, and we're through to the World Cup final.

Bottom left: Eusébio is consoled by his teammates. A wonderful player, a wonderful game.

Bottom right: Relief and delight from Gordon Banks and Nobby.

Top: We had some time to relax in between games. Here Jack, my mother Cissie, and I celebrate our passage through to the World Cup final.

Bottom left: Time for a spot of cricket in a friendly match at Roehampton.

Bottom right: A round of golf during a break in training the day before the final.

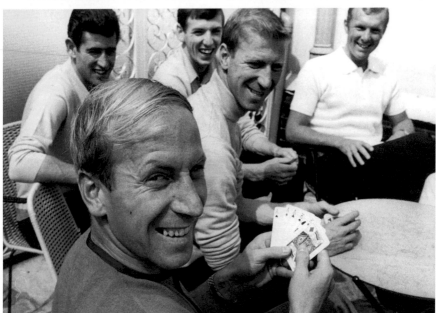

Top: A visit to Pinewood Studios and the set of *You Only Live Twice*. Jimmy Greaves (left) and Bobby Moore (right) meet Sean Connery and Yul Brynner.

Bottom: We enjoyed a few games of cards, this time I had a full house against (left to right) Peter Bonetti, Martin Peters, Jack and Bobby.

As it was, he would soon enough have plenty of reasons to feel vindicated in his confidence before the opening of the World Cup in eight months. And also, perhaps, in his decision to 'invite outside' one of his most persistent critics, Eric Cooper, who had a big readership for his billing as the *Daily Express*'s Voice of the North. He had written a scathing piece under the headline 'It's Hokey Cokey, Alf' after the draw in Amsterdam which presaged the arrival of Jack and Nobby.

Cooper's reference was to the nursery song which goes, 'You put your right foot in, Your right foot out, In out, In out, Shake it all about, You do the Hokey Cokey, And you turn around, That's what it's all about.' After his long months of careful analysis of the team's potential, and his hard decisions about the qualities of individual players, Alf, the relentlessly self-taught professional, was incensed by such open, and in his opinion ill-informed, mockery. Perhaps fortunately, Eric declined the invitation with thanks.

But then if Alf didn't get the chance to express himself physically, he was soon able to effectively stem that swiftly risen tide of doubt and criticism.

We would go another ten games without defeat before the World Cup curtain was raised, winning nine of them, with an aggregate of twenty-three goals to six, six clean sheets and claiming such formidable scalps as Spain, in Madrid, and West Germany at Wembley, when Nobby scored his one international goal.

What couldn't be defined by statistics, though, was the interior life of a team learning about itself, beginning to understand its own developing potential.

For me the arrival of Jack and Nobby brought an especially warm feeling. For one thing, I was being joined by two new

England team-mates in whom I had always recognised superb competitive instincts. For another, I could also tell myself that I had the company not only of a growing band of close and stalwart team-mates but of brothers, Jack, who had shared my youth and my hopes back in the North East, and Nobby, who I had already come to love with an intensity that still grips me to this day.

Both were so overjoyed by their selection they could scarcely contain their feelings. They were like young warriors called to action for which they had long yearned.

Jack, nearing thirty, made that emotional announcement to me when he burst into the United dressing room just after his Leeds United had beaten us in an FA Cup semi-final and some of my club-mates made it clear quite bluntly that he was in danger of overstaying his welcome. Nobby wore a blissful expression from the moment he got the call, right up to attempting to shake hands with our great United colleague Denis Law before the Wembley kick-off and being told, 'Eff off, you little English bastard.'

Afterwards, Nobby confided that the exchange had removed his last qualm about kicking his esteemed team-mate up in the air whenever the occasion demanded.

It has to be said, though, that not everyone in English football shared my enthusiasm for Nobby's elevation to a potentially key role in the World Cup crusade. Some, including many years later such a weighty figure as Brian Clough's European Cup-winning lieutenant and a future international manager Martin O'Neil, suggested that by picking Nobby, Alf was turning towards the cultivation of thuggery.

Right from the start, I saw that as a travesty of football judgement. Nobby played with passion, and an extremely hard edge, but in my view he always displayed the heart – and the tactical brain – of someone who both loved and understood the game right down to the core of his being.

I could give you a thousand examples of how graphically he conveyed his feelings for the game and the football club which had brought us together – and quite how deeply they were rooted in some of his earliest experiences.

He made me familiar with his Manchester. He took me down the streets of his native Collyhurst, where he was born in the cellar of his family's two-up, two-down terraced house during a bombing raid by the Luftwaffe. He showed me the old abandoned cemetery where he and his friends had played football amid the upturned gravestones. He showed me the football field made out of waste land by his father Charlie, an undertaker, and some of his friends. He took me into so much of his past that it made it that much easier for me to understand the force of his desire to succeed when he put on the shirts of Manchester United and England.

Most affecting, for me at least, was the detail of his memory of the most dramatic day of my own life.

Four years younger than me, he gave a haunting account of how it was back at Old Trafford when he and his fellow apprentices were told to go home and await the facts of an 'incident' involving the first team at Munich airport.

'The sixth of February 1958,' he said, 'was supposed to be just another shift at the football dream factory. It was a frosty morning, the kind that when I was an altar boy kept me in bed for an extra half an hour when I knew the stern Canon Early was saying mass. I took the usual 112 bus for the forty-five-minute ride from my home in Collyhurst to Trafford Bar. There the bus crew changed for the final leg that took me to the ground.

'Inevitably much of the talk on the bus concerned United,

particularly so that morning. The day before, the first team had qualified for the European Cup final, drawing 3-3 with the fine Red Star team in Belgrade. The team, despite its youth, was growing before everyone's eyes. On the previous Saturday they had beaten Arsenal 5-4 in one of the most thrilling games ever seen at Highbury. For so many people in Manchester they were young gods and when I heard the talk on the buses and in the street I swelled with pride.

'I knew these gods. I ran for their bacon sarnies. I had pleaded successfully for their autographs. I cleaned their boots. I watched, up close and enthralled, as they played in baseball boots on a stretch of concrete beside Old Trafford on Friday afternoons, twenty-two of them shouting and joking and showing bits of skill and creating a world I couldn't wait to be part of.'

Nobby's passion for the game and his love of United still glow in every line of his report and maybe the desolation he felt and expressed so vividly when he learned that the misadventure of Munich had brought such terrible consequences, and which so mirrored my own at the dreadful scene, was the first and most enduring of our bonds.

This is how he described the impact of the confirmation of all the devastating facts. 'I found out what happened on the way home when I changed buses in the centre of town. I went up to the newspaper seller and bought a copy of the *Evening Chronicle*. It was strange seeing the faces of Roger Byrne, Geoff Bent, Eddie Colman, Mark Jones, David Pegg, Tommy Taylor and Liam Whelan staring out of the front page. They belonged at the back of the paper. But they were dead. "Coly" was dead. He couldn't be dead. I cleaned his boots. None of them could be dead, but especially not Coly. But that's what the *Chronicle* was saying in big black headlines.

'I felt sick. Everything seemed normal enough. The streets and the shops looked just the same. The sun was presumably still up there beyond the low leaden sky.

'I knew no one would be at home. My mum and my dad and my brother Charlie would be working. I couldn't face the empty house. When I got off the bus I walked across Rochdale Road and down Livesey Street and into the church. You could just walk into a church in those days. They're all locked up now. I prayed and I prayed that the *Chronicle* had got it all wrong. I prayed and I wept. I sat back in the pew for a long time. It could have been an hour or two, I don't really know. There was no one else in the church.

'Then I went home. The house, as I expected, was empty. The lads were dead, or so I had read, but people still had to work. I put the dinner in the oven.

'The rest of the day and night is mostly a blur. I remember my father calling Jimmy Murphy, Matt Busby's right-hand man who hadn't made the trip to Belgrade, hadn't sat on the runway while the plane was refuelled and the wings froze over, and telling him that he had a car at his disposal. My dad ran Jimmy to all the funerals.

'That's all we seemed to be doing for weeks, going to funerals. I served on the altar for several requiem masses. Not Coly's. I went to his funeral and was surprised to learn that he wasn't a Catholic, not that it mattered. Coly was dead. It kept coming into my head but it wouldn't stay there. For a long time it was a shock which greeted each new day. It was devastation. I'd given his boots their last shine. I'd never see him moving upfield so smoothly, so quickly, despite carrying a bit of podge. That was his body type but it didn't affect his game.

'He could leave his marker with an easy change of pace and great control. He could really motor when he decided to go forward and I tried to copy everything he did on the field. Later, when I scored my first goal for United – against Newcastle – I was proud for lots of reasons but the biggest one was that I thought it showed a touch of Coly. I broke quickly and sent the ball into the top corner of the net. It was a nice goal for a kid to dedicate to his hero.'

In these words I believe we find the essence of my beloved Nobby. If he played tough, and overcame some formidable obstacles to any kind of athletic success, it never coarsened the nature of a man who, for all his ferocious reputation, ultimately always found it easier to love than to hate.

Most touching of all, for me, was his passion to play. My, he wanted to play. He was far more able as a player of insight and skill than many of his critics allowed, but inevitably it was the force of his tackling, and the absolute commitment of his approach, which drew most attention. In the World Cup he would endure, but survive, one great controversy and two years later he near miraculously avoided another when we were side by side at the Bernabéu against Real Madrid to win a desperate battle to make it to the European Cup final against Benfica.

What he did was guaranteed to offend the purists and it was also true that one or two of his team-mates were also left aghast. His job was to man-mark the quick and clever winger Amaro Amancio.

Amancio was something of a reincarnation of the great Francisco Gento in his speed and crossing ability and he was also extremely subtle – on and off the ball. After scoring a first-half goal which helped wipe out our lead from the first leg – by the interval they were winning the game 3-1 and looking good enough to make irrelevant the fact that they had failed to score in the away leg at Old Trafford – Amancio struck another cruel blow. He kicked Nobby hard on the thigh as most people's attention, including most crucially that of the match officials, centred on our goalkeeper Alex Stepney clearing our lines.

Nobby's thigh tightened ominously and he feared that he would finish the game a badly hobbling passenger, quite unable to curb the menace of Amancio. As that apprehension hardened, it was then that he repaid the winger in kind. With the most serious action elsewhere, he knocked Amancio down before running to the referee and pointing out that the Spaniard was down. 'He's injured, ref,' said Nobby most earnestly.

The great stadium howled its displeasure but Nobby's gamble that, like Amancio earlier, he would escape the gaze of the referee and linesmen was a winning one and, whatever the morality of what he did – he could, of course, as a good altar boy, quote from the Bible about an eye for an eye, a tooth for a tooth – there was no doubt it was a huge contribution to our progress to the final. That was confirmed when Bill Foulkes, who formed a superb partnership with Nobby in central defence, made a rare foray upfield to score one of two late goals, the other one coming from David Sadler.

On the way home Nobby confided that he was still appalled by the possibility that he might have been sent off. 'Can you imagine the headlines?' he said. 'However, I knew my thigh was tightening despite the heat treatment at half-time. I reckoned I just had to take the chance.'

There was no censure from Sir Matt Busby. He had reached his goal of a place in the European Cup final and, no doubt, he realised that Nobby's decision was a big, perhaps even the most vital, contribution. The Old Man, as I came to refer to the founder of the great Old Trafford tradition, always preached on behalf of a beautiful game, always sought to surround himself with the most gifted players. But he was also a practical man who grew up in the Lanarkshire coalfield after losing his father on the Somme. So, perhaps, no one knew better that amid all the beauty sometimes it was necessary to inject a touch of iron.

No doubt Alf had considered such a reality when he called up Nobby. He had also requested a number of character references and all of them, including the one I offered, spoke of his exceptional determination to succeed as a top-flight player.

Nobby had conquered some considerable concerns about his physical capacity to play at the highest level. He was tough, but he was also small and not the least of his problems was extreme short-sightedness. That he found a solution, which brought so much relief he had to restrain himself from dancing down Manchester's thoroughfare of Deansgate some years before his unforgettable jig of celebration at Wembley, was largely through the perception of our Irish goalkeeper, Harry Gregg, the hero of Munich.

Harry was a fiercely emotional and often combative figure but, as Nobby would have great reason never to lose sight of, he also had an extremely kind heart. He saw, more clearly than anyone else at the club, or in Nobby's life up until that point, that his problem represented much more than an inconvenience, and an embarrassment, that went back to his days of rubbing his eyes against blurred vision as he tried to read the exercise books in his primary school classroom.

The extent of Nobby's crisis, which he had come to believe was the reason for his only sporadic first-team appearances in the early sixties and the loss of his place in the 1963 final against Leicester City, became apparent to Harry during a card game as the team travelled by train to an away fixture.

Afterwards, he said to Busby, 'You know, boss, you just have to do something about Nobby's eyesight. The kid is living his life half blind. He's really struggling. He was putting down the wrong cards. He just couldn't read them. We can only imagine how it is affecting his play.'

It was much later when Nobby revealed the scale of his anguish – and his fears. He said, 'You come to terms with a problem like that and, certainly back in those days, you just hoped that you would be able to get by. Deep down, though, I knew I had a terrible problem. Between my debut in 1960 and my omission from that Cup final and flirtation with a transfer request, I would have one good game and then slip back into the reserves.

'The problem came to a head in my own mind during a match against Everton at Goodison Park. I went to receive a throw-in and I suddenly realised I was guessing when it came to the timing of the ball and to where and to whom I was going to play it. I was given a man to mark and in the flow of the game I frequently lost sight of him. It was a terrible shock but maybe out of fear of what I would be told if I raised the problem with Busby and was sent to see an eye specialist I kept quiet. I would try to get along in the fog.'

Hearing those words gave me a new insight into quite the amount of difficult terrain Nobby had covered by the time he reported for England duty at Hendon Hall, his contact lenses carefully in place for what he deemed one of the most important appointments of his life.

Nobby's problems registered strongly in someone like me who had always taken his physical gifts, if not for granted, as assets supplied in the cradle, and came with the solitary demand of making the most of them, which of course for me would always be as much a pleasure as a duty. For Nobby there was no such luxury and I could only admire his determination all the more. He had got the better of what might easily have been an insurmountable barrier to his highest hopes.

Once as a boy he had been alarmed to discover that his father's undertaking duties had required a body to be kept overnight in the cellar where he had been born. He was reassured by his mother, Kitty, who said, 'Nobby, love, it's not the dead ones you have to worry about.'

If that gave the boy some reassurance, it was nothing to the uplift he felt when he left the eye specialist's surgery with his new contact lenses.

Again, his recall of that liberating experience touched me deeply. Nobby remembered how the world had suddenly become a new and wondrous place. He reported, 'First, I discovered in those posh consulting rooms that there was no easy cure. I had to wear big, hard contact lenses and squirt blue lubricating fluid into my eyes. I also realised when I walked out on to Deansgate that I would have to relearn the most basic steps I had made in the game. They put the big things in my eyes and told me to go out and have a walk.

'I'll never forget walking down Deansgate that time. Everything was so clear. Suddenly, Manchester was a brilliant place of clean lines. The sky was the most vivid blue. The clouds were white and fluffy. The ends of the buildings were clearly defined. Everything was so sharp. But then I did find myself stepping off the curbside a foot too soon and when I started playing again I was guilty of some horrible mis-calculations.'

It was a hard period of rehabilitation and a lesser man might not have made it. It took him some time to adapt to the contact lenses which were in an early stage of their development. He complained that his eyes dried out for a lack of oxygen and often he would have dark panda rings around them. He fell away as a first-team contender for a while but, step by step, he came back and before the end of '64 he had with growing assurance brought his game to a vital mix of clear vision and the sharpest of timing.

Still, though, it seemed to me that everything was just a little harder for my friend. It seemed to be his fate that nothing he wanted to achieve would be simple or straightforward. He had to battle it out, prove to himself and those who sat in judgement of him that indeed he deserved any success that came his way. So it was when he made his final step into the England team.

The door was opened to him by Alf in February 1965 when he picked Nobby for the Under-23 team to play Scotland in Aberdeen. He would be pitched against an impressive Scottish team which included such stars as Billy Bremner of Leeds United and Charlie Cooke, but then quickly enough it was clear this was the least of his challenges. The complication was that United were due to play an important league match the night before the Under-23 game and Matt Busby said that he needed one of his key defenders. Nobby was required to tell the England manager, who it seemed likely was considering him for a place in his World Cup squad, that he had to be scratched from his team.

It was a terrible dilemma for Nobby, and one compounded when his wife Kay, the sister of Johnny Giles and at difficult times no less feisty than her brother, insisted that the manly thing to do was defy the esteemed manager of Manchester United. That was the agonising decision Nobby made before calling Busby – and hearing the great man's phone crash back on its cradle when he was told that his player was going to take his chance with England.

Unfortunately, Nobby's torment did not end there. At half-time in Aberdeen, Alf pointed out to him that Cooke was creating a lot of problems and he was certainly in need of some close attention. This Nobby applied with his usual zeal but again the situation was not as straightforward as it might have seemed. In the turmoil of his decision to reject Busby's command, he had travelled to Aberdeen without the fluid for his contact lenses, and it was a critical omission. When Nobby thought he had left Cooke in a heap after a fierce tackle, he received a tap on the shoulder from his team-mate Norman Hunter.

'What do you think you're doing?' Hunter asked. 'I'm doing what Alf asked,' said Nobby. 'I'm attending to Charlie Cooke.'

Hunter's reply was chilling. 'No, you're not, you've just flattened Billy Bremner.'

Nobby and the great Scottish midfielder would regularly chuckle over the incident and my friend told the story himself once again when we travelled over the Pennines to Billy's funeral in Doncaster more than thirty years later. After the game in Aberdeen, Nobby explained the problem to Alf and assured him it would never happen again.

What he could never do, of course, was give anyone, in any situation, a categorical guarantee that he was immune from the possibility of some kind of mishap off the field.

Once he came close to demolishing a hotel room we shared in London. He did it innocently, with the demeanour of a victim of outrageous ill fortune. First, he pulled down a set of curtains while drawing them in the morning to inspect the dawn. Then he bumped into, and knocked down, a radio attached to the wall. I packed my bag as quickly as I could, not such an easy task given the tears of laughter which filled my eyes.

On another occasion they came in a gale when he described the repercussions of a collision he had while driving down Market Street in Manchester. When he bent down to inspect the damage he inadvertently head-butted the other driver. As he told it, once again he was simply trapped by another conspiracy of fate.

Because of this clumsiness that was guaranteed to provoke so much hilarity – the sports writer Hugh McIlvanney once commented, 'by comparison with Nobby, Inspector Clouseau was blessedly adroit' – the impact of his efficiency on the field was so often all the greater. It was evident, paradoxically enough, in the brilliance of his timing in tackling and unerring ability to read the flow of a game.

Early in his career he determined these were his greatest strengths and there was no doubt they were the qualities that Alf found so compelling. When Nobby received his call-up to the Under-23 team in Aberdeen, and was so clearly on trial as a potential member of the World Cup squad, he spoke with our Old Trafford colleague Wilf McGuinness who did some work for Alf as a trainer. Nobby asked Wilf to point out to Alf that the greatest momentum in his career had come with his switch to central defence and that it was here he might be of most help to England.

Though sceptical, Wilf said he would speak to the boss. Predictably, the word came back that Alf had his own ideas about how best to utilise Nobby's virtues. Nobby also had to understand that to win a place at the heart of the defence, rather than become its forward shield, he must surpass both Bobby Moore and the formidable Norman Hunter.

So Nobby played his game of brilliant foraging, of winning tackles and supplying the ball to his forwards at speed and with great accuracy. No one knew better than me the value of such service. Or valued higher the fact that, certainly in my belief, Nobby would not have made it to the England team under any other command than Alf's. Possibly the same was true of my brother Jack. It was Alf's genius to see certain players in certain situations where their strengths could be uniquely effective. It was the manager's great triumph to recognise substance over mere style.

Both Nobby and Jack had come through serious career difficulties, Nobby triumphing over his faulty eyesight and Jack having to battle so hard to convince his Leeds manager Don Revie that he could become one of the great professionals of his age. The result was in that spring of 1965 they came to the England team really wanting to play.

Sometimes on the field their relationship smouldered to the point of an explosion. Jack always remembered the first time he learned of the consequences of failing to impress Nobby with the consistency of your performance. He recalled: 'Once, when I lost my concentration for a second and made a mistake, all I could see was this little face coming at me from about thirty yards, breathing smoke and fire, and I remember turning away and thinking, "Oh, bloody hell, I've upset Nobby Stiles." '

No doubt he had but the depth of their respect for each other was never under serious threat and that included the time they squared up to each other quite ludicrously during a training session.

Both of them put in huge performances in the battle against Scotland, denying their opponents any chance of fully exploiting their two-man advantage in the second half. Gordon Banks was particularly taken with the fury of Nobby's game, which might have been a ninety-minute celebration of the fact that his error of mistaken identity in the Under-23 match had been quickly dismissed by Alf as he admired the intense commitment of his new player.

Banks noted, 'Nobby came into the game like a tiger. The way he tackled his Manchester United team-mates Denis Law and Pat Crerand made Alf realise here was a player totally committed to the England cause.'

There was indeed an instant rapport between the manager and his new player. Later, Nobby reflected, 'When I went out in that England shirt with the three lions it was brilliant. And I cannot say enough in favour of Alf Ramsey. I would have died for him. He was such a man of his word. I could not see a single weakness in his approach as a manager. He treated you like an adult. He never hectored or laid down the law – and he was an Englishman through and through. He hated the Scots. I remember just before I made my debut asking Budgie Byrne what was the difference between Alf and Walter Winterbottom.

'"The difference is," said Byrne, "when we're playing Scotland, Alf will say, 'Get into those Scotch bastards.'"'

But then if Alf appealed to Nobby's most warlike instincts,

he also had the ability to make clear the detail of his expectations. Like me, Nobby would soon enough note the difference between the styles of the men who would do most to shape our careers, Matt Busby and Alf Ramsey.

Busby would make his demands, tell you what he wanted to see, and he could be wonderfully inspiring at times, and especially when the team was under most pressure to deliver an outstanding performance. But he didn't explain any of it in the manner of Alf.

You listened intently to Alf because you knew it would be a big mistake to misinterpret anything he said. When we went to a room in Hendon Hall or some foreign hotel, usually after a light meal of poached eggs on toast, we always left the pre-game talk feeling secure in the knowledge that we had been perfectly prepared. We were insured against unwelcome surprises – and never in doubt about quite what was expected of each of us.

It was a state of mind that I knew, as surely as anything I had in all my life, would be both enlivened and strengthened by the arrival of my brother-in-arms, Nobby, and my other brother Jack.

6. Bond of the Blood

When Jack came to the team that spring day, and proceeded to display the qualities that had persuaded Alf to pick him before younger and perhaps more polished contenders, he provoked in me a burst of pride that ran very deeply. It went all the way back to our shared roots, and my first understanding of who I was and from where I came.

Our Kid's triumph was that of someone I thought I knew so well but who from time to time had made me feel that in some ways I didn't know at all. And down the years until then there had been plenty of evidence that he had felt pretty much the same way.

We had shared everything and at times could agree on hardly anything, at least not beyond the touchline of a football field.

Almost everyone who grew up with us in the North East said that in many ways we were indeed quite separate. Yet here we were, suddenly and at a relatively late age, pitched together again. As boys we had shared so much we had been obliged to share a bed. Now we would be together in the dressing room of the national team.

He had gained a status I had seen him grow into over the years and, despite the view of some hard critics, which at one point included his Leeds United manager Don Revie, that he would never achieve it, I had been increasingly impressed by his determination to make his mark at the highest level.

At Elland Road he had had many rows and scrapes but he had come through all of them, whole and tremendously competitive. For me it was evidence of an extraordinary ability to become strong at points which in someone less resilient might have been permanently broken.

Jack had marched on in his refusal to stop believing in himself, even when he had come to see the point of listening to some people who might have something valuable to say, and his success filled me with something more than straightforward admiration. I have often reflected that maybe it also meant that a certain warmth, respect and, yes, love, would always be retained in a relationship with my brother which might otherwise have suffered potentially irreparable damage.

Perhaps if it hadn't happened, if Alf had formed another view that for all his battling qualities and strength Jack just wasn't made for the international game – a view that circulated widely within English football with the news of his selection – the paths of our lives would have drifted increasingly apart.

Already there was considerable tension in our relationship. I had gone my way and he had gone his. But now we were joined together again. We could examine ourselves and each other in the kind of opportunity that may never have presented itself again, had Jack not managed to convince Alf that he had something vital to offer. We might have gone through our lives, and finished up in our old age, quite apart once we had journeyed out beyond the streets and the pitheads of Ashington.

The mission of the team, after all, was to value each other's strengths and compensate for any weaknesses and in such a challenge maybe brothers are given something of a head start. I feel the gift of this most strongly today when we meet and talk about our lives and our families, and, more frequently now, our aches and pains and sometimes our regrets that the time of our greatest, most thrilling experience in football seemed to pass so quickly.

We also, I think, in our different ways offer our thanks that the divisions which once spilled into the open, and made us appear in the eyes of the world brothers at war rather than the ones who embraced so warmly on the most wonderful sporting day of our lives, have softened down through the passing years. And to the stage where we know that, in the end, we have more to celebrate in each other than set us apart.

There were, to be honest, some points in our lives when such a perspective seemed remote, if not impossible. So often it could be said that we may have been united by our blood but not our natures. This may have been exaggerated to some degree, as is the case so often in lives which are at least to some extent under the gaze of the public, but then again it would be wrong to minimise the differences between us.

It was not true that as a kid I preferred to stay home and clutch my mother's apron while Jack responded to the various calls of the wild. I loved the outdoors, too, and most particularly in the company of a football, but there was no doubt he was much more extrovert, much less restrained in his behaviour. If he had a thought, a sudden impulse, he acted upon it and he shrugged and laughed if the consequences were not as he had assumed they would be. I was more self-absorbed and I tended to seek the shadows in all but the action and expression that came to me when I played football.

On the football field I was certainly not averse to a little acclaim. I enjoyed being hoisted on to the shoulders of my school team-mates after a particularly good performance and I wanted to shout out my pleasure when Joe Armstrong, the famous scout of Manchester United, said after one trial game that I should see my future at Old Trafford. But then I tended to make football my safest place, one around which I could set comforting boundaries.

Football, for a long while, never provided Jack with such an underpinning. If he played, it was with the same relish that he packed his fishing rod and laid his bait. For him it seemed to be just part of his boisterous life. For me football was the core of it.

When the first degrees of fame brought me notice beyond the security of the pitch, my overwhelming instinct was one of retreat. There was, for example, the occasion infamous in our family when I demurred when our mother Cissie insisted I signed a stranger's autograph book. The incident made me shrink in embarrassment. My mother was angry with me, couldn't understand my reticence, and I wanted to hide in the furthest corner. For Jack it would have been no more consequential or disturbing than a gust of wind ruffling his hair as he marched along the sand dunes or a river bank.

Jack always knew who he was and what he wanted at any given moment and, more than anything, that was not to have to conform to other people's expectations. He was his own, somewhat unruly, boy and he would be the same when he became a man.

His arrival in the England team re-conjured for me so much

of our boyhood and not least those days when we travelled to Newcastle to see the beacons of talent, men like Stanley Matthews and Tom Finney and Len Shackleton.

There were days when he would often rebel against his duty to look after his kid brother, and this was especially so when he craved to be free to roam across the land and seascapes he loved so much. These were days when I automatically assumed it was more likely I would receive a clip on an ear than a brotherly hug.

They never included, however, those times when we pooled our earnings from a grocery round and made the pilgrimage to see our football heroes. Then, both of us inhabited a world of unbridled excitement which came to a climax after we lunched on pie and chips and then walked up the hill to St James' Park.

Before the kick-off, we were filled with the most wonderful anticipation. Then, when the drama was spent, when the great men had done their entrancing work, we filled the homeward journey with our analysis of what we had seen. I remember, particularly, how deeply we scorned the various theories on how best to contain the genius of Matthews.

'Keep your eye on the ball,' defenders were warned before each game. 'Keep your balance, jockey him, keep your patience and do not lunge in. Do not let him lure you into false moves as he shimmies, tauntingly, over the ball.' So it went and at each new piece of advice we laughed and shook our heads. As far as we were concerned they might as well have been explaining how you nailed down the wind that swept along the Tyne.

Not the least wonder of those occasions was that we were able to tell ourselves that because we belonged to a quite formidable football clan we could take some proprietorial pride in the great spectacle that always filled us with such delight. We were touched, in the most intimate and familiar way, by something that meant so much in the lives of so many people.

Our grandfather Tanner, my first coach who was also a hard-headed, sometimes ruthless trainer of professional sprinters, spent some of his last days, when his eyesight had dwindled, hearing me read the football results from the local evening paper – and urging me to work at every scrap of the talent I had been given. Because if I didn't it might just lead to a lifetime of regrets.

Not everyone got on with Tanner – many felt he was a hard and unforgiving taskmaster – but I adored him. He seemed to make it a personal mission to hammer out my pathway to the football life.

He trained me to run, build in those early days on the natural pace which would always be one of my greatest assets. Most of all he talked about my duty to exploit all of my gifts; that not to do so was more than carelessness. It was the sin of neglect. You could never achieve anything, truly, if you did not work for it. When you did that you gave yourself the confidence to believe that you deserved everything that came to you. But of course it wasn't always easy. At times it hurt.

Tanner underlined the great reality and pride of my young life. It was that if football was the game of our people, if everyone played it in the backstreets and the park and sometimes even fresh from coming off shift at the colliery, it was also the game of our family. It was a gift that should never be spurned or neglected.

Any recollection of those times inevitably returns me to the night when I went with Jack to the cinema in Ashington to see a film entitled *The Red Shoes* starring the beautiful dancer Moira Shearer. Well, that's not quite true. We were drawn to a Pathé News report which would feature the England debut of Jackie Milburn, our mother's cousin, against Northern Ireland in Belfast in 1948.

Unfortunately, most of the town had read the prominently displayed poster advertising the news film and when we arrived at the cinema we had to join in at the back of an extremely long queue. By the time we reached our seats it was the footwork of Moira Shearer filling the screen rather than that of our second cousin and hero of Newcastle United, 'Wor Jackie'.

At the end of the feature film an usherette told us that our tickets were for the first show only and that we had to leave. We protested bitterly but it was only when many of the audience shouted that we were indeed connected to the local hero that the usherette relented.

So we stayed and joined in the cheering that greeted the brief clip of Jackie running on to the field. Most of the short newsreel was filled by an exquisite sixty-yard run by Matthews which ended with a goal and it was this that set us dancing on the cobbles as we went home to our house in Beatrice Street.

Now, seventeen years later, we were treading together another field for England. It was, we agreed, a remarkable turn in our family's involvement in football and a source of immense pride to, more than anyone, our mother. Yet if Jack and I could also feel extraordinary exhilaration at the unique distinction of two brothers playing together in the national team, the fact was that our relationship had indeed been beset by certain complications.

To be honest, they have taken most of our adult lives to

resolve since Jack, in my view, unfairly took our mother's side in what amounted to her refusal to accept my wife Norma – and in a way that I believe would have brought hurt to any son, however loving. All I can say now, truly, is that in all the pain that came with the kind of dislocation which I know from time to time afflicts so many families, I never lost sight of my debt to a mother who, I know, cared passionately about her sons.

Though it is a myth, helped along by newspaper stories and photographs that accompanied my emergence as a schoolboy candidate for stardom with Manchester United, that my mother gave me my first lessons in football, I have never forgotten her passionate interest in and support for my early steps into the game. Nor would I ever begin to discount the way she brought four sons up through the war years on my father Robert's modest wage from the pit.

Her passion for football was always mirrored in her pride over the fame of her cousin Jackie and the fact that her four brothers, Jack, George, Jimmy and Stan, all made good and long careers as professionals.

She urged her sons, and the fact was I needed a lot less bidding than Jack, to sit at their uncles' knees and learn about a life that represented to her a sure-fire escape from the hardships and dangers of a working life spent underground. And then there was the delight with which she greeted the news that Jack and I would be playing together for England. She left no one in doubt it was the great fulfilment of her best hopes.

No, I never questioned any of this even when I felt myself obliged to defend the feelings and status of a wife whom I loved dearly and who would always do so much to enhance my life.

My mother encouraged me to spend some of my school holiday time with her brother Stan, who was playing at Chesterfield. On visits home to the North East, Stan and his brothers would take me down to the beach and encourage me to show off my skills. My mother would watch over us, so often clucking with pride. And when I came back from Chesterfield she wanted to know every detail of the footballer's life. For her it was more than a way of earning a living. It was an escape to an existence so charmed it could barely be imagined by so many lads obliged to ride a colliery lift each working day.

It became clearer to me as the years passed that none of the strife that had come with my attempts to have Norma seamlessly absorbed into the life of the Charlton clan could ever ultimately break the ties of blood and experience that bound me to Jack.

We went to different schools, and went different ways – my obsession with football was initially so much greater than Jack's, no doubt because my talent for it was more obvious in our boyhood – but in a way that only compounded my respect for the fact that in the end he made so much of himself in the game.

My delight at his selection by Alf was underpinned by the fact that I had regularly driven across the Pennines to watch him playing for the fast-emerging Leeds United. I knew he had had some problems with Don Revie but then I could also see how he had come to convince his manager that he had a vital part to play in the development of one of England's great club sides.

I loved the way he was involved in the game. His passion to succeed was reflected in every move he made. I also noted how he had refined his game, how his timing – and his impact in both penalty areas – had made him such a powerful influence on a team which was setting an extremely hard pace at the top of English football. So I would drive home thinking, 'Well, Our Kid is really making something of himself in the game.'

Revie had at first seen a stormy, not always disciplined figure, someone of strong opinions – and emotions – who would often express his frustrations in the most forceful way. My former United team-mate Johnny Giles, who became so integral to the success of Leeds, once said of Jack, 'He made a fantastic contribution to the development of the team and he deserved all the success that came to him, but if I'm honest I have to say he wasn't always the team-mate who made you feel most comfortable.

'He never spared his criticism if he thought you had done something wrong and in the dressing room we said of him, "The thing about Jack is that if he isn't always right he is never wrong."'

It was a remark that certainly triggered the memory of some of the more tempestuous moments of our youth, as did Johnny's recall of the time Jack became so disenchanted with the flow of cards on the Leeds team bus that he picked up the pack and threw it out of the window.

We were brothers who, according to many of the people we grew up with, often suggested that football was the one bond left unbroken by our often sharply different natures. Even the game we loved, me quite exclusively and Jack sharing his affection for it with a lifelong passion for fishing and hunting, could provoke flashpoints.

One of the more explosive came after I'd watched him play for his youth team on the Ashington Colliery Welfare Ground.

I had been very impressed with his performance, his strength in the tackle and his effectiveness in the air, where he generated so much power with the thrust of his long neck, but his effort was flawed by a careless mistake which cost a goal.

I pointed out how a 'stupid' mistake had marred an otherwise terrific performance. His response was to hit me on the head which such force it would always serve as a warning against saying to Jack something he might deem the wrong comment at the wrong time.

It was also true that he was not often too thrilled when told that he had to look after his kid brother during time he had allocated to hunting or fishing. Reluctantly he would allow me to tag along in his wake as he pursued the rabbits and waited for the fish to bite.

This meant that football, our lifelong inheritance from our mother's line, would always form the strongest aspect of our relationship. For me it was my life, for Jack it was an important part of it and, ultimately, the means by which he escaped his horror at the prospect of a lifetime of work in the pits. He briefly experienced the ordeal, then signed for Leeds United in what he considered the most liberating act of his life.

The pit was my father's life and sometimes I would meet him at the pithead at the end of his shift. We would walk home, talk about his day and my hopes for the future. But if my father was largely unmoved by the appeal of football, and often became embarrassed when people he didn't know so well wanted to talk about the progress of his sons in the game, it was not as though he didn't leave us a legacy of his own.

Though he would sometimes comment about our play, offer a criticism or perhaps a little praise, it was clear to us that it was all coming second-hand. What he did give us, though, was something utterly authentic and Jack and I would always agree that it was indeed a valuable gift.

It was to do with how a man should tackle life and all its difficulties. He had to do it as uncomplainingly as possible, he had to meet his responsibilities to his family and he had to get on with any work that was available.

In his life this meant going to the colliery each working day, and I don't think either Jack or I ever lost sight of this. We always had a strong sense of it when he came home at night, sometimes with fresh scars from the colliery, sometimes with a few lumps of coal he had collected while walking his little horse along the shore.

If Jack took more of his nature from our mother than our father, if he was much bolder and less self-conscious about what people might think of him if he behaved in a certain way, and said precisely what was on his mind, in the end he was faithful enough to the idea that sooner or later it was essential to make the best of your situation. Jack did face difficulties at Leeds but when he appeared for England duty he had resolved them quite brilliantly.

On my trips to Elland Road I had been increasingly impressed by the development and the authority of his game, and another admirer of his achievement in turning all his prospects around was Ian St John, the fine, brilliantly combative centre-forward of Liverpool and Scotland.

St John had the chance to observe Jack extremely closely on his debut for England. Afterwards, he reflected, 'When I first saw Jack in the Leeds team I wasn't overly impressed. I thought he could be rash in a way that put his fellow defenders in difficulty. But that day at Wembley when he first appeared for

England I was quite amazed at the extent to which he had transformed his game.

'He had reinvented himself. He was now playing to his strengths, in the air and in the tackle and in his ability to read the game. He deserves real credit for turning around his career, a career that was going nowhere. But I do think Don Revie was vital as well. I spoke to Don many times and he said that when he first became manager at Leeds, Jack was a big dogmatic bugger who didn't care to listen to anyone's opinion but his own. But eventually the penny dropped and he became a real player.'

When Jack and Nobby were picked for England the prevailing critical response was that it was an act of desperation. They were, the theory went, rough-hewn players who wouldn't have heard the call to England duty from any other manager but Alf. I was inclined to agree with the latter point but only in a way that acknowledged the insight that went into the selections. Alf had the vision to see the best qualities of both players and as we moved closer to the World Cup there was a growing consensus, both inside and outside the camp, that the team had been quite immeasurably strengthened.

One of the principal beneficiaries, my brother would say – and I couldn't argue – was me. Jack declared that a huge factor, an absolute key to success, was the introduction of Nobby. He said, 'Nobby could win the ball and allow my brother Bobby not to have the responsibility of having to pick up and mark and hold up the people in the back four. Nobby gave the ball to Bobby and let him play.'

George Cohen echoed that point. 'It's not recognised that Nobby was a very good distributor of the ball, but he fed Bobby Charlton time and again. Bobby could see Nobby go into a tackle, was confident he'd come out with the ball, and moved into space knowing that Nobby would find him. That was a very good partnership. It became the axis of our midfield, it made everything we did more coherent.'

For Jack there was an equally warm welcome from his new team-mates. Gordon Banks was particularly appreciative of his physical authority, saying, 'Jack was strong and commanding in the middle. We used to get on at each other during matches but this was purely to keep each other on the alert. The sometimes rude and brutal things we yelled in the heat of battle were always quickly forgotten once the final whistle was blown.'

Ray Wilson, with whom I had made such a strong bond, spoke of an instinctive understanding with my brother. He said, 'Me and Big Jack were mouthy players and it's very important that people talk. We never used to break, we tried to keep the back four solid, we never tackled until they got round the penalty area and the other lads put them under pressure, so they couldn't squeeze the ball through.'

What we were seeing then in the team, and from the distance of today the picture is no less vivid, was a pattern that unfolded with increasing clarity from that April day at Wembley to a biting cold night in Madrid near the end of 1965. It was no less than the smelting of the finest, most efficient defence in the history of English football.

Detaching the defeat by Austria at Wembley in October – one over which Alf would be so quickly vindicated in his claim that it was a passing aberration – the statistics alone tell a story of extraordinary, fast-gathering meanness.

In six games, finishing with the match at the Bernabéu which would always be remembered for almost entirely different reasons (Alan Ball being not the least of them), we conceded just three goals. We shut out the talented Hungarians, who were led by the world-class Ferenc Bene at Wembley, we yielded one to the Yugoslavs in the always fierce battleground of Belgrade, and left West Germany and Spain scoreless in Nuremburg and Madrid. Sweden were beaten 2-1 in Gothenburg.

This was exactly the statement of tough frugality Alf had hoped for when he called up Nobby and Jack. There was still plenty of time to fashion his optimum strike force, but first he had to close the gates. Now, with each new performance, you could hear them tightening.

For me, fortified by the presence of Nobby and Jack, and with Alf making it increasingly clear that any worries about my defensive frailties in midfield had been removed at the stroke of writing down Nobby's name on the team-sheet, it felt as though I was taking some first, sure steps into a promised land.

The critical pressure was for a spectacular performance but what was being produced, the players had now come to believe, was a convincing blueprint for success in the great tournament. The pleasure, and gratitude, which came to me with the reinforcement of Nobby was heightened by my long and admiring analysis of quite what he brought to the game.

I'd never, and never would, have a relationship with any player on the field quite like the one I shared with Nobby. When Jack quailed at the idea that he had upset the little man in the heat of the action, it reminded me of an early assessment I had made on the nature of Nobby's fearlessness. My conclusion was that there was only one man on earth who had the power to inspire in him a little dread.

It was his father, Charlie, and I discovered this at half-time one night at Old Trafford when Nobby had briefly lost his head and earned a booking. As we walked up the tunnel and turned towards the dressing room we passed the point where fans could get closest to the players. It was then I heard Charlie bellowing Nobby's name. When he heard the cry 'Norbert' my friend walked towards his father with the bearing of a contrite and fearful schoolboy summoned by a ferocious master.

He knew precisely what to expect. It was a lecture on the behaviour required when you represented a great football club like Manchester United. It was not enough to play strongly, to battle for every ball; you also had to be in command of everything you did and all of your emotions. Nobby couldn't always meet such a demand but the certainty was that no one had a more developed idea of what he had to do to help his team in all circumstances.

He was certainly not lacking in attacking skill and intuition but his early conclusion was that his surest asset was an ability to win the ball and put it at the service of a more creative player. From this, I benefited so hugely I have to say it was one of the cornerstones of my greatest success with my club and my country.

The result was that when you received the ball from Nobby you were bound to say, 'Hell, the little fellah had to spit blood to win this ball, I just can't waste it.'

I never forgot that one of my foremost responsibilities for both United and England was to make myself free to receive the ball from Nobby. His job was to defend, which he did like a tiger and with brilliant perception of how the game was flowing, and maintain a steady supply of possession.

Neither Jack nor Nobby meekly accepted any restriction on their right to shape a game, Jack with his dominant presence in either penalty area, Nobby with his zealous prowling of the ground in front of defence.

Nobby, the combative altar boy, and Jack, who was never happier than when he had a shotgun or a fishing rod in his hands, were not everybody's idea of a holy alliance. But for both Alf and me there was never a question mark against their status. Right from the start, we agreed, they were an unqualified blessing.

7. Olé, Olé, Olé

Madrid on 8 December 1965 was so cold it made walking down the wide and elegant Gran Via an unaccustomed ordeal. Eight years before I had strolled along there in the spring sunshine before later watching in awe the unfolding majesty of Alfredo Di Stéfano at the Bernabéu.

It was the most riveting individual performance I had ever seen and on that soft, sweet-scented night, when my eyes followed every stride of the great man, I felt as though I was being taken to the very boundaries of what was possible from one player on a football field.

Now there was ice in the wind coming down from the Sierra and that seemed like the most appropriate accompaniment for the chill of apprehension that came with the fact that at a crucial point in the shaping of England's team we were facing one of Europe's better sides in their own fabled fortress. We had made some good, if occasionally erratic, progress through the year but here we were under a critical examination, one that could well tell us whether we were a team which at last could begin to contemplate with some confidence the climax of a long and testing journey.

Bringing a fine edge to the challenge was that we had been spending our training hours in Madrid working on the detail of a new strategy which Alf believed could well be crucial to all our hopes of moving on to a higher and more secure competitive level. He had never been so fastidious in the outlining of his game plan – and making clear the expectations he was placing on the shoulders of every player stepping out into the Bernabéu.

England had never won anywhere in Spain, so it was not so easy to imagine that in a few hours our campaign to win the World Cup would be touched in the great stadium by what felt like several degrees of white heat.

In 1957 I was a travelling reserve for Manchester United's European Cup semi-final against Real Madrid, a mere spectator. This new experience, by the most extreme comparison, made me feel I was suddenly at the heart of something huge and thrilling.

After we had beaten Spain 2-0, and Alan Ball, playing his fourth international at the age of twenty, had produced one of the most phenomenally committed performances I'd ever seen at any level of the game, Alf left the dressing room much more quickly than usual.

There was none of the normal brusque, one-on-one debriefing as he mingled with his troops. He didn't linger to point out individual mistakes or to take a player through the pivotal points of his performance and, occasionally, perhaps offer a light pat of congratulation for something particularly well done, or, maybe more frequently, a frown of censure. He certainly didn't pepper us with his sometimes biting one-liners, as he had George Cohen in our final training session before this match in Madrid.

Alf had taken part in a seven-a-side game and been the victim of a clattering tackle by George. He went down heavily on to the frozen ground and George and the rest of us were aghast as he slowly and rather shakily got to his feet. 'Fucking hell, Cohen,' he said, 'if I had another fit right-back you wouldn't be playing tomorrow night.'

But then if he was less voluble and eloquent after the match, neither did he seek to disguise his satisfaction.

I had a sense that he wanted to be alone for a little while so as to better absorb the meaning of what he had seen. Surely everyone had to believe it was confirmation of his claim that England could indeed win the World Cup. We had the players, we had the system – and now, suddenly, there was the kind of recognition which could hardly have been imagined when Jimmy Hill was telling the nation to pack away its dreams for at least another four years.

Certainly Fleet Street was agog at the style and the innovation of England's performance. The style was strong and quick and filled with authority. The system was about to enter the history of the game and for all those who would later claim that Alf's 4-3-3 was a tactical blight on English football, a discarding of romance and colour and what had always been presumed to be the unshakeable, everlasting appeal of dashing, elusive wingers, there were others, and certainly I was one of them, who either saw or lived it, who were convinced otherwise. We believed that in the right hands, and with the right personnel, it could deliver all that you wanted – and with more certainty than had ever been felt before.

I went on the record with my enthusiasm and, looking back and rereading my words, I sound very much like someone who had suddenly seen a very bright light in a once murky room. I told a reporter, 'Before Alf we never really had a plan away from home and this new development was really something. When he told us about the switch to 4-3-3 he emphatically made the point that we were not going to become a defensive team, that the three up front wouldn't be alone. When we had the ball the three up front would become six.'

The English media heaped praise on both the manager and the players. The headlines hammered home the theme of a major breakthrough. However, it was one thing for Desmond Hackett, the volatile voice of the *Daily Express*, to rhapsodise over our performance. It was quite another that professional opinion across the world was both intrigued and positive.

Hackett's piece, though, certainly made agreeable breakfast reading. He wrote, 'England can win the World Cup next year. They have only to match the splendour of this unforgettable night and there is not a team on earth who can master them. This was England's first win in Spain but it was more than a victory. It was a thrashing of painful humiliation for the Spanish. Gone were the shackles of rigid regimentation.

'The team moved freely and confidently and with such imagination that the numbers on their backs became mere identification marks on players who rose to noble heights. England's football was as smooth as the brush strokes of a master – precise, balanced and as lovely to watch as the ballet.'

There was no provocation here for Alf to invite a sometimes scathing critic outside. But more gratifying, no doubt, was the homage paid to him – and England's performance – by a fellow professional, the Spanish coach José Villalonga.

Villalonga's body language on the touchline had become quite desperate, as had that of the Spanish full-backs Severino Reija and Manuel Sanchís who held up their hands in bewilderment as they marked empty space normally occupied by traditional wingers – and we attacked from all points of the tactical compass. As it was happening, I said to myself, 'This is fantastic. But we don't have wingers and their full-backs are standing out there like lamp posts. They are doing what they have always done but everything has changed. And Alf has changed it.'

It was, despite our steaming breath in the cold Castilian night, the most encouraging invitation to believe that we had indeed achieved an extremely warming new dawn. Ramsey's Way suddenly seemed like the most inviting thoroughfare.

Joe Baker, the star of Hibernian and then Arsenal, whose thick Scottish accent did not disguise his commitment to his native England when he put on the white shirt, scored early and played with impressive bite before having to leave the field injured after thirty-five minutes.

When he did so he was replaced by Bobby Moore's superb and ferocious understudy Norman Hunter, a development which prompted Ball, whose enthusiasm and relevance to every phase of the action cut a great swathe through our opponents, to produce a huge grin from beneath his red thatch, place his hands together and say, 'For what they are about to receive.'

It was not, though, brutal tackling that most disrupted the Spaniards. It was the sharpness and the range of our attack, the speed with which it was transformed from the most efficient of defences.

Roger Hunt, who was making a rare appearance in the absence of the sick Jimmy Greaves, scored the conclusive goal after I linked in a sweeping passing movement which started with George Cohen and was carried forward by Moore. The effect was of the kind of killing sword stroke so familiar to those who patronised the nearby Plaza de Toros.

The Spanish coach said, 'This England team was phenomenal tonight. They were far superior to us in their experiment and their performance. No team in the world could have lived with the force or the variety of their attack. We tried to adapt to the situation, we did all we could, but I realised long before the end of the game it was never going to be enough.'

For Alf the Madrid morning was full of such reinforcement and not the least rapturous – or lyrical – was that provided by my friend Geoffrey Green, who wrote in The Times of the post-match mood the man of the moment helped create over a little liquid refreshment.

Alf had explained his thinking on 4-3-3 to a group of reporters and then invited questions as the champagne was poured.

Geoffrey reported to his readers, 'As the champagne corks popped so the temperature rose and the verbal exchanges sharpened and slurred. The giant crystal chandelier overhead sparkled like the Milky Way and Alf was on cloud nine. Laying his glass aside every now and then – every quarter hour on the quarter hour I would judge – he cupped his hands in front of an enigmatic smile to murmur, "This precious jewel." Each time he repeated the action I tottered to my feet, raised my champagne goblet and gave a Russian toast, "Here's to the four corners of this room."

'So the small hours unwound happily. It was only the next day, following a massive dose of Alka Seltzer, when I came to realize two things. The room I had been toasting was entirely circular; and Alf's "precious jewel", caressed in imagination, was football.'

Alf, of course, was rarely given to public caressing of any

sort, and he was still less inclined to count his victories in the long run of friendlies that, as the World Cup host nation, was our sole diet after elimination from the Nations Cup in Paris at the start of his reign. But he did hoard in his mind anything he considered to be superior performance from individuals and the team.

In his estimation, until we played our opening World Cup game, results were meaningless and performance was everything. Here he was thrilled by the execution of his best hopes. Like an early fan of the Russian Revolution he was inclined to believe that he might have seen the future, and that it worked.

He had already been hugely encouraged by the swift acclimatisation achieved by Jack and Nobby. They displayed a fine understanding and implicit acceptance of his demands and both had performed impressively in Madrid. And now Alf had another player to place at the core of his hopes.

It was the astonishing, boyish, irrepressible Ball. As he had with Nobby and Jack, Alf had watched him over the months with a growing interest and, he would reveal later, excitement. It was not so much the liveliness of his play and the skills that accompanied the vision and the urgency but the overwhelming sense that he was perfectly comfortable with all the demands placed before him. He flowed like an electric current wired to every corner of his team.

Alf saw Ball in the salty air of Bloomfield Road, Blackpool, and when he came to the football strongholds of Manchester, Liverpool and London. The more he saw him, the more he loved the passion and the industry and the sharpness of wit brimming from his prospective recruit. It was no insult to the fine skills of the boy with the high-pitched voice and the unquenchable desire to succeed, which had been cultivated by his old pro football manager father, that Alf quickly saw in him potential as his ultimate foot soldier.

Alan was a player he could trust to never stop running, never wilt in his duty to police the efforts of both himself and his team-mates. Many years later Nobby, for whom supreme commitment was assumed to be an endless personal resource, reported his shock at a command he received from Alan midway through one particularly hectic phase of action. 'I had just made a couple of big, really draining runs, I was exhausted, wondering where my next breath was coming from, and for a second I had my hands on my hips. Bally ran up beside me and yelled into my ear, 'Run, you bastard.'

'Bally' never tired of telling the story of one of his early encounters with Alf. He swore that his account was true in every detail and there was no doubt it did smack of an authentic example of Alf's sometimes brutal teaching style. This, anyway, was Alan's version of the conversation . . .

'Alan, what happens when a man takes his dog for a walk?'

'The owner throws a stick and the dog runs after it and fetches it back and drops it at his master's feet.'

'Quite so, Alan. Now I want you to think of yourself as the dog, the stick as the ball and the dog's owner as Bobby Charlton.'

Bally would shake with laughter when he told the story, which he did long after he had proved himself one of the outstanding creative midfielders in the history of English football and had broken the British transfer record along the way when he moved from Everton to Arsenal in 1971 at a cost of £220,000.

My response to Alf's parable of the dog and the stick was

that I liked to think of it as not so much a comment on his exaggeration of my standing in the game and his team, but his refusal to leave anyone with the smallest illusion about one of their essential functions in his grand plan. At the same time I was always eager to say that Alan had quickly outgrown anyone's idea of merely a potential champion at Crufts.

Bally had come in seven games earlier in another formidable stronghold of European football, Belgrade. Then, he was still a few days shy of his twentieth birthday but Alf had seen all he needed. He believed that the young player had enough natural-born nous and competitive steel to prosper in the place which eight years earlier had created a road block in my own international career and, effectively, kept me out of a World Cup.

Alf made the announcement of his selection directly to the player during a training session the day before the match. Again he had studied Ball's game, his mannerisms, intently and when he took him to one side he said, 'Are you all right, young man?' Ball chirped back, 'Yes, I'm fine, boss', to which Alf replied in classic fashion, 'Well, in that case stop kicking the ball around, I want to talk to you. Do you think you are ready to play for England?' Again Alan responded, unblinkingly, 'Yes, boss.'

'Then you are playing tomorrow,' Alf said. First Jack and Nobby, now Alan Ball; Alf was gathering his people, his elect, together with a growing certainty – and a necessarily quickening pace.

My enthusiasm was no less in this latest case than in all the others. It was, plainly, another instance of Alf being very sure of the instincts and the character of a player who for some time had been under quite exhaustive examination. Also, it was one more emerging example of mutual trust, Ball saying at the end of his career, 'Alf was complete. He was tactically aware, thorough, had his own idea of how the game should be played, was approachable and could always put you right.

'I never found a flaw in him and I've played with a few managers: Ron Suart at Blackpool, Harry Catterick at Everton, Bertie Mee and Terry Neill at Arsenal, Lawrie McMenemy at Southampton. That day in Belgrade Alf told me not to worry about how I played, "just play," he said.

'He promised me I would play enough times to see if I would make it. He dispelled the idea that anyone would get only one chance.'

I first encountered Bally while playing for United against Blackpool at Bloomfield Road. I had heard a lot about him, how vital he was to his team's momentum, and all of it was confirmed.

He was fascinating to watch, so alive, so aware of everything that was happening around him. It was amazing to see these qualities in someone so young. He wasn't naturally fast, he was denied that great asset, but the compensations he produced were huge. He was a less elegant, but no less impressive, version of Bobby Moore in his instinct to always be in the right place at the right time

In this he also reminded me a lot of Nobby. His football brain worked overtime at moments of maximum pressure and if he wasn't quick he was aware of the speed of those around him and he played off it beautifully. He was never at a loss for an option, however tight the situation.

In the course of the next few years I was disappointed when he didn't join United, as much indeed as when we failed to sign Gordon Banks. His energy, his football intelligence, would have made him quite integral to our strength. Although our styles were quite different, in a way I suppose he reminded me quite a bit of myself when I made my first steps into football, though my passage was no doubt easier. He was rejected by his local club Bolton Wanderers, who considered him too small, too easily brushed aside. There can rarely have been a greater miscalculation in the history of the game.

Football was for him, as it was for me, more than a calling. It was his life. His father Alan was besotted by the game, someone who seemed never happier than when talking about and, indeed, inhaling all of it quite whole. The influence he exerted over his son was very strong. It was a rare day when Bally didn't call home for a council of war.

Apart from his natural balance, and his ability to control his performance despite its unvarying passion, he had an extraordinary combative nature. He saw points of conflict incredibly early, he anticipated them and responded ahead of the rest. But never stupidly. You could be in a very tight situation, needing a little time and space, and you looked up and he was there.

If Alf was assembling a team of champions, here was a substantial portion of both its heart and its intelligence. In the build-up to the World Cup this became increasingly clear and it was dramatically evident in Madrid.

At the Bernabéu it was the most striking single indicator that we were indeed moving towards establishing the core of our team. Nine World Cup finalists started the game and there is no doubt that in one way or another all the claims on that status were strongly enhanced in the ensuing ninety minutes.

Only sympathy, rather than any small degree of reproach, could be dealt to the two who didn't make it: Joe Baker and

George Eastham. It was not that they failed, and indeed Baker had been particularly impressive before he was hit by injury, simply that in Alf's relentless analysis the counter-claims of Geoff Hurst and Martin Peters would eventually triumph. And who could say that errors of judgement had been made?

Appropriately, when you considered the style and the manner of their impact on the team, it could be said they came with late and, I certainly believed, unanswerable runs.

Soon enough, though, it was clear that whatever line-up and set of tactics Alf unfurled for the raising of the World Cup curtain in six months, there was no question that the victory in Madrid would be presented by him as prima facie evidence that he may have found a way to win the tournament and that henceforth wingers, extremely talented individuals like Peter Thompson, Terry Paine, John Connelly and Ian Callaghan, were banished from his sight. No, he insisted, the performance against Spain did not amount to an indelible blueprint. It simply gave him, and the core of his team, an option that in the right circumstances might prove not only workable but potentially devastating.

He could hardly have been more explicit about this in the wake of Madrid, saying, 'I think it would be quite wrong to let the rest of the world, our rivals, see exactly what we are doing. I think it is my duty to protect certain players until the time we need them most. In Madrid it was a step, and a very big one, in our education as a football party. My job will be to produce the right team at the right time and this does not always mean pressing ahead with a particular combination just because it has been successful.'

Sometimes football managers are playing games when they make such pronouncements, throwing up smokescreens and hoping to send rivals haring off in wrong directions. But Alf's football dogma did not lend itself to such diversionary tactics. He was more concerned with building his own body of evidence in the matter of his best options, and all that he did between Madrid and the announcement of his World Cup squad of twenty-two the following June was confirmation of the truth of his assertion that he remained flexible about who and how he would play.

He didn't, as some imagined he might in the first flush of his triumph in Spain, abandon wingers. Three – Terry Paine, John Connelly and Ian Callaghan – would get into the squad and there was a place for one of this endangered species in three of four games we played before gathering in the Lilleshall training centre in Shropshire.

There, we worked intensely and under strict discipline before making the four-game sweep through Europe which carried us to the dawn of the tournament. Before the fleeting visits home Alf allowed us almost begrudgingly, and with perhaps an echo of our conversation in Rio two years earlier, and the first of the tour games in Helsinki, five players were told that they hadn't made the cut.

At various stages of the long road all of them had made strong cases for their inclusion, most notably the gifted Peter Thompson, who had performed so impressively when we lost heavily to Brazil in the Maracanã two years earlier, and Budgie Byrne, who around that time had scored a memorable hat-trick against Portugal in Lisbon. They left us, along with Thompson's Anfield team-mate Gordon Milne, a clever, talented midfielder operator, the fine, strong Chelsea forward Bobby Tambling and Blackburn's stylish full-back Keith Newton.

It was hard to see such accomplished – and ambitious – professionals leave. Each of them had had good reason to nourish their hopes, and not least Newton who just a few months earlier had been awarded his first cap in our 1-0 win over West Germany at Wembley.

Inevitably, I speculated on what my own feelings might have been had I received that ominous tap on the shoulder. I knew I would have been devastated because I had come to love my life with the England team. Each game had become a wonderful challenge, a test not just of any natural talent I might have but also my ability to be in charge of it, develop it according to the needs of the team and a manager whose judgement I had come to respect so highly.

As a youngster I had seen the international game as a luxury, something of a bonus, a quite glamorous distraction if you like, from the club football which imposed such heavy physical demands in return for a livelihood which in enjoyment and satisfaction I had always believed couldn't be rivalled in any other walk of life. By now, though, playing on the international stage, running on to the fields of places like the Maracanã and Bernabéu, had become an element of my lifeblood. I could only imagine the empty feeling my rejected squad-mates carried away from the Shropshire village Alf had turned into one of the great testing grounds of our careers.

It was also true that none of us had reason to believe that our tickets to play had been stamped unequivocally. There was never a point when Alf, by accident or design, conveyed this assurance and in the games that came after Madrid it was clear enough he was still steeling himself for some major decisions.

In the first of them, a 1-1 draw against Poland at Goodison Park early in January, he kept the 4-3-3 system, with Ball, Stiles and Eastham again working in the middle and Gordon Harris of Burnley getting a run in my place in the forward three. I had a twinge of injury and Alf was happy enough to take a closer look at a player who had become a major factor in the extremely impressive Lancashire team.

Six weeks later I came back against West Germany at Wembley, when Nobby Stiles stabbed home his only goal in international football and Geoff Hurst's debut was, strangely enough on reflection, less a talking point than the boos which rippled down from the terraces of an Empire Stadium disgruntled by a performance which carried little of the panache or certainty displayed at the Bernabéu.

Alf dismissed the jeers and the slow handclapping and preferred to dwell on the encouragement provided by Hurst's strong running and powerful physical presence. If the champagne that came with the Madrid honeymoon had been enjoyable, it had not exactly turned his head. Back in the dressing room he said to us, 'Listen to them moan out there. But I will tell you this, they'll go mad if we beat West Germany by one goal in the World Cup final.'

Peter Thompson was one who was not lifted by Alf's defiance and later he reported that he had left the stadium cast down by the fear that he had missed an opportunity to make a convincing case for the enduring value of an out-and-out winger. Many years later he still felt the pain of that time, saying, 'Bertie Vogts marked me. I had about five kicks and they were all in the warm-up. In the dressing room afterwards Alf sat down beside me, put his hand on my knee and said, "a little disappointed, Peter." That hurt me so much more than Bill Shankly shouting and ranting back at Anfield. Alf was the exact opposite. I respected him so much. I still remember the hurt of those few words that day.'

Alf, as always, was moving along in pursuit of maximum, proven strength. Thompson's stumble had left the door ajar for

Connelly or Paine or Callaghan. Hurst had arrived beside the stoically enduring Roger Hunt, to challenge the hope of Jimmy Greaves that he would quite seamlessly reassert his primacy among England goalscorers after a long and draining bout of hepatitis.

It was no atmosphere in which I could afford to believe that my job was done, my case established. Perhaps it was motivation which was always a little more than subliminal and maybe it was that, and the usual stimulation of going back to where it all started for me at Hampden Park, which provoked some of my best form against Scotland in the next match. After Jimmy Johnstone and Denis Law responded to an early onslaught from Hurst, who opened the scoring with his first international goal, and two from Hunt, I stretched our lead to 4-2 with one of my more spectacular long shots.

We won 4-3 and most everyone agreed it was a spirited riposte to the critics who tore into us so ferociously after the German game. Everyone, that was, except Alf. Something in the Scottish air, or perhaps the water, always brought the sharpest edge to his demeanour. On this occasion he may have read a piece by a leading Scottish sports writer, John Fairgrieve, one which might have inflamed even someone much more equable than Alf about the possibility of losing anything north of Hadrian's Wall.

Fairgrieve wrote in the *Daily Mail*, 'There are those who contend that Alf Ramsey is an unappreciated genius. There are many more who believe he is the biggest threat to his country's prestige since Bonaparte. My own view is that England do not have the smallest chance against Brazil or Italy in the World Cup in July. Against several other finalists, like Hungary and Russia and West Germany they could not be fancied at all. And if I was being really harsh, I would say that England are really lucky to be in the World Cup finals at all. Many Englishmen already believe this and say so.'

These were not sentiments to soften Alf's mood and another journalist discovered this when he airily expressed the view that the Hampden match, whatever its defensive shortcomings, had been a great one to watch. 'For you, maybe,' Alf almost snarled, 'but I thought there was some appalling football played. We must be much, much better.'

No matter that at times Law could hardly have attacked with more menace had he been issued with a claymore, or that the small and mesmerising Johnstone had produced some runs amazing in their touch and intricacy, England had conceded three goals. That they had scored four was beside the point as far as Alf was concerned. Much as he wanted to beat Scotland, in any circumstances, the victory had not been underpinned by the kind of performance that he now demanded as a matter of course.

Alf was conscious enough that in at one least one aspect of his argument his Scottish critic could not be convincingly contradicted. In England much of the euphoria over the triumph in Madrid had indeed become resubmerged in some of the old doubts.

This was the much-respected English sports writer John Moynihan, author of the classic and wonderfully evocative study of the post-war English game, *The Soccer Syndrome*: 'Perhaps we of the press and supporters of England would like more communication from Alf Ramsey and less of the attitude that the England side is his and his alone. Haven't we waited long enough for a team to win this competition?

'Ramsey is not always a man to arouse confidence in the task. Is he trying to build a team with or without Jimmy

Greaves? Is his plan a flash in the pan, relying on hard workers like Roger Hunt and Nobby Stiles, merely following the plough? England's team needs to be a team of eleven Rolls-Royces, average runners will not do. And surely he must play at least one established winger.'

Alf's response was coolly defiant when he picked his team for England's last game on home soil before the start of the World Cup, which was now just two months away. He said, once more, that all his selections were about strengthening his squad rather than entrenching a mere eleven players. He said every member of his group had to be able to step into any match, 'otherwise they are worthless to me'.

Pointedly he added, 'I have picked a team against Yugoslavia because I want to see what certain players and combinations can achieve.' With that latest Ramsey injunction buzzing in our ears, we put in an immeasurably better performance than the one that had irritated him so much at Hampden. Jimmy Greaves, back in the team after his debilitating illness, scored in the ninth minute. I scored my thirty-seventh goal in my sixty-fifth international with a powerful shot which nicely celebrated the fact that we had played with much of the assurance and the touch we had displayed in Madrid.

Alf was especially pleased with the performance of the slim twenty-two-year-old to whom he had given a first cap and the chance of a late run into the company of potential world champions. As it turned out, the making of a late, perfectly timed run quickly proved to be one of the young player's most compelling specialities. His name was Martin Peters.

8. Man in the Mask

Martin Peters was, right at the start, cast as the quiet one who might just pop out of the shadows clad in a black mask and a cape. He was certainly stealthier than Geoff Hurst, his West Ham team-mate who was two years older and two matches earlier had come into the team against West Germany with a game that was both intelligent and strong while placing little reliance on any kind of subterfuge.

Geoff was as he appeared at first sight: a force that never could be left unattended by the defender who was expected to contain it. He had power, some guile and a wonderful honesty. Martin's virtues were not so immediately obvious, or at least not so easy to instantly classify. It was also true that the young east Londoner came without the pervasive aura of his other club-mate and great influence, Bobby Moore.

Speaking for myself, this meant that it took as long as a few minutes to grasp fully quite what a brilliant addition he was to the cause.

What Martin had, it was clear enough long before the end of the Yugoslav game, was something to indeed gladden Alf's heart. If he had that stealth, if he could disguise a run, a sudden and biting intervention, his subtle style would never obscure his most striking quality.

It was a capacity to provide anything you would want from any midfielder, ancient or modern. He had a quite seamless ability to marry defence and attack. He read so quickly the requirements of either role – and he did it with astonishing consistency.

When a few years later Martin was moving towards the peak of his maturity – while still in his mid-twenties – Alf provoked some mockery with that headline-grabbing declaration that here was a footballer ten years ahead of his time. Martin may have been a little sheepish under the weight of that praise, but he had no reason to be so. My own view was that he had a talent that would have been sharply relevant at any phase of the evolution of football.

This was because it covered so cleanly all the requirements of the game: vision, the coolest execution, fine skill, and – something I could only envy – a devilry and control in the tackle that made him an opponent to be abused only at high risk.

He was a young football man for any season, any system and any epoch.

When his football days were over and, like Geoff, he had made a career in the insurance business, he gave a low-key and quite unemotional account of his progress into the England team. It is fascinating to go back to because, it seems to me, it perfectly reflects the style of his arrival. It was one of a young man ready to deal with any challenge which came before him.

He recalled, 'I'd played just once for Alf at the Under-23 level, against Wales at Bristol in 1964. Then nothing until 1966. Until three months before the Yugoslavia match I hadn't even been mentioned in dispatches. Then I had an Under-23 match against Turkey at Blackburn, didn't score and it came down the grapevine that Alf thought I couldn't head the ball.

'By then I'd had a varying three seasons – lost my place at West Ham in 1963 when they went on to win the FA Cup, got back the next season at centre-half, moved to left-back, then right-half when Eddie Bovington was injured and was then never out. Being selected against Yugoslavia was joining the elite but I'd never taken much notice of the national team, being more concerned with my club place, and playing for Ramsey didn't really enter my head until Geoff got in against Germany.

'Admittedly I was in the preliminary forty for the World Cup and apparently Greenwood was pushing Ramsey for me to have a go. Not that there was too much difference in the way England played, I found playing for West Ham aligned you for international football, though probably that's why they found it difficult trying to win the league. That first game I tended to let Bobby [Charlton] and Jimmy Greaves have the ball but later I started to do more what was instinctive.'

In every game it seemed to me that Martin worked himself near to death. He ran endlessly and in the process took pressure off the defenders, often less obviously than such as Nobby and Bally, but in all the crucial ways just as significantly. Sometimes I felt a shaming twinge because just as I relied so much on the tackling and passing service of Nobby, I was also forced to note the range of Martin's contribution to the team. The expectation on my shoulders was that I go forward, threaten whenever I could the opposing goal, and largely forget about almost everything else.

Martin defended and attacked with such great assurance

and this quality could not have been more evident in that first game against Yugoslavia at Wembley. He came close to scoring two goals. He tackled, he filled vital space which he glided into unmolested. He made chances, he headed off danger to our goal as though he had all the time in the world. It was a stunning debut in terms of both technique and awareness and it persuaded me that here was a player who could always be relied upon to keep his head.

On reflection I shouldn't have been surprised by his immediate impact. A little research would have gone a long way to explaining why Alf so strongly suspected that here was a young man promising to do anything you would want in a football player.

Before becoming England's first £200,000 player with his move to Spurs in 1970 – Alf's old team-mate at Tottenham and now manager Bill Nicholson had become quite as much of an admirer – Martin had played in every position for West Ham, including in goal when, in his third game for the club, he replaced his injured team-mate Brian Rhodes.

And now, as I revisit an inventory of my team-mates made years ago when I was first asked to try to assess their different qualities, the strengths they had which lingered most powerfully in the memory, I see again that the impression Martin first made was the one that would always be imprinted so firmly in my mind.

Martin, I said, was the newest boy on the team bus and he didn't have a lot to say, certainly nothing like so much as the cheeky chappie Alan Ball, but then he had a confidence that could hardly have become more tangible or enduring to this day, when like all of us he is obliged to deal with the frailties of advancing age. And this, despite his quiet manner, made it so much less surprising when he so quickly brought such a sharp and uplifting cutting edge to all that we attempted to do.

There was indeed much scepticism when Alf said that Martin was running so far ahead of his time but I have to say, once again, that it was born of a quite profound ignorance about what is most important in the game. Sometimes it seemed to me that he was connected to some separate system of thought that enabled him to drift into the action as though from nowhere, with a vital interception or strike on goal the frequent result.

Perhaps for some there was a temptation to believe he did it on a whim but the more you played alongside him, the more you realised how deeply he understood the game and the rewards that came with the most subtle movement. That first impression he made in the game against Uruguay was a calling card of unimpeachable authenticity.

What never ceased to amaze me, though, was the fact that Peters, Hurst and Moore could bring so much to the England team, provide such a constant and intelligent presence, and always look thoroughbred performers for West Ham, without carrying their club team on to a more consistently competitive level.

They had that success in the FA Cup and the European Cup Winners' Cup, and they were widely accepted as purveyors of much stylish football, but with great strength in key areas, with Moore an outstanding commander of defence, Peters so influential in midfield, and Hurst an unquenchable forager up front, you might have expected a more substantial and enduring dynasty. Instead, it was as though their great players were stamped with the legend Made for England, and only someone as pragmatic as Alf could consistently make their different strengths so integral to the successful working of a team.

This is not, for a moment, intended to belittle the achievements of Ron Greenwood, the West Ham manager who gave England three players of wonderful quality. His team wore their ambitions to play superior football on their blue and claret shirtsleeves.

That desire was deeply embedded in the thinking and the emotions of West Ham United and what I am saying, I suppose, is that football will always at some point demand a certain compromise between that which is beautiful and something else, something more gritty, more grounded in an understanding of what makes the difference between winning and losing.

I discussed this when referring to the night in Madrid when Nobby made his crucial, and some would say unacceptably cynical, contribution to Manchester United's passage into the European Cup final of 1968, and again I believe the debate is made relevant when considering the gap between the foundation Ron Greenwood had built for the creation of one of the great English club sides – and the relatively slim body of their total accomplishment.

I remember United playing an important championship game at Upton Park and the concerns we took on the journey to east London. The reality was that we won comfortably. Our fears that the combined quality of Moore, Hurst and Peters would imperil our title ambitions simply didn't materialise. It was impossible not to wonder why as we returned to the north. Was there a failure of competitive development in the West Ham team, did they lack the hard imperatives imposed by a Ramsey – or a Busby?

That had to be the ultimate conclusion. Busby had marshalled superb quality in his fabled Busby Babes and when the heirs of that team went on to be champions of Europe, George Best, Denis Law, before he was injured, and I were given a large portion of the credit for our football skills. Yet what Nobby displayed that night at the Bernabéu, and Busby countenanced, was something not possessed by the West Ham team which made such a huge contribution to England's World Cup hopes. Denis, Nobby, Paddy Crerand, Tony Dunne all had terrific talent in their different ways, but in Denis and Paddy's cases particularly it was often wrapped in the most silky of football skill.

Paddy was not quick – he once declared 'if I get any slower I'll be arrested for loitering' – but no one ever passed the ball with more beautiful and meaningful effect. Denis's instincts were ferocious. United also had the huge and often ruthless physical presence of Bill Foulkes at the centre of defence, where no one had a better, more acute helpmate than Nobby.

What I hope I'm presenting is not a picture designed to diminish any of the qualities brought to England by the West Ham trio – that would be impossible for any fair-minded judge – but one merely indicating their extraordinarily smooth absorption in Alf's grand plan. Their fusion in the England team was a huge factor in our belief that we could beat the world.

First Geoff, then Martin, gave us so much added buoyancy as we moved into the final phase of our preparation for the World Cup – and in the process made it abundantly clear to any discerning judge that, having made his defensive plan, Alf faced a few months of the most intense decision-making as he considered the claims of such strong new contenders for a place in his attacking scheme.

Ball and Peters had announced their threat to the corps of wingers, offered a new way of playing, and Hurst and Hunt had brought similar pressure to the great finisher Jimmy Greaves. As spring turned to summer, Jimmy, when out of the managerial earshot, could sometimes be heard humming the theme tune of the Michael Caine movie, 'What's it all about, Alfie?'

Though he had reminded Alf, in the unlikely event of it being necessary, that his draining bout of hepatitis had not diminished his superb and often uncanny scoring touch, he was also aware that the challenge he faced had its roots as much in Alf's philosophy of football as his assessment of individual skills.

The problem for Jimmy, it was becoming apparent enough, was that in Alf Ramsey's mind it was not so much all about how one player could from time to time hit sublime notes but perhaps how another, or maybe a pair of them, could strike a more consistent rhythm of effort and integration with his team-mates. Here, first Hunt, now Hurst, had proffered the most formidable credentials. Neither captured the imagination of the press box, neither threatened to surpass the exquisite mysteries of Jimmy's ability to ghost into the penalty area and pick a killing spot, but their promissory notes could be taken to any bank. Notes moistened by the sweat of non-stop and unswervingly relevant commitment.

Very quickly I made an assumption about Geoff which I never had to revise. It was that he had the ability to receive the ball in a forward position however heavy the attention of defenders, hold it for just quite as long as was necessary for reinforcements to arrive. He was, like Hunt, inexhaustible both physically and in terms of awareness of the movement of his team-mates.

His greatest threat to Jimmy's hopes lay, I had no doubt from when he arrived for the match against West Germany which followed our tactical triumph in Madrid, in how much he could contribute to the 4-3-3 system. Many years later the rise of Eric Cantona at United, in so many ways a quite different player, gave me a sharp reminder of one of Geoff's prime assets. It was that ability, aided by two good feet – his left one was always much more than passable – and an assured touch, to hold up the ball in an advanced position while taking all manner of punishment.

It was very clear that Hurst immediately felt at home in the team atmosphere that Alf had worked so hard to develop. Later, he recalled, 'Alf had this terrific ability to bring the team together, and that was partly due to his authority. He was the common denominator, the cement that bound us all together. He was all powerful and one of the things which made his job possible was the willingness with which we all accepted his authority.'

It was an understanding which quickly became refined to the point of becoming utterly implicit in almost everything we did on the final stages of the march into the summer of 1966.

There were many indicators that Alf's determination to finish the job, to make all of the hard work worthwhile, all the riding of criticism and doubts which had swirled up like sandstorms whenever our performance slipped below what was considered an acceptable level for potential world champions, had reached a new level of intensity. It was as though he already sniffed the aroma of success and some ultimate vindication and occasionally his deepest feelings erupted with great force.

My United team-mate John Connelly felt this strongly when he and Nobby Stiles and Alan Ball overstepped the line drawn by Alf so clearly much earlier in his England reign. I felt it when I was involved, relatively innocently I thought at the time, in that curfew-breaking foray into the West End in 1964.

John, Nobby and Alan had their critical moment after we assembled at the Lilleshall training centre for two weeks of something I can only describe as total immersion in the requirements that would be demanded of us if we were chosen to walk out into the World Cup final.

We reported for duty, and it is a phrase I do not use lightly – appropriately enough, Jimmy Greaves cracked – on 6 June, the twenty-second anniversary of the D-Day landings in Normandy. Our lives were not at risk, of course, but Alf had made it abundantly clear that our reputation for competitive honour and patriotism was.

The errant trio realised they were in trouble only when confronted by Wilf McGuinness, who had been recruited by Alf to the training camp staff, partly out of recognition of the brilliant way he had responded to a career-shattering injury with his work for both United and the England Under-23 team. They had slipped away to a nearby pub for a pint but had returned quickly in what they considered good order and also reassuring themselves that Alf had not imposed a specific ban on leaving the manorial Lilleshall premises. However, they were told by Wilf, 'You're in big trouble, lads, the boss knows you've been to the pub and he's blazing.'

Both Nobby and Bally were desperately contrite. They said they didn't realise they had gone out of bounds and had been in the pub only for the time it took to down their pints, which was just a few minutes. John's approach, though, was sharply different.

His feistiness was no doubt one of the reasons that had first made him appealing to Alf – and why he was still contending for a place in the great tournament as an orthodox winger – but Wilf, Nobby and Alan all believed he had horribly misread the situation when he declared, 'For heaven's sake, Alf, we're just talking about a pint here. We didn't realise we were doing anything wrong.'

Alf simmered for a moment, then rasped. 'All of you, get out of my sight.'

That marked the end of any socialising not expressly approved of by the manager and I always thought that it said a lot for Alf's respect for John Connelly's talent and combativeness that he survived his miscalculation and made it into the group stage of the tournament.

On reflection, it should have been clear enough to all of us that Alf had reached a fine point of disciplinary zeal. While discussing our pre-tournament programme – after Lilleshall we would have some fine-tuning on a three-match tour of Scandinavia and a final friendly against Poland in their gritty citadel of Chorzów in the minefields of Silesia – he told the press, 'I will take them out to the country and brainwash them about what we are going to do.'

His faithful trainer Harold Shepherdson, who had come to know him so well, later confirmed that Alf had now moved on to another level of resolve. He said, 'If there was a time when Alf could be said to have changed from second gear into top, and faced up to the last and hardest lap of all, it was when he met his team at Lilleshall.'

No one had a harder understanding of what it took to make a top professional than Wilf McGuinness. Before he broke his leg at the age of twenty-two, he was in the foothills of what was already shaping into an outstanding career. He played for United's first team before his eighteenth birthday and, despite the competition provided by the Busby Babes, he played enough games to qualify for a title winner's medal at the end of the 1956 season and when the injury disaster occurred he had already laid the foundation of an international career with two England caps. He was a ferociously committed player, a natural predecessor to my man Stiles. So Wilf knew a little bit about preparing yourself for the highest ground of football competition and he could not have been more enthusiastic about what he saw at Lilleshall.

Wilf recalled, 'The training was strong and physical for the end of the season. The players were all divided into groups and we passed on each group after fifteen minutes of hard slog. Every group was trying to outdo the other in the circuits and in the ball work. It was punishing work but the players really took to it. By the end of it they really knew they were fit. Alf wanted it that way. He wanted everyone to give everything they had. Les Cocker and Harold Shepherdson were ideal for what was needed. Les came from Leeds United and was a bit of a hard man. Harold had been in the job since Walter Winterbottom's time and was very experienced and well respected.'

The work was extremely hard – but, as Wilf said, it was also extremely rewarding. For me it was a little like approaching the end of a long journey, one that I knew deep down had made me a better footballer and, I hoped, a stronger man.

The mornings were devoted to the hard physical work and ball practice and a substantial amount of the latter was concerned with polishing tactics. If there was quite a bit of player participation in the debates surrounding that tactical approach, with Nobby and Jack particularly voluble during and after the action, there was never any argument about who had the final word. Alf delivered it with ever-increasing urgency – and precision.

In the afternoons we had no-contact sport before a soak in the bath and an early dinner, which was followed by either a lecture or a film. We went to our dormitory-style rooms around 9 p.m., where the beds were comfortable enough and by the second week far more tempting than any rash ideas of breaking curfew.

By this stage we had also gathered the nerve to fulfil Alf's demand that our practice sessions were played at something close to the intensity of real matches. This development came when Alf suddenly halted a practice game to complain that we simply weren't playing hard enough. We told him of our worries that we might risk ourselves or our team-mates so close to the World Cup. Wasn't this, we wondered, not evidence of our concern that at this late stage nothing should come needlessly between us and our best chances of success?

Alf was singularly unpersuaded and still less impressed. We were not, he pointed out, attending a holiday camp but the most important testing ground of our careers. What happened on the training pitch was not so much an aid to superior performance but its very foundation. So we fought harder for every ball, we picked up bruises and we accepted Alf's hard dogma that we had to go full out – and take our chances.

All twenty-seven of us were left standing and so Alf had to draw the fine line between those five who returned to their families, and whatever consolation that might bring in what would surely be the emptiest summer of their professional lives, and the twenty-two who packed for what amounted to the last of the most demanding auditions of their football careers.

Alf passed his regrets to the fallen and told the rest of us that we still had everything to play for and, by implication, that he didn't have to dwell on, everything to lose.

The final cut – I believed with some pride and relief – delivered the best-prepared group of players in the history of English football – right down to their toenails, in the care of which, the team doctor Alan Bass discovered with alarm, he had to educate the majority of the squad.

Here were the players who travelled to Heathrow airport for the flight to Helsinki for the start of the final reckoning . . .

Goalkeepers: Gordon Banks (Leicester City), Ron Springett (Sheffield Wednesday), Peter Bonetti (Chelsea)

Full-backs: Jimmy Armfield (Blackpool), Ray Wilson (Everton), George Cohen (Fulham), Gerry Byrne (Liverpool)

Half-backs: Nobby Stiles (Manchester United), Martin Peters (West Ham United), Jack Charlton (Leeds United), Ron Flowers (Wolverhampton Wanderers), Bobby Moore (West Ham United), Norman Hunter (Leeds United)

Forwards: Terry Paine (Southampton), Ian Callaghan (Liverpool), Jimmy Greaves (Tottenham Hotspur), Roger Hunt (Liverpool), Geoff Hurst (West Ham United), Bobby Charlton (Manchester United), Alan Ball (Blackpool), George Eastham (Arsenal) and John Connelly (Manchester United).

Everything was in place, including agreed financial rewards which seem so flimsy now when you set them against the ambitions we carried that summer and the levels of expectation building in the nation. The Football Association proposed that each player received a bonus up to £1,500 on a sliding scale, depending on the number of individual appearances in the tournament. We rejected the suggestion in the briefest of debates. We had travelled along the same road, made the same commitments – and if anyone doubted this they had needed only to watch a random work session in the Shropshire meadows – and the FA took our point. They accepted that each member of the squad should be paid £1,000 from a pot which today seems so bizarrely modest, and which would soon enough be confirmed as such when it was reported that the FA were required to pay a quarter of a million pounds of corporation tax from their net profits.

George Cohen, who had a better idea of business affairs than most of us, was also irritated later in the year when he received a summons to collect a case of Bollinger champagne and two others containing red and white wine which had been stored in the underground car park of the FA at Lancaster Gate in London. He reported, 'I remember driving into the car park and thinking, "My God, where is all this booze going?" You could have fitted the entire players' allocation into a couple of car spaces but the rest of the car park was filled to the gunwales. That was the kind of thing that came along regularly and it did put you on edge.

'Players played and took what they were given and the FA rode a gravy train which on this occasion had taken on a massive supply of champagne and the finest burgundy. All in all, I reflected, it was quite nice of the FA to remember us.'

Yet George's old outrage had reason to be fanned down the years – and maybe not least in 2002 when the England team flying to the Far East for the World Cup were given a week's stopover at a luxury hotel in Dubai with their families or girlfriends, and this after much clamouring for bonuses stretching into the millions.

However, George, like the surviving rest of us when we gather for our annual reunions, readily accepts that we inhabited another world back in 1966, and that not one of us would give back a day of the adventure which is still at the core of our experience. No, we say, we wouldn't trade it for the £200,000 a week commanded by today's Premier League stars.

It was, though, an experience which by the time we landed in Helsinki we knew well enough was likely to bring a twist or a tremor with almost every step along the way. Alf provided still another in the Finnish capital when he announced the team. He had promised to make changes, insisting that indeed every player still had plenty of time to make, or undo, his case, but it was something of a convulsion when the name of Bobby Moore was missing from the team-sheet.

It was unthinkable – at least to me – that Bobby should stumble out of contention at this late stage but then it was also true that he had contractual problems with West Ham and, technically at least, this might just have left him an unregistered, and thus ineligible, player at the start of the World Cup.

Bobby later theorised that Alf might have been prodding him towards a swift concentration of his mind on a difficult situation, one which had been complicated by a report that the Arsenal manager Billy Wright, aware of discord between the player and his manager Ron Greenwood, had made West Ham an offer.

If that indeed was Alf's intention, Bobby confirmed that his omission certainly had a cautionary effect. He said, 'Everyone in the squad was aware that different players would get an opportunity because Alf had said he would be trying to play everyone if he could during the tour. Yet it was a warning and I thought, "Oh, right."

'Alf didn't speak much about the captaincy, though he had asked, before I took over from Jimmy Armfield in 1963, whether I wanted the job, was I aware of the responsibility? It was a vote of confidence and support as much as anything when he appointed me. I didn't really influence him as a captain, it was such a good era and we knew various players could have come in because the backbone was established. He would have a quiet word with me about what he intended, to keep me informed, but only after he had made up his mind. He never consulted me on selecting a player.

'When he left me out in Finland he never said anything. Norman Hunter was playing well, his club Leeds were successful and I was in disagreement with West Ham. People, including Alf, may have thought my mind was on other things. It may have been his way of saying, "I know what's going on, show me you want it." It did create a doubt, showed me I had got to work at it.'

Bobby returned to the team for the next match in Oslo, which for me seemed like the last word in the way of a formality. But, then, I had never doubted Bobby's role in the team, the reassurance his presence brought, and there was no doubt I had come to take him for granted. I never thought anyone should play in his place. He had so much vision, so much time.

Alf also left out Jimmy Greaves, while giving Ian Callaghan his first cap, but if he had created a few fresh headlines, the game itself provided little fuel for more controversy. We beat Finland comfortably, 3-0, Callaghan was lively on the wing and Martin Peters scored his first goal for England.

In Oslo we overwhelmed Norway 6-1 and the restored Jimmy Greaves scored four goals, which made him England's top scorer with a remarkable forty-three in forty-nine games. It was a strike rate which said everything about his superb facility in front of goal and though the Norwegian defence was less than obdurate, Jimmy, understandably enough, felt that he had achieved a full-scale resurrection. He said that whatever the opposition you still had to put the ball in the net, adding, 'I felt after Oslo that I had cracked it, and when we beat Poland at the end of the tour I was sure that Roger and I would be the front two.'

Before the win in Chorzów we had beaten Denmark comfortably enough in Copenhagen and as we turned for home – and the start of the World Cup in six days' time – there was a powerful sense that we had announced ourselves as serious contenders. Not the least encouragement was another superb performance from Martin Peters against the tough, quick Poles. Ray Wilson, who was generally more voluble on the pitch than off it, confided, 'The last few days have convinced me that we can do it. I think we have moved into a different league.'

That was the message, and the conviction, Alf had sought to implant for three and a half years and often in the face of widespread and strident ridicule. But now he had believers in the most crucial place of all, the dressing room. The prize of a place in a team of champions had never seemed so real. It was as though we could close our eyes and almost touch it.

9. The Legacy of Dunc

That urge to reach out, to take hold of something made tangible by all the work and the self-examination which had followed the abrupt awakening on that winter night in Paris, was for me quite overwhelming in the early morning of Monday 11 July 1966 – the first day of the World Cup.

I opened the curtains of the room I shared with Ray Wilson, looked up to a cloudless blue sky and then quickly drew them together again because Ray was sleeping like a baby. I showered and dressed as quietly as I could and went down to the breakfast room.

I wanted this day to fly, I wanted to be in command of all of it – and the twenty days that followed – and to be able to say that this indeed was the time of my football life, one from which I didn't take a single regret.

I was twenty-eight years old and had played sixty-eight times for England, seventeen times more than the closest to me in experience, Jimmy Greaves.

I spanned the epochs of Stanley Matthews and Tom Finney, two of the greatest players the world would ever see, and this one newly inhabited by youngsters like Alan Ball and

Martin Peters, who carried no other weight of memory, or disappointment, beyond their own freshly minted ambition.

By the sharpest comparison, in an England shirt, and in the company of such as Johnny Haynes and Billy Wright, I had known moments of great hope often but invariably consumed by another reality – one of futility and despair that we would never move on to a truly competitive level in the World Cup, never know the surge of conviction that we had created new horizons that really could be achieved. On so many occasions I'd had reason to wonder if I was packing my bags on a road leading nowhere.

So, yes, this was my time, England's time. It had to be. Too many possibilities had been created, too much hard work done, for it not to be.

Our ancestors had introduced football to the world, rightly considered it a gift of great value, but the generations that followed made the critical misunderstanding that we would always own it, always be the arbiters of what was right about it and what was wrong.

One result, which in the next weeks had to be reshaped and swept away, was that we had barely scratched the surface of the game's greatest tournament, and if anyone needed some perspective on this scandal of waste and arrogance it was surely provided by Uruguay, whom we would be facing at Wembley in a few hours. Perhaps not just Uruguay, though; maybe we also had to beat the worst aspects of our football nature and chief among them was that complacency which came with the misapprehension that we were in some way innately superior, that if success had been delayed for so long it was, ultimately, still inevitable.

Four years earlier in Chile we had 'celebrated' our first

appearance in a World Cup quarter-final with, as I have already reported, a conspicuous lack of honour and self-belief. Some of us had believed that the goalless draw against Bulgaria in a match utterly lacking in character somehow represented a significant milestone on the way to redemption. Uruguay, with a fraction of our population, had by then been champions of the world twice.

Now, my team-mates and I could tell ourselves we would never have a better chance of taking the title before our own people in our national stadium; this was something for me to reflect upon at some depth over my morning coffee. At the heart of it there was more than anything a nagging feeling that a large debt had to be discharged.

We had, finally, the chance to deliver to the vast but long-frustrated following of English football something they could treasure, something which had long been the property of their counterparts in Uruguay, Italy, West Germany and Brazil. And if we couldn't do it, if we couldn't take this chance so generously proffered by the football gods, well, we would have the rest of our lives to ask how it was we failed our people and ourselves.

It meant that if the breakfast room was still to be filled by the chirruping of Alan Ball, the clatter of Nobby's cutlery or some debate launched boisterously by my brother Jack, I did not lack for companions.

They jostled in from my past. There were the schoolteachers who helped me along the way, Jimmy Murphy inviting me to have a sherry as he talked – sometimes it threatened to be endlessly – about football in his little office at Old Trafford.

There was my other mentor, Tanner, still exhorting me to do well, still demanding to know the Saturday afternoon results even as his life slipped away in that dimly lit bedroom.

There was the large cast of relatives, led by my mother Cissie, with my father Robert, quiet but I liked to think proud at her shoulder. And there were all the uncles, the football ones who gave me first understanding of the challenges that I would have to conquer if I made it as a professional. I thought of the days visiting with one of them at Chesterfield and the insights that accumulated so quickly, not least a sense of the tension that was so palpable around the fight for first-team places, which when relieved by the sight of their names on the team-sheet reminded me, at least a little, of the heady mood of the lads bursting out of the colliery lift at the end of their shift.

There were the other uncles, too; the ones who gave me so many glimpses of lives that had to be waged beyond the football field. The most colourful of them, without doubt, was Uncle Buck. He didn't follow his brothers into football but that didn't prevent his achieving his own degree of stardom. He was a poacher who enjoyed legendary status along the river banks and some said, though it was never confirmed to me with any certainty, that there were times when he used dynamite. That was enough to provide me with an extraordinary image: a river exploding with an array of beautiful salmon.

On my father's side I had the uncles Tommy and Dave. Tommy was gentle and extremely kind. He took me to a shop to buy me my first football boots, Playfair Pigskins, and as I pulled them on to my feet so eagerly I thought, 'This must be the best day of my life.'

Dave had a little boat which he moored on the Wansbeck River, where he ran out fishing lines and one day he ran aground, much to the consternation of Tommy, who was dressed in his best clothes, including the baggy pants that were in fashion then, and was supposed to be on his way to a wedding. He had got into the boat with grave misgivings after we had met Dave in the street.

Tommy had been right to be apprehensive when Dave told him that we would just have a small outing on the river. He made a bedraggled sight on the river bank after Dave had started to carry him through the water on his shoulders, then promptly discarded him when I shouted that the boat had shifted and was in danger of floating away. Dave and Tommy were just two of the characters who came teeming into my memory as I thought of who I was and all those who had helped me along to this day which would do so much to shape the rest of my life, one way or the other.

I thought of three lads in a boat – and another one who was still, eight years after his death, the one I always came to when I thought of who had inspired me most vividly and explained what you could do on a football field if you were blessed with great talent – and determination.

I thought of Duncan Edwards. Big, incomparable Dunc. I thought of him hauling that bed he had picked out in the national service army billet we shared in Shropshire after deciding the one I had been allocated was simply not good enough. Big Dunc, who I couldn't help believing with every fibre would have made a mighty contribution to this day. He would, I speculated, have been around the peak of his physical development and experience. He would have carried so much into England's most promising campaign to win the World Cup.

Inevitably, I suppose, my thoughts on this summer morning turned again to Munich, reminding me once more of what a crazy, hard and cruel world it could be. How sometimes it was near impossible to fathom or accept; but, then, what was the alternative to making the best of what was left, pressing on to the point where, if you were strong enough, and lucky enough, you might have a day like this filled with the greatest opportunity? There wasn't a serious option, of course. You accepted the worst of it, however painful and bewildering, and fought to make the best of the rest.

In this I knew there could be no better example, no brighter light, than the shining legacy of Big Dunc.

It was an inspiration that had served me so well, helping to lift me away from those first days when I struggled so hard and so painfully to know how I should react to what had happened in Munich. Then it was so overwhelming, so oppressively on top of you, squeezing the breath out of you, creating a horror so surreal you could never have imagined it waited in ambush. Not any of it, and certainly not the sight of my great friends and team-mates laid out in a neat row where they had been carried from the burning wreckage. Or the great man of football Matt Busby, bloodstained and terribly pale and me putting my jacket around his shoulders before I was guided into the back of a pick-up truck which was partly filled with coal and being driven to the hospital, with just a small graze on my head, and then passing out when a doctor gave me an injection. And then waking up in the ward and asking a German patient in the next bed who spoke a little English to read from the newspaper he held before him the names of those who had lived and those who had died.

I was back in England when the news came in that Duncan, whose strength in his fight for life against such heavy odds had staggered the German doctors, had lost his battle two weeks after the crash. My mother told me and it was as though all the lights in the house had been turned off and I would never see the sun again. I went to see a doctor and he talked about what would, I suppose, be described today as grief management but it is a phrase that I still find difficult to understand. You do not manage grief because in my opinion there is no way you can do that. It comes over you in waves and you just have to hope that there is a day when it no longer engulfs every moment of your existence. Old friends came to the house. Young lads brought their footballs and on occasion I went out into Beatrice Street for a kick-around. And all the time I wondered if the game would ever have again its old and joyful meaning.

There were so many to grieve over but at the heart of it there was always Duncan. When my mother gave me the news of his death I knew straightaway I would spend every day of the rest of my life honouring him, and that dedication was never as concentrated or as strong as it was at the dawn of this World Cup.

I could see him lugging on his shoulders that great bed across the barracks dormitory. And I could feel again the emptiness that came when he took his regular leave for first-team duty with United and sometimes, when I saw a plane in the Shropshire sky, I would say to myself, 'Maybe that's Dunc and the boys', and I longed to be with them.

Once I went back with him to his home in Dudley in Worcestershire and as we went through the front door his mother said, 'Duncan, I've just attacked someone who came in here to do some burgling.' She had whacked the fellow and while she had none of the power of her son she obviously had more than enough of his will. I realised now that Duncan had got so much of it from his formidable mother.

She had a chart on the wall which listed all of Duncan's games, his movements of the past and future, and the details were prodigious. Once, with army games, too, he had played 100 games in a season.

I have been back to Dudley many times to speak of their hero and mine, and sometimes when I'm told he was one of the greatest players I think to myself, I suppose almost jealously, yes, but do you realise quite how good he was, do you have any idea of how great he would have become?

That feeling came back to me so strongly on that day in July 1966. England would have so much strength at its disposal in the next three weeks. We had the security provided by Gordon Banks in goal. We had the superb leadership of Bobby Moore. We had the calm but also fierce defence of Cohen and Wilson and Jack Charlton and the radar-tactical perception and tackling of Nobby, the insatiable appetite of Alan Ball. Jimmy Greaves, arguably the most acute finisher in the history of English football, still believed it was his time. Martin Peters had brought the promise of new and brilliantly innovative talent. Roger Hunt and Geoff Hurst had made it clear that they were prepared to run for ever.

Unfortunately, though, we didn't have Duncan Edwards, which, as I ran back once more through all the great players I had seen, and played with and against, I had to conclude was a loss which could scarcely be measured. He would have given us so much going in against the knowing, obdurate defenders of Uruguay. He was, I kept coming back to it, the best player I ever saw.

Today, it is still astonishing when I bring back into focus the profile of his brief, meteoric career. He was sixteen when he played in the First Division for the first time in April 1953, against Cardiff City, the youngest in history. Less than two years later he was an England player and there is a picture of him taken in training before the game against Scotland which astounds me in what it says about the confidence he carried on to the international stage. Astounding, at least for someone like me, who, three years later when Duncan had been lost in Munich, joined the great names of the English game with such trepidation. Duncan is portrayed laughing in the company of Tom Finney and Billy Wright. It is not the picture of two legends and a boy. It is of three men going about their business, relaxed and utterly sure of themselves.

Duncan was twenty-one when he died. Now, in 1966, he would have been twenty-nine and running the show, at least that part which came after Alf sent us on to the field. He really was a beast of a player. Beast; yes, that is the word that always came into my mind when I saw him play. From fifty, sixty, even seventy yards, he could send the ball wherever he wanted it to go, right foot, left foot. One pass might go like a perfectly thrown lance, direct and to the inch of his target. Another might curl beyond a defender and into the path of a team-mate who had made himself space. He was huge in defence and always creative and strong in midfield but in my book he was always a striker, always filled with the power and the skill to destroy a defence.

Thousands of British servicemen saw perhaps the ultimate evidence of this in Berlin's Olympic Stadium in May 1956, when England beat the reigning world champions West Germany 3-1. Still only twenty years of age, the scale of Duncan's performance was quite breathtaking. At the end the army lads ran down to the field to touch their hero, to celebrate one of the most thrilling performances, no one needed to tell them, that they would ever see.

Duncan *was* England that day. He was their power, their drive, their ability to take apart piece by piece the team which had shocked the world with their ambush of the sublime

Hungarians in the World Cup in Switzerland two years earlier. Fritz Walter, who had led the Germans so forcefully to that triumph, scored a late goal but it had been made as inconsequential as all else the Germans did after Duncan struck twenty minutes into the game.

He collected the ball on the edge of his own penalty area and beat five Germans before driving the ball home from thirty yards. It was the kind of intervention which destroys the will of opponents and by then it had become an integral part of Duncan's modus operandi. He made anything seem possible and when I thought of the degree of command he showed in the stadium where the great black American sprinter Jesse Owens once spread-eagled Hitler's master race theories, I also recalled with a smile the change of strategy Duncan once imposed on the normally uncompromising Jimmy Murphy.

Apart from his stunning feats in the senior game, Duncan had three times led United to winning campaigns in the FA Youth Cup. Before the end of that extraordinary run, Jimmy became concerned that the rest of the team were becoming overly dependent on their masterful captain. This led him to a decision which amazed the team before a tie against an impressive collection of young Chelsea players at Stamford Bridge.

Said Jimmy, 'I think it would be good if on this occasion when you have the ball you look for some other option than simply passing the ball to Duncan.' At half-time we were trailing by a goal and Jimmy said, a little sheepishly, 'Remember what I said about finding other options, well, forget it. Give the bloody ball to Duncan.' So we did – and we won.

I always felt safe when Duncan was around, on and off the field, and on this morning when I had such optimism about

England's chances I also thought how much less of a challenge we would be facing if he had been spared to lead us.

In the years that followed I learned that conviction went much wider than I imagined. I have been involved in many ceremonials dedicated to honouring Duncan, including opening a museum in his name in his home town and placing a blue plaque outside his old digs around the corner from Old Trafford, in Stretford. I have seen statues unveiled and his name evoked countless times when the talk has been of supreme football achievement, but perhaps it was the intensity of the feeling triggered by his absence in 1966 which touched me most.

He had played a vital part in the qualifying drive for the World Cup in Sweden in 1958 and no one doubted that he would have given England so much more authority and impact in the finals. In 1966 that sense remained strong in the minds of many leading football men. Stanley Matthews, no less, had once described him as a 'rock in a raging sea', and many years later Terry Venables, a midfield star of Chelsea and Tottenham who would become England manager, said, 'Had he lived it would have been Duncan not Bobby Moore leading England in 1966.'

Tommy Docherty, a future manager of Scotland who had felt the force and the scale of Duncan's game out on the field, was most emphatic of all. He declared, 'There is no doubt Duncan would have become the greatest player ever. Not just in British football, with United and England, but the best in the world. George Best was something special, as was Pelé and Maradona, but in my mind Duncan was better in terms of all-round ability and skill.'

Looking back, I suppose Duncan was bound to invade my

thinking on the day that signalled what seemed certain to be the defining phase of my career, which had started in the shadow of his greatness – yes, greatness, because if it was unfulfilled along the peaks of club and international football, it had been established, come what may, in a way that I knew would never wither in either my mind or my heart.

There were so many people who accompanied me that day through the rituals of preparation – I took optional training on a nearby pitch because I always believed it was vital to loosen up at least a little – and in all the reverie that can come when you try truly to concentrate your mind, I should not have been surprised that Duncan's presence would be so pervasive.

Most of all, I suppose, I reflected on the fact that fate had denied him the chance to finish his work. It was his tragedy, and English football's terrible loss, but maybe tonight we could make a start on filling some of the place he had left so empty.

His inspiration, I prayed, might just keep us safe.

10. Staying Alive

It was not as I hoped it would be that first night at Wembley and perhaps not as the nation had been led to expect. Still less was it a monument to the spirit and meaning of Duncan Edwards, but then the Uruguayans, as anyone might have guessed, were in no mood to usher me or anyone else towards any swift confirmation of our highest hopes

Easy rides have never been offered by South American football teams, never have and never will be, it is not in their nature, and the Uruguay we encountered had come – you could see it in their eyes even as the opening ceremonials unfolded – with a single, ruthless purpose. Plainly, they intended to delay, if not utterly wreck, the party.

Alf had been careful to play down the pressure on us before we had to make our first statement of the World Cup. Defeating Uruguay would be a good, positive start, it would enliven the hopes of the nation and calm the media, but it was not something we had to pursue at all costs. It was important to go forward with a degree of caution.

We also had to remember that his first selection was not an indicator of anything more than his instinct for what might work best against the inevitably, and classically, loaded Uruguayan defence.

Because it was so obvious they would retreat en masse behind the ball, Alf had decided to invest in the width of attack offered by a traditional winger, John Connelly, rather than the tactical inventions of Martin Peters. And if chances were going to be sparse, and had to be seized upon hungrily and with maximum efficiency, Jimmy Greaves had shown enough of his old sharpness to keep his place at the expense of Geoff Hurst.

As always, Alf had announced the team on the eve of the game. He always said it was crucial that a player had plenty of time to compose himself before any challenge, and certainly that of greeting the start of a home World Cup. He stressed that the work had been done, nothing had been left unattended. He was pleased with our preparation, our response to all that he had asked.

Now we just had to play, with discipline and an understanding that we would have an extremely long time to regret any failure.

For me it was another instance of Alf striking the right note between gung-ho optimism and any excess of self-doubt. Certainly I felt that along with my team-mates I had been brought to a proper understanding of what was in front of me, and what I was expected to deliver. It was, I suppose, a final underpinning of the trust that had been built, brick by brick, down the years.

Indeed, by now I had reached the point where I saw in Alf all the most important qualities which had been lacking in the leadership of England since the Football Association had deigned to accept an invitation to compete in the World Cup of Brazil in 1950, by which time it had grown from the first tournament hosted by Uruguay twenty years earlier into the competitive pinnacle of the world's most popular game.

Alf knew the game so deeply, understood the demands it made on all the different personalities who often had in common only the degree of their talent and the insecurities placed upon it by the pressure of the highest level of competition. Alf could relate to the fears of a player because he had known them so well. They had kept him awake in the night, brought beads of sweat to his brow. This didn't make him anyone's idea of a favourite uncle – he wasn't made like that – but you always knew there wasn't anything you feared as a footballer that was unknown to him.

His understanding was a huge asset for us all and, again, I mean no disrespect to the knowledge and intelligence of Walter Winterbottom, something that had been so plainly missing in Chile four years earlier, when always you searched vainly for a breath of the unity that was now so implicit in all we carried towards the game with Uruguay.

I felt this most strongly when, after my workout and writing a few letters back in my room and then a brief stroll among well-wishers in the Hendon streets, I joined my team-mates for my favourite light meal of poached eggs at 4.30 p.m., a time ordained by the team doctor Alan Bass as it permitted optimum digestion in the three hours before the Wembley kick-off.

On the bus to the stadium there was, as usual on the approach of the most important matches, rather more reflection than talk but the tension grew swiftly enough when we reached the stadium, saw the banners and the expectant faces, and filed into the dressing room. It was then that my pal Ray Wilson and I put in place a ritual that would serve for the rest of the tournament and, when I think about it, was in some ways quite as bizarre as anything contrived by George Cohen.

As room-mates we piled all our gear in the same bag, which Ray would always carry to the dressing room. Twenty minutes before the start, after my rubdown, Ray handed me my boots, one at a time. He then passed me an ammonia inhaler, a sniff of which I liked to think had the effect of clearing my head. It had to be the same one with the top broken and I was obliged to use it just once. Then, when the buzzer sounded, we all shook hands, and some like Nobby and Bally yelled some exhortation, before walking out into the corridor and up to the pitch.

Finally, the waiting was over. The trial runs in South America and Europe and here in the great stadium were done and evaluated and Alf had reminded us of his first stirring declaration, 'Gentlemen, most certainly we will win the World Cup.'

We, like so much of the nation, were primed for the launch of a great adventure and, as I had when I looked out on to the day that morning at the hotel, I longed for a first confident, impressive stride, quick evidence that we had the means to move forward more positively than we had ever done before.

Unfortunately, Uruguay had their own and quite different picture of the immediate future. It was one which would go some way to explaining the extraordinary achievements of their past.

From the first kick they announced their intention to create blanket defence and no football nation on earth, except perhaps Italy through the ages, have such a vocation for draining the life and the optimism out of their opponents. For them it is not a brutal matter, an unbroken chain of destruction; it is a branch of art – a dark one no doubt – but, coupled with an ability to strike suddenly and with the most polished skill, it had not only twice made them world champions but was also central to their belief that the possibility of a third triumph was never too far away.

They had lovely skills but their method was both cynical and brutal. It said you just had to swarm behind the ball, make your tackles, cover the dangerous ground, needle the opponent next to you in any way you could, a crack on the ankle, a judiciously aimed stream of spit, and wait out the moment when you were able to sweep through the anger and the frustration that you had built in the opposition with your version of torture by a thousand cuts.

I fancied before the end of this game that the Uruguayans, like all the South American teams I had encountered at home and abroad, were producing something they probably practised in their sleep. Indeed, before the end of this World Cup I would once again be haunted by how it was that some of the most gifted football nations, who could unfurl passages of beauty that might have graced the Bolshoi, saw systematic skulduggery not as some desperately contrived intrusion into the game but an implicit part of it. If football was a reflection of life, they seemed to be saying, it had to have all of it, the good, the bad and the downright ugly.

But then it seemed that when the game was over they also believed that, unlike in real life, the worst of the behaviour, the direst of the crimes, could easily be washed away.

Naturally enough, we were all disappointed by the goalless draw but Alf was quick to point out that if we hadn't covered ourselves with glory, nor had we significantly weakened our chances of qualifying from the group. Uruguay were always going to be the toughest opponents at this stage of the tournament and his biggest fear, he confided, was that the attacking skill which lurked in the trenches of their defence might just produce a killing counter-attack – and a huge increase in the pressure which inevitably rested on a host nation. As it was, we had survived such a disaster – and could anticipate rather easier pickings against our other group opponents, Mexico and France.

In this sense we hadn't dropped a point but gained one and that argument was strengthened considerably two days later when the teams considered least likely to make it to the knock-out stage from our group, France and Mexico, drew at Wembley.

We could also take some satisfaction, against the background of considerable national disillusion, that Uruguay's deeply entrenched defence had not totally disguised the fact that some wearers of their blue shirts were players of certifiable world class. Most notably these were Julio César Cortés and Pedro Rocha, who in their next game scored the goals in the 2-1 defeat of a French team which had gone ahead with an early goal – and then paid a heavy price when the Uruguayans were obliged to abandon their tank-trap defence in search of at least two goals.

John Connelly came closest to penetrating the Uruguayan cover when his header dropped on to the crossbar. That would be a poignant memory for him because had he scored he might have profited from the extra space that in all likelihood would have been conceded in Uruguay's need to hit back. As it was, he felt the life of his game being stifled quite relentlessly and later he spoke wistfully of his growing sense that he was playing his last game so early in the tournament.

He said, 'We really gave their full-backs stick in that match but somehow we were not getting over the crosses. I was surprised and glad to be back in the team because I knew Alf had an admiration for Peters, who was a very good player. I'd played fairly well in my matches against Scotland, Norway and Denmark – you know when you're going well. But Uruguay was a bad one to come back for. They were determined they weren't going to lose.

'I hit the bar and scraped the post. I was told later I got a bit of criticism on television, that the commentators had some laughs. It's all right for them, they stay on. The crowd had applause for Bobby Moore, playing at the back with Jack, and I remember thinking, "He should try it up here." Up front we were three against eight some of the time. I couldn't believe it: in the next match against Mexico there were so many people going forward. If we'd scored against Uruguay, maybe the team would have stayed the same.'

Maybe it would; maybe the same piece of football history would have been written in another way with a slightly different cast of characters.

Certainly John Connelly was a fine player and a good colleague and when he died in 2012, the third member of the squad to leave us after Bobby Moore and Alan Ball, it was no less wrenching because he hadn't played a more prolonged part in the tournament.

I liked his honesty, his straight manner which came so clearly from his roots in South Lancashire, and that was as evident on the field as off it. And, of course, he was right to reflect on what might have happened had he launched England's World Cup campaign with a goal prised out of the steel jaws of Uruguay's defence.

None of us, after all, had been encouraged to believe that we were immovable parts of the grand plan. Bobby Moore had his brief convulsion of concern in Scandinavia when his name was missing from the team-sheet. Martin Peters, who had taken his chances so superbly in the last strides of the build-up, and played so well in the final friendly in Poland, no doubt must have secretly felt that he had done enough to make the opening game. Similarly, Geoff Hurst might have believed that his hard running, his swift understanding of Alf's priorities, had earned him the chance to set the ball rolling. For myself, I couldn't count the times over the years when Alf had given me a chiding word, a frown of reproach for mistakes I had made, especially on the defensive side of the game.

So, yes, there was a fine line we all had to walk and none of us could make any presumptions about our status until the team for our last game of the tournament was picked. When I think of this reality, I have also to say once more that it was one of Alf's achievements that he installed this fundamental understanding so surely. He never said that if a John Connelly was overlooked in favour of someone like Martin Peters, it made him a lesser player or someone who had failed a crucial test. No, every situation threw up new demands, new situations, and if you had made it into his final squad, if you were there to be called into action at any stage, well, you had proved yourself a footballer worthy of high regard. Most certainly, you had won his confidence.

John Connelly also had the warm regard of all his squad-mates when, three years before he died and forty-three years after he played against Uruguay, and came so close to making a breakthrough against the most defiant and technically accomplished defenders, he went to Downing Street to receive his World Cup winner's medal from the prime minister Gordon Brown.

This was the result of pressure on the world authority, Fifa, that such medals should be awarded not just to the winners of the final but all those who had contributed on the field.

Those of us who had already been recognised in the honours system felt the same pleasure in the year of the millennium when Alan Ball, George Cohen, Roger Hunt, Nobby Stiles and Ray Wilson arrived at Buckingham Palace on a spring morning to be presented with the MBE by the Queen. We also applauded George's adherence to protocol when the Queen, while handing him his medal, said, 'It's been a long time.' He later reported that the response he suppressed was, 'Yes, Ma'am, and quite a lot has happened.'

What he had in mind, no doubt, was that he had three times been required to fight cancer with great courage and, along the way, rebuild a business that he had gone into when his playing career was cut short with savage abruptness two years after the World Cup. He had also had to sell a beautiful house in Kent and fund a pension plan with the sale of his World Cup medal. He had to deal with the tragedies of losing his mother when she was run down in a Fulham street by a juggernaut truck and his brother in a violent incident at the night club he owned, a tragedy over which George fought a long and frustrating battle for legal redress.

Yet in all my many and always warm meetings with George since 1966 I never once saw him with his head down or his shoulders slumped. Always he had, along with his wry sense of humour, the demeanour of a man determined not to let the worst of fate get the better of him.

That was the kind of attitude which, to my mind, typified

the spirit of the team. I also recognised it in John Connelly, when I travelled to see him in Burnley, where he enjoyed the best part of his club career and then returned as the amiable proprietor of a fish and chip restaurant. He never moaned about his World Cup fate, never dwelled for more than a fleeting moment on the personal glory that was lost when he so narrowly failed to beat the Uruguayan goalkeeper Ladislao Mazurkiewicz.

He said, 'What really have I got to complain about? I had a good career in football and I have plenty of reasons to feel proud. How many lads out there would have been pleased to have had a few of my experiences?'

The briefest glance back at John Connelly's career provides an emphatic answer to that question. He played twenty games for England, scored seven goals, and right up to that last game against Uruguay, one that could not have been designed less favourably to the needs of an orthodox winger, he played as if all might still be before him. Along with the World Cup medal he received at Downing Street, he won championship medals with Burnley and Manchester United.

As it happened he was England's first casualty of the World Cup but it was not a status to weigh down a man who played his football, and lived his life, with everything he had.

Certainly he wasn't alone in his disappointment as we travelled back to Hendon Hall bracing ourselves against an inevitable tide of criticism. In the morning the papers were apparently filled with extreme scepticism over our prospects, making the flamenco snap and high praise of Madrid a forlorn and distant memory. I say apparently because Alf was adamant that no one should so much as glance at a newspaper at breakfast, let alone digest the considered opinions of such as

Desmond Hackett in the *Express*, Frank McGhee in the *Mirror*, or even the toastmaster of Madrid, Geoffrey Green of *The Times*.

I doubt, though, that anyone could have portrayed our difficulties more vividly than did George Cohen many years later. He recalled, 'The Uruguayans were as stubborn and difficult as Alf imagined and predicted they would be. We couldn't get round them or through them. Connelly found himself running into blind alleys, as did Wilson and I when we tried to steal a little ground on the overlap. Bobby Charlton was unable to get within firing range, Roger Hunt threw himself against a brick wall. In the end we were relying on Jimmy Greaves to thread his way through some blue-shirted resistance, but it didn't happen.

'The South American coach Ondino Viera made no pretence to any ambition beyond survival. He had a sweeper, the captain Horacio Troche, behind a back four and everyone else, including their most creative players Rocha and Cortés, in withdrawn positions. Body-checks and high tackles were commonplace and, ironically enough, Nobby received one of the worst. But he scarcely blinked and carried on. We ran relentlessly but only into an ever-deepening deadlock.'

Though Alf had banned us from reading the papers, not everybody followed his instructions and the following day no one had any doubt that we had to win back the belief of the people, and, perhaps, a little of our own. If Alf had read the newspaper criticism, and I suspected he had because like most football people he found it difficult to resist the temptation in the wake of any performance, good or bad, he firmly rejected the idea that we were suddenly in crisis.

He said that most certainly we could have played better but

then it was also true we could have played much worse. He said he was happy with the defensive performance, it had been solid and watchful and never looked in danger of allowing a sneak goal that might well have been both psychologically and tactically disastrous. As for the attack, well, it wasn't the best day but he added, 'You will rarely find opponents more capable and dedicated to making your lives difficult.'

Some newspapers agitated for us all to be returned promptly to the training field to work on new tactics. Didn't we know the nation expected much better than our first offering? It just wasn't good enough.

Fortunately for us there was no more chance of Alf enrolling in the Robbie Burns Society than of following the dictates of Fleet Street. He deemed that what we needed most was not a return to the treadmill but a brief break from football. It was just as well, though, that one of the newspapers had not witnessed the degree of relaxation achieved by some of the lads at a reception for the team staged by Hendon town council.

Nobby reported later that a few of the players, having become bored by the ceremonials, and partaken eagerly of the wine that accompanied the buffet, sent some of the local dignitaries home with prawn cocktail and potato salad that had been slipped into their suit pockets. Such laddish behaviour, had it found its way on to the news pages, might not have hugely enhanced our image as we prepared for the next match against Mexico.

However, those pranks apart, Alf could say that the day had gone exactly as he had hoped. While West Germany were overwhelming Switzerland 5-0, Brazil surviving the brutal tackles of Bulgaria to win with goals by Pelé and Garrincha, and the USSR pointing North Korea back to their mysterious homeland, or so it seemed, we were briefly returning to the world beyond the touchline. Alf was certainly in one of his mellower moods and had arrived at the civic reception with no hint of the pressure that had gathered around him so sharply from the moment the first boos had rippled down the Wembley terraces.

We went to the reception after a visit to Pinewood Studios arranged through a contact of Alan Bass. Alf, the movie buff, was particularly pleased to meet such eminent film actors as Sean Connery, Yul Brynner, George Segal and Robert Morley. He would later confirm that the Scottish brogue had never sounded so pleasant to him as when Connery made a short speech in which he said that our match against Uruguay had done nothing to deflect him from his belief that England would win the cup.

It just happened that Connery was taking a break from playing James Bond in *You Only Live Twice*. In the morning on the training field, and with a much sterner face, Alf would make clear his opinion that we had used up one of those lives.

John Connelly, of course, had some reason to spend the rest of his life envying our generous allocation.

11. The Sweetest Goal

It was once said I was a scorer of great goals rather than a great goalscorer and to dispute this might suggest a degree of immodesty, something I would wish to avoid at this more reflective stage of my life. However, it also happens that as I look back I see an element of truth in the fine point of a clever and, let's face it, not exactly ungenerous assessment.

No one, anyway, had to tell me that I wasn't Jimmy Greaves or Gerd Müller. No, I didn't inhabit football exclusively to score goals in the way of those natural-born predators. I always knew that to score was the point of it all, the ultimate objective, and everything I did along with my team-mates was in the hope of achieving that.

But I didn't change colours like a chameleon when there came a sniff of a goal, didn't believe that only in the act of putting the ball in the net was I truly defining myself as a footballer.

Some might see evidence of that in the fact that I obviously relished so much swinging long and arching passes across the field and there were certainly times when it was suggested to me that a shorter, more direct ball might have carried more telling effect.

The charge sometimes aired, and never more so than when Jimmy Murphy was setting me his relentless drills, was that I was a little in love with the ornamental for its own sake; even, I blush to mention, that it was not unknown for me to step back, a little like an artist contemplating the effect of his latest brush stroke.

Whatever the truth of that, as a professional I could never ignore the reality that scoring a goal had to be more than some occasional extension of my role as a midfield playmaker and sometime left-winger – and the fact that I had scored more for England than anyone, until I was surpassed recently by my Manchester United and England successor Wayne Rooney, will always be a source of great pride and satisfaction.

Now I can only hope for him, as he contemplates the possibility of his last World Cup finals in Russia in 2018, that he knows the kind of moment that came to me on the night of 16 July 1966.

I hope that he gets to enjoy the charge to the spirit that accompanied the goal I scored against Mexico after two hours and six minutes of the hardest toil and growing frustration in our first two games of the 1966 tournament.

The impact it had on my confidence, my understanding that we might just win the World Cup, has never dwindled down the years. I can re-conjure it as easily as I might this morning's stroll among the autumn leaves.

Some judged it to be the best of my career. I'm not so sure about that but I do know it was one that I, and also it seemed the team and the football nation, greeted not so much as a triumph as a deliverance.

Suddenly, everything we had worked for, and dreamed about, seemed possible. It was, surely, a moment to build upon and have it nourish all of our hopes.

Certainly, it left me in maybe the most blissful state of mind I had ever enjoyed out on any field and the fact that I was experiencing it in a place which I had loved so much since I first discovered it as a schoolboy international, and been so entranced by the old towers and, most magically, a playing surface that I thought might have been transplanted from some football heaven, just made it all the more perfect and exhilarating.

On the old film of the game there is some rather strange evidence confirming my exalted mood.

It shows that when the referee blew for half-time, with the stadium still buzzing in the wake of England's breakthrough, one of the twenty-two players returned to the dressing room so quickly he might have been attempting to qualify for the Olympic 100m final. Yes, it was me.

Why? It was because when my shot whipped past the Mexican goalkeeper Ignacio Calderón, releasing tension that had started to grip us five nights earlier in the first half against Uruguay, I suddenly felt that I could run for ever. Nor had I ever felt better, more confident in my skills and my pace and my sense of direction.

The game seemed easy again. When the break was signalled, I suppose now, I just wanted to confirm to myself that I was indeed, at the age of twenty-eight, in the best possible condition. Inevitably some of my team-mates speculated that I was in great need of the bathroom. What wasn't in question, however, was the general and joyful assumption that we were, finally, on our way.

In terms of ability, and football sophistication, the Mexicans plainly lived on a different and a less stylish street than the Uruguayans but in one respect they might have been wearing the light blue of the South Americans rather than their own plum-coloured shirts. They wore the same legend across their hearts, the one that said, 'No Pasarán – They shall not pass'.

That we did breach their defence – and in the thrilling process believed that truly we had set ourselves up to play with much more poise – was something for which I received lasting praise.

However, whenever I see a flash of the old film showing my leap of celebration or hear some reference to the goal that ignited our campaign, I think immediately of Roger Hunt, my companion on that first trip to London to meet the man who promised that we would indeed win the World Cup.

Roger was in so many ways the epitome of Alf's ideal of the selfless team-mate, the man whose commitment to the hard, and often less glamorous and noticed work, was ultimately the difference between winning and losing.

If the theory ever had to be embodied in a single, important strike, the one against Mexico would surely serve well enough. There is no hardship, certainly, in recalling again every detail of it.

The goal was set in motion by Martin Peters, who was replacing Alan Ball after the Uruguayan impasse (the other change was also a case of tactical like for like with an orthodox winger, Terry Paine, replacing the ill-fated John Connelly).

Playing with great confidence, Martin broke up a rare attack from the Mexicans – who had started in almost identical fashion to the Uruguayans when Isidoro Diaz booted the ball into our half while the rest of his team-mates retreated into defensive positions – and played the ball to Roger, who immediately passed it on to me.

He had found me in a nice little pocket of space just inside my own half. It was a situation in which to apply another tenet of Murphy's law, in this case the one that insisted that when you found yourself briefly unattended by defenders with a mission to close you down, the best approach was to use up that space as quickly as possible.

'If you find yourself in some space,' Jimmy often told me during our Sunday morning sessions, 'make sure you cover the first ten or twenty yards as quickly as you can.' He pointed out that this served two purposes. It discouraged front players from attempting to track you and at the same time created a degree of doubt and confusion in the minds of the defenders.

On this occasion Roger was the perfect ally. As I moved into the Mexican half I saw that he was darting one way and another to make a series of distractions, and the more he did it the closer I found myself to Calderón's goal.

Roger's diversionary tactics had prevented the Mexicans sending in a single challenger to my possession of the ball. Had they done so, I would likely have laid it off, probably to Peters, and then gone again. Instead I found myself in the kind of firing range that was never yielded by the Uruguayans.

I hit it sweetly enough from around twenty-five yards and again Murphy's law was applied: hit the target and hit it hard.

At the distance of fifty years it would be easy to skip on to the next challenge facing us, the final group game against France, but that would be another disservice to a Roger Hunt so widely, and undeservedly, cast as a mere workhorse. It was Roger who most effectively got on with the job of seeing off the Mexicans and confirming our progress into the quarter-finals.

It also helped that at half-time Alf was in his best business mode. He said that the goal was delightful but it still counted up to just one. The Mexicans, now obliged to attack, were not without threat. Their striker Enrique Borja was clever and persistent and plainly capable of exploiting the additional support from his team-mates that the new situation so urgently demanded. He had given Mexico the lead in their opening game against France, one of thirty-two goals for the national team, a record which would stand until 1997. There was also some creativity, and plenty of energy, from Diaz and Aaron Padilla.

So, of course, Alf was right to wage another battle in his war against complacency, and in this case the threat of downright euphoria. As always, no one listened more attentively than Roger. Without his ceaseless application, his insatiable willingness to run in pursuit of any possibility, we would not have drawn any benefit from the move which brought the decisive second goal with fourteen minutes to go.

Again Martin Peters was involved. We traded passes out on the left before I played the ball into Jimmy Greaves, whose shot could only be pushed away by Calderón. Hunt was there to deliver the killing stroke. No Pasarán? Roger might have quoted General Franco, who said after taking Madrid during the Spanish Civil War, 'Hemos pasado – We have passed.'

It would prove, though – despite the fact that we fancied ourselves against the French team which did not seem anything like the force which had given Alf such a sobering first experience of international management in 1963 – something less than a trouble-free rite of passage.

Inevitably, Alf carefully measured his praise after the victory which made for much more agreeable reading in the morning papers that found their way into our hotel more easily than after the Uruguayan roadblock.

Yes, he said, we had played better than we had against

Uruguay: there was more rhythm, more certainty and patience in the build-up.

Again, with our second clean sheet, we had been watchful and composed in defence and our goals had come with some fluency. But, then, we also had to remember that we had not disposed of one of the heavyweight contenders.

If we had not beaten Mexico we would surely have been, despite our home advantage, relegated from the group of favourites in which Brazil, their frailties yet to be exposed, still figured prominently alongside such as Argentina, Portugal, Hungary, USSR, West Germany and an Italy still three days away from being destroyed by the shock troops of North Korea.

Instead Alf could proceed against France in the knowledge that another of his players, barring injury, had guaranteed himself a place in the rest of the campaign. It was Martin Peters. There had been that great surprise when he was left out of the Uruguay game. He had been superb in the climax of our preparations against Poland in Chorzów and now after his performance against Mexico, in which he played a part in both goals and was never less than a source of sharp action and consistently applied intelligence, it was unthinkable that he would not line up against the French.

It meant, we can see it so clearly in retrospect, that Alf now had much less than a handful of decisions concerning the players who might make the difference between winning and losing it all.

The questions he was asking himself most intensely can be itemised easily enough. They involved four players: Alan Ball, Geoff Hurst, Roger Hunt, and, given his long-won reputation, most agonisingly, Jimmy Greaves. At this point, before Jimmy picked up an injury against France which would endanger his place in the likely quarter-final, Alf's biggest issue concerned Ball.

Could he continue to leave out such a tirelessly committed, and now smouldering figure? Alan's room-mate Nobby reported that he was taking his exclusion extremely hard and Alf's fear might have been that the young player's hurt and frustration could turn into outright disaffection. As it developed, that never became a factor and perhaps in this Alf's instincts were working more acutely than those who worried that the setback of being left out against Mexico might destroy in Alan one of the most remarkable forces of motivation any of us had ever seen.

Still, Nobby's concern was understandable enough. Many years later he recalled, 'Bally was shocked when he was left out for the Mexican game and there were occasions when it was clear to me how much he was hurting. Once he came up to our loft of a bedroom at the hotel after collecting some winnings from a local bookmaker's office and threw a few fivers on the floor. Then he did a dance of mock celebration and shouted some insults in the direction of Alf, a man I knew he respected, perhaps even loved, and that, with the look on his face, told me that really he was breaking inside. Fortunately, though, it turned out that he had a lot more resilience, and self-confidence, than anyone could then have imagined.'

Whatever his private evaluation of Bally's situation, and measurement of the effect his continued exclusion might have, Alf decided to roll the dice, one last time in the tournament it would prove, in the direction of an old-style winger. On this occasion it was the fine Liverpool winger Ian Callaghan who got the nod, but with only the same result as those of John Connelly and Terry Paine. All three wingers were fine, talented professionals but what they couldn't do was indefinitely hold up Alf's growing conviction that in 4-3-3, the magic formula unveiled in Madrid, lay his best chance of delivering the World Cup.

No doubt the most complicated question of all was to do with Jimmy Greaves. He made that statement of great confidence after victory in Poland, when he said that as far as he was concerned there was no doubt that he would share with Roger Hunt duties up front, but the course of the first two matches had not strengthened his case. Hunt, as usual, had run quite relentlessly and against Mexico he had been, as I said, increasingly relevant to all that we attempted.

By comparison, Jimmy was a much more peripheral figure and, most crucially, he had failed to score. For Jimmy and his elite breed that was the equivalent of being denied oxygen. He kept his place against France but his pensive expression suggested that at least a little of his natural swagger had gone missing.

It would be further eroded in the French game and soon enough his fate would become an increasingly and passionately debated national issue. However, twenty-four hours before he walked out on to the pitch at Wembley and into the first phase of the great, unfolding crisis of his career, and, perhaps, his life, another story of threatened grandeur had already reached a brutal climax. It was the terrible sight of Pelé, the world's greatest player, being kicked out of the World Cup.

The tawdry, violent story had started a week earlier when the Bulgarians targeted Pelé in a series of shocking tackles, most of them launched by Dobromir Jetchev, who was eventually booked after pushing the great man to the point of retaliation. Pelé was bruised and battered so severely he was unable to play in Brazil's next match, a 3-1 defeat by Hungary, and he was clearly far from fully fit when he returned to Goodison Park as his nation's last hope of survival against Eusébio's Portugal.

There was an awful certainty that it would end badly for the great man, who I had watched invade the imagination of the world in 1958 as the eighteen-year-old sensation of the Sweden World Cup and who, less than a year later, redoubled the awe I felt for him when we faced each other before a vast crowd in the Maracanã. On that occasion, Johnny Haynes and I both hit the woodwork but it did little to make us believe that we could overcome the genius of the nineteen-year-old who performed with such poise and authority it was as though he had invented a new way of playing. He was so quick and so strong, he worked astonishing patterns in alliance with the great midfielder Didi, and always there was the sense that he would create more time and more space than anyone around him.

It was a mystique the Portuguese, a team I had come to admire not only for their talent but their decency, were allowed to kick to pieces that dreadful night on Merseyside. Pelé hobbled off the field, shaking his head, it seemed to me, with a combination of anger, frustration and sadness. The Portuguese moved on to the quarter-finals and Brazil, authors of the beautiful game, went home with their wounds and their disillusion.

Back in the Hendon Hall Hotel, I could only mourn the meaning of their departure – and fear for the future of the game I loved if a team as gifted as Portugal could so shamelessly assign their defender João Morais the job of, effectively, crippling the world's best player. Of course, there is a line that will always be drawn between the best ideals of the game and the most cynical reaction to the highest of talent.

Before the end of the tournament some would say there were times when England crossed that line – indeed, soon enough the claim would threaten the place of my friend Nobby – but I would always believe that what we saw at Goodison Park, first from Bulgaria, then Portugal, was something more than excesses of zeal and some misjudgement. For me it was a systematic attempt to subvert the point of the game. It was anti-football prosecuted by a team possessing the shining lights of such as Eusébio and Coluna, and certainly it was impossible to imagine as I went to my bed that four years later in Mexico Pelé would once again be anointed as the probably eternal claimant to the title of the world's best player.

Better still would be the fact that Pelé did not have a protection unit around him as he achieved the most stunning resurrection. He was accompanied by the beautiful talent of such as Gérson and Tostão and Jairzinho. That would have been greeted as a fantasy had the possibility been aired when Pelé was being helped out of Goodison Park.

I still see him on his travels around the world and it is still the same old sharp excitement when he appears in any room, usually fashionably late and quite conscious of the impact he still carries. He's had a tumultuous life, a number of marriages, and from time to time you hear that he is still obliged to go out to earn some money as he flies from one continent to another.

Given the meaning of his career, you sometimes wonder how that could be so but then Pelé, who was playing brilliantly among the best and the hardest of his football-obsessed country when he was just fifteen, had maybe more reasons than most to believe he deserved to enjoy the fruits of his success.

He was born in poverty, he worked as a servant in a tea shop before becoming, along with Muhammad Ali, one of the great men of the twentieth century, and so today he remains a symbol of what can be achieved if you have the will, and the passion, to go alongside the highest talent. There will always be challengers for the mantle of a Pelé in a game which has found its way into every corner of the world and today there are many believers in the historic supremacy of Lionel Messi, as there were for that of Maradona after his extraordinary domination of the 1986 World Cup, but for me Pelé will always occupy the highest terrain.

Unlike my friend and hero, Duncan Edwards, Pelé was able to complete the course he had set himself. It was one on which he proved he was equal to every legitimate challenge. That the one that besieged him fifty years ago in England could not be so described was a passing sadness for me as we strived to win the World Cup. However, what he achieved for himself and, in my opinion, the rest of football four years later was, as I look back, nothing less than the brilliant cleansing of one of a few rather large blemishes left by the year of 1966.

It would, however, be wrong to suggest that I was weighed down too heavily in the wake of the Brazilian exit. Alf, of course, had been convinced they would not be a threat after seeing them labour against Argentina at the Maracanã two years earlier. He said that, Pelé and Garrincha apart, they were a team which had grown too old on the vine and was in desperate need of some judicious pruning.

Pelé plainly nursed not only his wounds but also his agreement with the Ramsey theory. Before flying home, he declared with a rare bitterness, 'I suppose our directors put their faith in the old dictum "God is a Brazilian", forgetting that God also helps those who help themselves.'

Alf, as always, believed that certainly there was still more we could do on our own behalf before the collision with the French.

He did not see them as a potentially deadly threat, and certainly not the kind of team which, five years before embarrassing us in Paris, had moved fluently to the semi-finals of the 1958 World Cup before encountering the emerging Pelé's Brazil and then, thanks to the prodigious finishing touch of the tournament's top scorer, Just Fontaine, overran the newly deposed world champions West Germany 6-3 for third place. But this new France were quick and this was something we had to consider in our preparation.

Alf said we had good stamina and it was an advantage we should attempt to further develop. There was an echo of his message at Lilleshall; we needed to bring more speed, more intensity to the training field. We also had to work on the building of our defensive wall when facing free-kicks from dangerous positions.

It was the same old Alf in the same old routine and for me this was less of an imposition than a comfort. I had the heightened encouragement of the breakthrough goal. I also had a still-strengthening faith in the judgement and leadership of the man in charge.

For at least two of my team-mates my feeling of wellbeing would very soon be a most enviable state of mind. One of them was Jimmy Greaves, fretting that his superb overall scoring rate had again tailed off in World Cup finals action. Now it stood at just one goal in six matches.

For a man who lived his football life to score goals, and had been doing it so brilliantly, so instinctively, since he scored as a seventeen-year-old making his debut for Chelsea against Tottenham at White Hart Lane, this was the most unwelcome and untimely pressure. How could it happen to a man who would finish his England career on the stunning mark of forty-four goals in fifty-seven games? It was a question that lay just below the surface as Jimmy went into the French game – and Geoff Hurst ached to get his chance.

Another issue was also about to emerge, though this is maybe a mild way of putting it. It was more in the way of a detonation. It concerned the further involvement of Nobby Stiles and, as a potentially devastating repercussion, perhaps even that of Alf.

This meant that while we would, thanks to Roger Hunt's two goals, brush past France, there was none of that inclination to celebrate that came after the defeat of Mexico. Then we talked about deliverance. Now we contemplated the threat of a major disruption – and maybe even a hint of doom.

12. Nobby's Trial

Heaven knows, it was not one of Nobby's most secure tackles and no matter how many times you played it back in your mind, or however much you loved him, it was impossible to disagree with George Cohen's account of the incident which brought our first full-blown crisis of the World Cup.

Nobby – there was no way around it – was in trouble and that was very bad news not just for him but us all. Apart from his work on the field, he had become a barometer of the mood of the squad.

The big question was both moral and practical. It asked whether he had committed on the fine French player Jacky Simon a huge but innocent (at least relatively innocent) miscalculation or a crime just as heinous and as calculated as those that had been inflicted by Bulgaria and Portugal on the great Pelé.

What was certain in the wake of it was that Nobby, who had so quickly become such a force in the team, such a point of intensely concentrated ambition, was walking around with the face of a condemned man. Where before he breathed conviction, now he was passive, almost as though he was resigned to seeing all his hopes crash around him.

The explosive eruptions between him and my brother Jack were in abeyance. So in training were his yells and exhortations. He was as glum as his room-mate Bally fretting about his chances of a recall to the team against Argentina.

Nobby had always played on the edge, always accepted that if he was to perform his difficult trade successfully he had to live with certain risks. Now the worry was that he might just have fallen the wrong side of the line.

George, who could never be counted among the squeamish in even the most challenging of situations, was not able to offer much comfort, no more than any of his team-mates. He was quite clinical in his recall. He said he winced and uttered a blasphemy when he saw the tackle go in.

Revisiting his account is the most vivid reminder of how one split-second misreading of time and space by a player in whom Alf had come to place so much faith – and affection – might just have made us leaderless at a most pivotal stage of the long campaign.

The drama, reported to the public in shocking headlines which included 'Stiles Horror Tackle Brings England Crisis', would take several days to unfold and as it did so it became increasingly clear that Nobby was fighting for his World Cup place and, perhaps ultimately, his international career. It also emerged very quickly that in Alf he had an ally who was prepared to risk, both on the player's behalf and that of the principles he had shaped for himself over the years, all that he had worked for since being appointed England manager.

George's evidence, while scrupulously accurate and quite

dispassionate, hardly challenges the belief that there was immense pressure on Alf as he made the case for the defence.

George said, 'He was in trouble with the authorities for a foul on the Frenchman Simon which, whatever its intent, looked horrible. Earlier he was involved in a collision which left Simon's team-mate Roby Herbin limping.

'Nobby was playing his usual game, committed and sharp, but when he lined up Simon for a tackle while the Frenchman was waiting to control a throw-in which just seemed to hang in the air as though shot in slow motion, you had the sudden apprehension that Nobby was coming in terribly late.

'Simon was a good, skilled player and he must have seen in the corner of his eye that Nobby was bearing down on him. A less confident player would have tried to lay off the ball more or less anywhere but Simon was more ambitious than that and he attempted to sell Nobby a dummy. Unfortunately, he didn't sell anything. He just bought himself the tackle from hell, one that from the moment of its inception was destined to land somewhere between the Frenchman's thyroid gland and his crotch.

'I remember grimacing and saying to myself, "Jesus – that looked bad."'

Not bad enough, however, for the Peruvian referee Arturo Yamasaki to reach for the red card we all feared. More remarkable still, Yamasaki also kept the yellow one in his pocket while administering a brief lecture to Nobby. Meanwhile, Simon got to his feet groggily and played on, much to everybody's relief, because if the referee had shown the same kind of tolerance displayed by his colleagues at Goodison Park towards the Bulgarians and the Portuguese, there was no Pelé limping away from the scene of the crime and so, as we breathed again, we could say the consequences were not so dire.

At least it was pretty easy to think so before we learned that the Fifa observer sitting in the stand had made his own decision to caution Nobby.

That was the trigger for an escalation of the problem which was confirmed the following day when Alf was called to the FA headquarters in Lancaster Gate and told that he had to jettison one of his favourite players. With that tackle, said the FA committee men, Nobby had gone beyond the pale. The FA could not countenance such behaviour – and nor should the England manager. There was no alternative: Nobby, who had brought so much passion, energy and tactical nous to the team, had to be banished.

Could it really be that the little lion of our team was about to become a sacrificial lamb, a victim of Fifa's belief that the great tournament was on the point of being irretrievably scarred by a sub-text of violence and intimidation?

Alf had woken up the morning after the defeat of France with the idea that his major challenge still lay in the need to sharpen our overall performance. Though Roger Hunt had again produced a major contribution, with both goals in the 2-0 victory, and was pointedly excluded from any criticism, the rest of us were left in no doubt about the manager's dissatisfaction.

'Against France we could get away with it – but if we put in another performance like that, teams such as Argentina or Portugal are capable of creating a much different story,' Alf said. 'We must increase the pace of our game – starting in our next training session.'

Instead, we went through the motions under the supervision

of Harold Shepherdson and Les Cocker as Alf answered the urgent summons from the FA.

Nobby, the eternal activist, had never been so distracted. Later, he gave his own detailed version of the tackle that went so grievously wrong, saying, 'As I first recalled the build-up, we were attacking along the right with George Cohen on the ball and Simon, a very good player, tracking him. When the French goalkeeper, Marcel Arbour, gathered up the ball and threw it out to Simon, I was already on the move, watching the ball looping down and lining up my tackle.

'George remembers it differently. He said the ball reached Simon via a throw-in and I came in so late the Frenchman just collapsed in a heap in front of the Royal Box.

'What I have to say in my own defence was that my intention was to hit the ball – and him – just as he turned. It is not a foul if you go through the ball (before colliding with the opponent), hitting it with all the force you have and that takes you through the player. That is a hard but legal tackle and it is what I intended to do.

'Unfortunately, for Jacky Simon and me, on this occasion he did not dwell on the ball. He moved it on first touch and I steamed into a man without the ball.'

From whatever perspective it was viewed, the conclusion had to be that Nobby was indeed at risk, especially in the atmosphere left by the assaults on Pelé.

The much respected Joe Mercer, manager of Manchester City who eight years later would take temporary charge of England, was serving on the World Cup TV panel and he told the nation that Nobby had committed a tackle so terrible it shamed all of English football. His fellow panellists Danny Blanchflower and Billy Wright both nodded in agreement.

Only Jimmy Hill, who in the past had offered that withering dismissal of England's World Cup chances, supported Nobby in his perilous position. Yes, he said, the tackle could not be condoned but he didn't believe it was malicious. Nor should it be forgotten that the player had fought so hard for his country.

Plainly, Alf had a huge task as he attempted both to save Nobby and retain his own authority. As he faced the array of committee men, he was told that he had a duty to England – and to the good standing of the World Cup – to discard arguably his most committed player.

Alf's response was consistent with everything I had come to see in him and believe about him. His most constant exhortation had been for loyalty to the team, to an understanding that if we did not work for each other, did not feel for our team-mates in their most difficult situations, we were nothing more than a collection of individuals destined to fail.

This was a lofty declaration but when it mattered most to one of his players he was as good as his every word.

I would come to believe that the ones he uttered to the FA hierarchy that summer morning may well have been the most important of his reign as England manager. He said, 'Well, gentlemen, most certainly Nobby Stiles can be thrown off the team but I must tell you I see him as a very important player for England, one who has done very well for the team since he was selected, and that if he goes, so do I. I should tell you that you will be looking for a new manager.'

Some broad outline of Alf's defiance did leak into the newspapers but it was only some years after he had retired from football that he confirmed the detail of it, saying, 'It was quite extraordinary. It seemed that they could not accept Stiles as an international and made it clear that they didn't want him. I just told them that if Stiles was to be dropped they could find a new manager. And I meant it. I would have walked out there and then.'

It was hardly the distraction Alf or any of his team, and least of all Nobby, needed before the challenge looming at Wembley against Argentina – the team that most of us, deep down, feared most, and especially those of us who had seen them play with such poise and skill, and their traditional ruthlessness, against Brazil in the Maracanã two years earlier.

Nobby's face was increasingly taut and by the time we had our Friday morning training session – the prelude to Alf's announcement of the team – I had never seen on it such a haunted expression. It was as if his whole life had reached a crossroads. In one direction lay the chance of glory, in another only oblivion and a degree of shame, a terrible fate for the former altar boy who each morning of the World Cup would go dutifully to mass.

The fact that I felt so concerned, and saddened, for my friend in his desperate situation might be seen as something of a contradiction, if not downright hypocrisy, following my expression of revulsion for the treatment received by Pelé. However, I did feel able to make a distinction.

Though I would never, playing in the style that I did, be able to close my eyes to the destructive force of violence in football, I could still see a difference between that which was cynical and programmed and something else which came from a certain style of playing, a physical aggression which was certainly part of Nobby's professional make-up – and absolutely central to the role in which he made his living.

No doubt it was also true that Nobby had acquired the reputation of being an extremely combative player, someone to place along such formidable figures as Norman Hunter and Tommy Smith. The reality was that every First Division club had at least two such players. Yet, as Nobby waited so fearfully to know his fate, I could say quite emphatically that in all the games I had played alongside him I had never seen him doing anything that smacked of the vicious or the vindictive. Yes, he was willing to get his hands dirty, as he did so crucially in Madrid, but the truth of that case, as in so many others, was that he was returning a transgression in kind.

Above all his other virtues he had a superb and unshakeable competitive honesty. Indeed, I would have sworn in any courtroom that I had never seen him do anything designed to injure a fellow professional. He played a hard game and he never whined on the rare occasions an opponent got the better of him. Malice had no place in his nature.

It was an appraisal that Alf shared quite implicitly – as he proved in an exchange during that training session on the eve of the great quarter-final challenge against Argentina.

All you could hear was the sound of distant traffic when Alf walked across the Roehampton training field to Nobby and went straight to the heart of the issue in his most succinct style.

He looked Nobby in the eye and asked him, simply, 'Did you mean it?'

Nobby replied, 'No, Alf, I didn't. I mistimed the tackle.'

Alf nodded and said, 'You're playing tomorrow.'

Had he switched on an electric current he could not have created a more stimulating impact among the players on that training field. Here, surely, was the conclusive evidence that Alf had a belief in his players that was beyond any compromise.

George Cohen, the most precise and eloquent witness to the

episode, would say later, 'Nobby said that he would never forget the day the manager of England stood shoulder to shoulder with him against the FA and their Fifa friends. Nor would any of his team-mates. Ramsey had talked so many times about the value of loyalty to the team and now he had showed us what he meant. At that moment no team in the history of football's greatest tournament had ever been so united behind the man who led them into battle.'

For Nobby his deliverance had come on a huge and warming tide. After recounting his brief conversation with Alf, he reflected later, 'It was an unbelievable wave of relief that swept over me when Alf said I was playing against Argentina. I was training again rather than going through the motions. And then Alf made a statement to the football world and the nation. He said that Nobby Stiles was a great young Englishman who was proud to play for his country and had done it very well.

'He said I was not just a good player but a great player. I saw him on the television and heard him saying it. I felt tears coming to my eyes and my skin felt prickly and I thought, "Alf, thank you very much."

'Later I called my wife Kay, who was staying with her family in Dublin and she wished me all the best for the Argentina game. Her brother Johnny Giles and their father Dickie, a very prominent figure in Irish football, also came on the phone to tell me that I had now to just concentrate on my performance in the next match and put all the other stuff out of my mind. All that was over now and the most important thing was to play to my limits. These were surely among the most important days of my career – and my life.

'Kay reinforced her phone message with a telegram and

many years later I found it, faded and crumpled at the bottom of a drawer. It sent her love and said, "You can do it."

'The day after Alf had given me the all-clear, as the team bus went up Wembley Way, I felt another surge of my spirit. Alan Ball nudged me and said, "Nob, look at that banner." It was a huge one that declared, "Nobby for Prime Minister." Another one was less lofty. It said, "Go and get the bastards." I felt I had been reinstated in the eyes of the nation.'

That was the wonderfully restored mood of my friend Nobby and I couldn't have been more delighted. I'd felt at least a little of his pain and now I could see all of his love of life, and his natural optimism, flooding back.

Yet even as I rejoiced with my team-mates over Nobby's survival there was reason enough to be reminded of football's habit of giving to one while taking from another. This truth was now deeply etched into the pensive expression of Jimmy Greaves. His reality was that if Nobby had come back from the crisis created in the game against France, his own position had worsened seriously.

At the end of the match against France he discovered, after rolling down his socks and removing his shin-pads, that he had sustained a deep gash in his shin. The team doctor administered five stitches and with each one Jimmy had fresh doubts about his ability to stay the course. The injury would certainly cost him his place against Argentina and, coupled with his failure to score in any of the group games, plainly weakened his prospects of withstanding the challenge of Geoff Hurst.

Geoff had been very impressive in training, reinforcing the good impression he had made in his flurry of outings in the run-in to the tournament, and with Alan Ball also recalled in place of the last of the auditioning wingers, Ian Callaghan, it was clear enough that Alf had returned, and perhaps permanently, to the 4-3-3 juggernaut that had purred so impressively in Madrid.

However hard he sought to maintain his normally jaunty and self-confident front, Jimmy's eyes said that he saw some discouraging writing on the wall and events would soon enough give substance to his sense of foreboding.

Later, Alf confirmed that Jimmy's injury was an irrelevance to his selection decision, saying, 'Jimmy Greaves had not shown his true form to substantiate his position in the team and would not have been selected for the Argentina match even if he had avoided injury in the French game.' At today's distance it seems so much clearer. Jimmy's disastrously timed injury was for Alf, however harsh this sounds, something of a convenience. In retrospect, it seems so obvious. Alf had by then decided that Geoff Hurst was indeed his man.

Soon enough there would be another national debate about the fate of an England player but again it would be Alf, and he alone, who would conclude the argument. He had saved Nobby even, looking back you have to believe, as he decided that Jimmy's time had come and, almost certainly, gone.

The situation left me with difficult and contradictory feelings. As I saw it, Jimmy's failure to make any significant impact in the three group games had left Alf with a choice between two or maybe three players as we moved into the challenging terrain occupied by the front-line contenders. There was a common belief, cultivated particularly by London-based sports writers, that in the end it would be a question of Hurst or Greaves. But the reality was that Alf had also put Hunt into the equation.

According to this theory, Hurst had qualities which might reanimate the scoring genius of Greaves, the restatement of which might just ultimately be the decisive factor in our becoming world champions.

Anyone who played with Roger Hunt knew that behind all the selfless running, the endless graft, there was also a tremendous instinct for finding a weakness in the opposing defence. Jimmy had given him his own vote of confidence after the victory in Poland and Roger had only built on his reputation for strength and reliability in the first three games of the tournament.

Reviewing his career record from the distance of today, it seems all the more odd that so many observers, from inside and out of the game, were so inclined to damn him with the faint praise that he merely owned strong legs and a willing heart.

His scoring rate for England would have been impressive without his vast accumulation of work on behalf of his team-mates, all those times his selfless running and aggressive inclinations had opened up a defence to plunder by someone like Jimmy or me. There was, of course, the most recent shining example of that in the game before Jimmy was injured, when Roger helped me so vitally to score the goal that broke Mexico.

His own scoring record was excellent. For England he scored at the rate of more than one goal every two matches (eighteen goals in thirty-four games) and in helping Liverpool to become one of the great forces in the English game he scored 245 in 404 appearances. Always he played with an abiding passion, a refusal to ever accept the possibility of defeat.

Against this impressive body of work – and the clear evidence that the particular skills of Geoff Hurst might have been made for the 4-3-3 system – it was no surprise that behind his breezy manner, his tendency to play the joker in the company of his closest companion in the squad, Bobby Moore, Jimmy became an increasingly brooding figure. When he scored four goals against Norway, he might have believed that he had put the weakening effects of hepatitis behind him, and even that his aura was fully restored.

His great problem, of course, was that he was required now to operate in a system which could hardly have been less sympathetic to the special needs of a supreme individualist who offered one specific contribution without any other guarantees. Jimmy lived by goals, they were his glory and his justification, and without them he was making no contribution to the system – Alf's system.

If Jimmy didn't score, as he didn't in those three group games, he became the most vulnerable of us all. Without the lifeblood of his goals, his very existence as a contender was in peril.

This must have been so hard to accept – and I could certainly understand his pain as it became increasingly obvious to him that playing a part in the climax of this World Cup, something which perhaps more than most of us he had come to see as a defining moment in his career, was no longer an assumption he could comfortably make.

Yet there was no way anyone could dismiss, dislike or devalue Jimmy Greaves. With United I had played against him so many times and I had always thought what a great man he would be to have on your side. You would have someone you knew could conjure a goal from nowhere.

He proved that when he came on to the international scene with a facility to score goals that was simply stunning. He scored two in his first game for the England Under-23 against Bulgaria in front of his own fans at Stamford Bridge. There, it was accepted as another formality in his swift invasion of the records set by his legendary predecessor Tommy Lawton.

The inevitability of his success was broadcast again when he played his first game for England in Lima in 1959. Jimmy alone escaped criticism on that tour of Latin America which saw us beaten by Brazil, Peru and Mexico. He scored our goal in the 4-1 defeat by Peru and not for one moment of an experience which might have been so discouraging did his performance suggest he was out of place.

In the end, though, it seemed that his misfortune was that if he had so many times proved himself a decisive factor for his teams Chelsea and Spurs (and even in his short, unhappy misadventure in Italy he scored nine goals in twelve games for Milan) he was not a Ramsey man. He had a genius for scoring goals but Alf, in his ultimately stubborn way, wanted something more.

He wanted another, less sublime but more consistent contribution. He wanted someone who had the humility to understand that nothing he could do would take him beyond the system that he believed was our best chance of success. On reflection, I suppose, humility did not come so easily to someone who could make the game's most difficult – and important – art seem so effortless.

George Cohen has admitted that from the moment Jimmy lost his place against Argentina, ostensibly because of his injury sustained against France, he found it hard to hold eye contact with his fellow Londoner. He explained that he had a strong sense that however quickly Jimmy recovered he would find that the die had been cast and he was the loser. When I consider this I do wonder if I might have been more understanding, and felt more compassion for someone whose talent I admired so much – and whose problem of alcoholism, many of his closest friends believed, was only deepened by the great crisis, and disappointment, of his professional life.

Certainly in all my subsequent meetings with Jimmy, with whom I played for England for seven years before the parting of the ways, I was saddened by the knowledge that he had sustained hurt which clearly he could never quite put aside, even in his years of great success as co-host with Ian St John of their hugely successful TV show.

Now, as I look back once more I have to return to an earlier conclusion. I repeat it here because, in all honesty, any changes or modifications would at best be merely cosmetic, if not hypocritical.

I said, 'The truth is that when he came to decide on the fate of Jimmy Greaves, my faith in the judgement of Alf Ramsey had become virtually unconditional. I also have to confess that when I look back I feel I might have been more sensitive to the pain of a great player who had been my team-mate for so long.

'My reserve at the time was rooted in the trust I had developed in Alf's instincts and judgement on form and ability, and if that sounds like an easy stance to take, given my rarely interrupted run of seventy-two caps for England to that point, I can only say that under Ramsey I never believed my selection was automatic.

'I know too that when he stood at the front of the bus on the way back from the Roehampton training ground and said, "The team for tomorrow is . . ." I never heard mumblings of disbelief or outrage. No one ever said, "Alf, can I have a word with you?" Of course, I would have been disappointed if my name had been included but I do not think I would have felt outrage or betrayal. My uppermost thought would probably have been frustration that, in the opinion of a tough but extremely analytical football man, I had failed one of the many tests he had set us all.

'Most of all I believed that without Alf we could not have been standing so close to the ultimate prize. He had made us winners and in this process there would, inevitably, be deep personal disappointments. That Jimmy should suffer one so deeply, and carry it down the years, is a sadness that I came to understand, maybe because of my own charmed position, only when the first anger had gone from his wounds.'

What was not in doubt, as Nobby picked up his stride again and Alan Ball called his father to tell him so joyfully that he would be returning to the action, Geoff Hurst prepared for his first World Cup experience and Jimmy, nursing his gashed shin, could occasionally be heard humming his plaintive tune, 'What's it all about, Alfie?', was that we now faced our most demanding test.

Argentina, dangerous, superbly gifted and deeply enigmatic, had come through their group with West Germany and promised to test more than our skills and our organisation. They would stretch us to our limits, from our ability to play football all the way to our understanding of what was right and what was wrong.

13. Tango in Hell

When we beat Argentina, when Geoff Hurst read perfectly the intentions of Martin Peters and got in at the near post to score our goal, we knew, finally, that we could win the World Cup.

If we could get by a team that was a combination of all that was beautiful and ugly in the game, one that had marvellous skill and apparently bottomless cynicism, we could indeed go all the way. We could see it clearly now. Once we had wiped the spittle from our eyes.

My feelings of bewilderment and eventual relief over the events of that Saturday afternoon of 23 July 1966 have never left me – and never been more intense than during meetings with Antonio Rattín at football occasions in his impressive home city of Buenos Aires and across the world.

The captain of Argentina, who took so long to leave the pitch after being dismissed by the German referee Rudolf Kreitlein in the thirty-sixth minute, made a most poignant gesture of departure as he finally allowed himself to be shepherded towards the dressing room before his final act of defiance: sitting down on the red carpet reserved for the Queen.

He reached out a hand and grasped a corner flag, then slowly released his grip. It is an image that speaks of a thousand regrets and whenever I see it played back it only increases an old confusion. How, I ask myself once more, could such a richly gifted team – one capable of outplaying Brazil in the Maracanã – make such a travesty of a quarter-final of the World Cup?

Rattín, I have discovered down the years, is a man of charm and natural friendliness. He made a political career when his football days were over and sat in his nation's parliament. He speaks of his love and reverence for the only club he played for, his boyhood heroes Boca Juniors, who once had the young great Alfredo Di Stéfano in their ranks.

I tell him of the time Di Stéfano gave me a tour of his home town, showed me the bridge in the poor neighbourhood of his youth from where he would jump on to a passing train and then alight, often perilously, at the Boca Stadium before climbing over the barriers to see his beloved team. I tell him of my admiration for so much of Argentinian life, the style and tango rhythms of Buenos Aires, and when I do he seems not to retain a hint of animosity over the extraordinary breakdown of values that so besmirched the game's most important tournament and triggered fifty years of enduring bitterness. It is as though, when he embraces you, he is saying that it never happened. Or, at least, that it was just a passing episode made inevitable by the pressures of the game at the highest level.

But, of course, it did happen – and even when it was supposedly over, when the game was won and lost and we faced our next challenge against a strong and brilliant Portugal – we could still hear them beating at our dressing-room door and someone saying, 'Bloody hell, it's the Argies – they want to come in.' And my friend and room-mate Ray Wilson, with a very hard expression on his face, responding, 'Let them.'

Perhaps we shouldn't have been so surprised that the match slipped so quickly beyond the control of the German referee. There were strong rumours that the South Americans were convinced that Fifa had urged on match officials a certain tolerance of the more robust style of the European teams. The battered Pelé was said to have believed the rumour – and more firmly when he came to inspect his wounds.

It was also true that in terms of fouls awarded, we had the higher count. However, I will always insist that if we played aggressively, and in our traditionally physical style, we never attempted to subvert the values of the game. We didn't litter our game with sly nudges and kicks and torrents of spit. Our captain Bobby Moore, unlike Rattín, did not attempt to referee the match from the first whistle.

After watching Argentina draw with West Germany in a goalless group game, Bobby later reflected, 'We accepted in our guts it was going to be hard, maybe brutal.' For Geoff Hurst, tasting his first World Cup action, there was swift justification for his captain's foreboding. He reported, 'At any moment, for no reason, you thought you might be attacked from behind. Twice I was kicked on the ankle, off the ball, and when I swung round there was a ring of blank faces.' Bobby's account would be equally horrific. He said, 'They did tug your hair, spit at you, poke you in the eyes and kick you when the ball was miles away and no one was looking.'

A more philosophical quote was attributed to Nobby, who was still rejoicing over his emergence from the Jacky Simon convulsion. He was reported as saying, 'Apart from the violence, I came through with no problems.'

My own perspective was somewhat different and perhaps best illustrated that, in my anger and frustration, I made a rare visit to a referee's notebook. The truth – at least my truth – was that in the ten years since I had made my debut for Manchester United against Charlton Athletic I had never seen, close up, such a corruption of what I believed to be football's true meaning.

In my travels with my club and my country I had certainly been the victim of foul play and been obliged to wipe spit from my face. But never before had such offences arrived so quickly or so relentlessly. What I found so appalling was that this was a team so plainly capable of producing all that was best in the game. They had a wonderful rhythm on the ball and then they could explode into the most brilliant action.

They had a clutch of players unquestionably of world class.

Rattín, as I had seen in the Chile World Cup four years earlier and in the match against Brazil in Rio, was one notable example. He was tall and commanding and had a lovely touch and the sharpest vision as he sought to dictate the flow of the game from midfield.

Silvio Marzolina was a defender of the highest class, strong in the tackle and silky on the ball. Ermindo Onega had subtle craft and a biting instinct. Oscar Mas gave them width and pace. With Rattín devoting himself to his superior game, and marshalling his impressive resources, rather than arguing with Kreitlein so constantly, there is no doubt we would have been stretched dangerously close to our limits. As it was, even with Rattín gone it was a great relief when Geoff Hurst settled matters with thirteen minutes to go.

After the game, and ironically enough in view of his inflammatory use of the word 'animals' and his attempt to

Top: Alf Ramsey talking to reporters on the eve of the World Cup final.

Middle and bottom: Cheered on by the crowds as we head to Wembley for the most important match of our lives.

Top left: Some of the wonderful crowds supporting us at Wembley stadium.

Top right: Lined up for the national anthem on that historic day, 30 July 1966.

Bottom: And off we go, all of us aware of what we need to do.

Top: Celebrations as Martin Peters gives us the lead.

Bottom: And we're 2–1 up in the World Cup final!

Top: Franz Beckenbauer and I were rarely apart from each other.

Middle: A missed chance to put the trophy beyond West Germany's reach.

Bottom: And with just a minute to go, West Germany equalise.

Top: As we gather ourselves for extra time, we remind ourselves of Alf's words, all that time ago: 'Gentlemen, most certainly we will win the World Cup'.

Middle: And it's in! At the time, I was sure of it.

Bottom: Geoff Hurst completes his hat-trick and we have won the World Cup!

Top: Ray Wilson parades the Jules Rimet trophy around the stadium.

Bottom left: Collecting the trophy from Her Majesty the Queen.

Bottom right: The final score, England 4, West Germany 2.

Top/bottom left: Winners of the World Cup.

Bottom right: While us players were at a banquet, our wives and girlfriends celebrated, along with my father.

The wonderful crowds that greeted Our Kid and me on our return home to Ashington.

stop the swapping of shirts, Alf made strenuous efforts to prevent any more spillage of anger, especially any physical expression of it.

When Ray suggested we should swing open the dressing-room doors and let the afternoon reach its natural conclusion, my brother Jack was clearly of the same mind and no doubt there would have been plenty of support for that approach from Nobby and Bally.

George Cohen might also have been drawn into an affray. He later admitted that already that afternoon he had gone beyond the line he always tried to draw separating emotions and a strict professional control.

With his usual precise recall, he reported how quickly the match had degenerated – and how, in the end, he had, against all his best instincts, found himself part of some of the worst of it.

He said, 'There was no question in my mind that this game against Argentina had the potential to be a classic but knowing their style, their extreme cynicism, you could only fear the worst, and especially now that the stakes had become so high with the brutal expulsion of Brazil by Portugal.

'The man I had to mark, Oscar Mas, was difficult. He was quick, mobile and clever and in the early going he administered a nasty shock. He gave me the slip as he went inside and I was perturbed to see that Jack Charlton didn't have him covered. Gordon Banks had to make a save, fortunately not a difficult one because Mas mishit his shot. It didn't happen again but it was a sharp warning of the need for total vigilance. You couldn't break your concentration for a second because they were playing it slow, slow, slow, and then very quickly indeed.

'They were niggling from the start. They made everything

difficult, arguing with the officials, stalling over free-kicks and at the heart of all the mischief was Rattín, a tall, domineering figure who spat out his disgust – frequently literally – when things didn't go quite to his satisfaction.

'The first confrontation of the slight and, to me it seemed, timid referee and the swaggering Rattín warned of the problems to come. Rattín towered threateningly over the referee and increasingly he was voicing his complaints. Rattín was a natural bully, you could see that, along with his beautiful ball control and excellent positional sense.

'The catalyst for a sporting disaster was a minor dispute over a free-kick. Rattín spoke aggressively to the referee. He was stoking the fire. The game was running out of control when Rattín was sent off. He was hellishly awkward but some of his play coming out of defence was just heavenly. It was Bobby Charlton's job to cover his breaks into midfield but Rattín was in the mood to take on the entire team.

'If you went anywhere near an Argentinian there was every chance he would just fall down. Tackles were flying in – and so was the spittle. Our front men, Hunt and Hurst, were taking most of it. There were some amazing things going on up there and even in defence we were getting hit late and dangerously.

'Nothing particularly nasty happened between Mas and me. The truth was that when necessary I could do a bit of the naughty stuff myself. I never wanted to be that sort of pro but sometimes circumstances force you into behaviour you wouldn't normally even consider.

'In fact, I did put the boot into one of the Argentines. It was Artime, who had been one of their more intimidating characters. I caught him hard and he almost did a cartwheel – right in front of the Royal Box.'

George was right about the threat Rattín might have legitimately presented, and the difficulties he could have made for me, had he simply got on with his naturally accomplished game.

Unwittingly, I was part of the ultimate flashpoint. Rattín fouled me twice in a few minutes, the second time with an absolutely undisguised trip. He was booked and I could see clearly enough he was on the point of losing all control. That happened when Kreitlein also booked his team-mate Alberto González. We later learned he was demanding, in Spanish, the presence of an interpreter and Kreitlein was dismissing his request, in German.

It was now that my bewilderment was complete. Here was a superbly equipped team, smooth in their skills, clever in their tactics when they applied them to the business of playing football, who appeared to be caught in some collective hysteria. Where was the authority of their coach, Juan Carlos Lorenzo? I couldn't imagine that for a second Alf would have tolerated such anarchy.

Some apologists for the Argentine behaviour stressed the fact we had the higher foul count but that for me was never more than a grotesque misnomer. They were a quick, highly skilled team eminently capable of inducing mistimed tackles and no doubt we were guilty of some such mistakes. No doubt we also sought to follow the old Busby principle of letting them know we were there. However, the referee was quick enough to reach for his whistle and on this issue Rattín could have had no reasonable complaint.

Much more significantly, there was no semblance on our part of a conspiracy to intimidate the opposition. We played in our own way but always acknowledged the laws of the game.

Rattín and his men seemed to think they could run everything over the heads of the officials and once again we had seen an example of the classic disconnection between the beauty of the South American style and some of its more ruthless expression.

Some accused the referee of being weak to the point of incompetence but to me his reading of the situation, and his reactions to the approach of the Argentines, was sound enough. If he didn't bristle with physical authority, that was no reason for anyone to assume that he could be easily brushed aside. In the most vital matter, the question of who would have the last word on who controlled the match, there was no question that he won the argument.

One consequence of that was that it helped us to win – and make a massive stride forward. Again, though, Alf was less than ecstatic about our performance, though he did agree that we had kept our heads well enough and if our execution was sometimes less than perfect we did show the best of intentions.

For me, though, and I've no doubt some of my team-mates, there would always be the unanswered question of what might have happened if a wonderfully gifted team had borrowed a few of the instincts of their neighbours Brazil. They had already shown that they had the beating of the world champions of 1958 and 1962 and they had done it in Rio. What they hadn't produced, though, was anything like the Brazilian faith in their own quality, their own ability to play the game not just more beautifully but more effectively than any other team on earth.

That philosophy had foundered under the brutal treatment Brazil had received from Bulgaria and Portugal but as they took home their wounds they could at least tell themselves that they had not compromised their belief in how football should be played. By comparison, Rattín's team left England shamelessly donning the clothes of martyrs. Rattín, I was appalled to learn, had on his return been invited to the presidential palace, where he was received as a hero who had been denied his just reward.

That, in my opinion, would always be a travesty of the truth. Nor would I forget an apprehension, which was at its strongest before Rattín was dismissed but lingered on up to the moment I heard the final whistle. It was that at some point Rattín and his talented colleagues would find the grace to remember that they had been given a destiny to play football at the very highest level with confidence and great flair – and not to cheat, not to seek out every cheap advantage they could find, not to scavenge through one of the most important matches they would ever play like a bunch of muggers lurking in a backstreet.

When the game was over, along with the first rush of anger and disbelief, I could only be grateful for the kind of leadership I had received with both United and England. The game plan of Argentina was an abomination which would have been thrown out of the nearest window by a disgusted Matt Busby or Alf Ramsey. In their different ways, they lived by one great article of faith. It was that you had to build a team you could trust.

Busby, the Old Man, said the greatest joy in his career was to send out players he believed in utterly, and then sit in the stand with the assurance that he had done his work as well as he could. He once reported that he felt sorry for some of his rivals who seemed so anxious before a game, so uncertain about the outcome. Some of them, he noted, would perhaps take a shot of Scotch before a big match, but though he was partial enough to a 'wee dram' he never felt the need for such a recourse.

'It was calming enough,' he said, 'to know that nothing was beyond the ability of your players and that, whatever the result, you could tell yourself that they had played to the limit of their abilities.'

It seemed to me that the Argentine coach Lorenzo had at least half a dozen reasons to embrace such a philosophy but there was not a sniff of it as the match wore on and the accomplished, if often shameless defence of his remaining ten players seemed geared to the possibility of exploiting rules which today seem quite incredible. Had Peters and Hurst not worked the breakthrough, we would have played thirty minutes of extra-time and, if there was still deadlock, we would have tossed for the right to a place in the semi-finals.

When Rattín left it meant that more than ever Argentina concentrated their greatest efforts on preventing us scoring. However, this did not banish all of our anxiety when they got hold of the ball. They had such talent that if one of us made a mistake, left a little unguarded space, they might yet bring the heavens crashing down on us. Sure enough, they conjured the heart-stopping prospect – with just fifteen minutes to go. Onega, whose skill and perception had given me concern from the start, sent the flying Mas away with a beautifully weighted long pass. I could hardly steal the courage to look as the winger flashed his shot just wide of Gordon Banks's goal.

Mostly, though, it was attrition and on occasion dangerously so. Rafael Albrecht, who had come back from his suspension for a bad foul on West Germany's Wolfgang Weber in the group game, hit Jack dangerously from behind when he was jumping at a corner and Hurst also raised the temperature when he stopped Roberto Ferreiro with a high tackle as he ran strongly out of defence.

When the match was over, when deliverance came, there was a sight amid all the rancour and tumult that would never lose its power to move me. It was of Jimmy Greaves embracing his squad-mates and, most significantly and graciously, Hurst the scorer and Hunt, his magnificently committed helpmate. Jimmy knew, surely, the implication of their performances. They had gone relentlessly into those Argentine trenches, they had turned and battled, held up the ball and taken the hits. They did it without a whimper of complaint and each time they emerged with the ball Jimmy must have known that his greatest hopes were receding a little further.

He must have known he was heading for some of the most difficult days of his life. Yet whatever his private thoughts, and perhaps even a growing resentment of the ultimate judgement of Alf, they were suppressed in our moments of triumph. That was something, forged in the great crisis of a superb career, I would always respect.

Perhaps in retrospect the most damningly acute assessment of Jimmy's fading prospects came from Ray Wilson. My friend was among the least publicly voluble members of the squad but when he spoke most of us tended to listen and this was also true of Alf. His head would turn when Ray made a telling aside. Now his personal perspective on the Greaves–Hurst debate could hardly have been more explicit.

He reflected that while Jimmy was no doubt a great player, a unique scoring talent, he was also 'bloody useless in the air. The chances we were going to get at Wembley were going to be mostly in the air because the other teams were so outrageously defensive. There comes a time in that situation when you have to start hitting 50-50 balls. And that's where Geoff was so good.

'You could hit balls to him and he would hold on, or knock them down for people like Martin Peters or Bobby Charlton. The change from Jimmy to Geoff certainly suited me because it meant that if I was under pressure, with two opponents against me, I could get it to Geoff and he would keep it, putting their defence under pressure. Jimmy couldn't do that.'

Ray's full-back partner George Cohen also came out of the Argentina game with redoubled respect for the efforts of the men in front – and he noted that for Alf it had been one of the most crucial aspects of our success.

George said, 'Alf knew we could play better but he also recognised the extraordinary and at times sickening nature of the challenge we had faced. He said he was very "gratified" by several aspects of our effort. He particularly liked the willingness of Hurst and Hunt to keep going into the trenches where their markers were behaving so atrociously. He also recognised the difficulty we had faced in maintaining any decent tempo when the Argentines so cynically stopped the play whenever we moved into anything like a dangerous position. His mood for several days after the game was more than anything a mixture of rage and bewilderment. Rage that our players had been placed at such risk by Argentina's methods – and bewilderment that the South Americans should so disfigure – and reduce – their own luminous talent.

'That latter mystery ran most deeply in my mind – and it still does. When I think of the whole extraordinary affair one strange little incident always comes back. The memory is of Oscar Mas, the man who had given me that anxious moment at the start of the match, tapping me on the shoulder and pointing to the big scoreboard. It showed the score from the Portugal–North Korea quarter-final at Goodison Park, one that had brought a great gasp from the crowd: Portugal 0 North Korea 3.

'Mas's expression said to me, "Oh, no . . . it's a strange game, a strange life, isn't it?" It was indeed. Here was a potentially great Argentine team selling itself, and the game it might have graced magnificently, so desperately short and at Goodison Park, my favourite ground, a bunch of obscure North Koreans were running through one of European's most powerful football nations. If we got through this Wembley ordeal, would the North Koreans be waiting, without fear, to spring another ambush?'

No, George's nightmare scenario was pushed back along with Rattín's warring, unscrupulous troops. Eusébio's power and skill and ambition returned the world – and its great football tournament – to its axis and those amazing shock troops had to return to their misty, mysterious land north of the 38th parallel content with the scalp of only one great football nation, Italy. Portugal would be our last obstacle on the road to the World Cup final.

We would have to subdue the impact of Eusébio and in this hugely pivotal matter it was clear that Alf saw another vital role for Nobby. There was a burst of ironic laughter when my friend reacted to his manager's matter-of-fact statement that his job was to remove the great man's potential influence on the game. 'For this one match or his whole career?' Nobby asked, straight-faced. The dismay he had displayed so deeply just a few days earlier was, we were all reassured to see, already consigned to ancient history.

There were, apart from Eusébio, new points of danger now. Portugal had a fine combative midfield, shaped majestically by their captain Mário Coluna, another football prize from their

African dominions, and Jaime Graça. Along the flanks, José Augusto and António Simões could be relied upon to supply the tall and always threatening José Torres with plentiful opportunity in the air.

Alf pointed out that there was one more certainty. Despite the shocking surprise of their bruising assault on Pelé, Portugal would not make the Argentine mistake of shunning the value of their own marvellous gifts.

In many ways, Alf suggested, we had overcome our greatest challenge. Argentina had taken us to a strange and potentially treacherous place. But we had survived. Now we could play, to our strengths and on our own terms. It was a bit like taking a great gulp of fresh, invigorating air.

14. Reaching for the Light

First, though, before the exhilaration of a real game against real opponents, and the adrenaline surge that would drive away all the bad feelings, there was a need to pause, to walk not just to the corner stool but back through the ropes and into the crowd. It had become an overriding imperative on the Sunday morning after victory over Argentina.

In truth, that still felt more like an escape than a triumph, one that left me gripped by an extremely intense desire to get away from the World Cup, if only for a few hours.

Alf had permitted us more than the usual post-match nightcap when we returned to the hotel; indeed, if not explicitly but in his demeanour, and his swift ordering of a drink for himself, he gave the clear impression that we were all in need of something extra to take away the hard edge of our mood. But then soon enough it became clear that what we had experienced, and been so bewildered and angered by, was not so easily left discarded at the bottom of a spent beer glass.

It kept welling back into our minds and emotions and filled each stage of the rising pitch of the bar-room exchanges.

Many attempts were made to lighten the atmosphere with

that frequently rough humour of the professional footballer and in this, inevitably, Jack and Nobby and Bally were to the fore. Most of the jokes, though, had a tough, sardonic element and whatever laughter they brought was brittle. It could, I suppose, hardly have been otherwise with the anger still so raw.

Nobby was especially emotional. He had carried into the game all the additional weight of his Jacky Simon ordeal and many years later his account of the day was no less vivid than it had been in the bar. He recalled, 'The manager's team talk was low-key, practical. "Don't get involved in anything off the ball," he said. "Walk away from everything. Just get on with the game: remember at all times what you have to do – win the World Cup for England."

'There was quite a lot to walk away from. Argentina had wonderful skill and a technically brilliant captain in Antonio Rattín but they were spoiling from the first seconds. We had to face a tide of petty needling – and spittle. The spitting never stopped. Time after time they gobbed in your face and when you went down in the tackle they were grabbing your boots and yanking your legs. You just had to keep telling yourself not to take the bait.

'I remember how, after I had hit the ground and was getting up, the Argentine I had gone down with got hold of my boot, lifted it and then fell back as though I had hit him. You knew then it was going to be a very hard day and this was confirmed when Bobby Charlton got booked.

'For me, of course, it was the day of all days when I couldn't lose my head. The need for self-control had been reinforced by Alf's assistants Harold Shepherdson and Les Cocker. Separately they got hold of me before the game – Cocker even pushed me against the dressing-room wall – and told me that I just couldn't let Alf down.

'Shepherdson said, "You'll never know what Alf has gone through for you." I said he shouldn't worry, I knew what Alf had done and there was no way I would let him down now.'

Nobby had been encouraged in the pre-match talk when Alf invited opinions on how we should deal with the clever playmaker Onega. The overwhelming reaction was that he should be man-marked and that the job should go to Nobby. My friend was particularly pleased that the ever-astute Ray Wilson led the vote on his behalf.

Now, we all knew that Alf was right to speak of the semi-final with Portugal as a great and thrilling opportunity as much as a challenge.

Yes, they would have those wonderful attacking players Eusébio, Coluna, Simões, Augusto and Torres but then a few months earlier in their own Lisbon citadel they had also been supposedly key figures in the Benfica team torn apart 5-1 by Nobby's and my Manchester United.

George Best did most of the damage that extraordinary night – and had been promptly elected to the status of the fifth Beatle by Fleet Street – but I had been pleased enough by my performance against a side that had twice been champions of Europe earlier in the decade and were still one of the most formidable forces in the game.

I scored the final goal and left the beautiful Benfica stadium convinced that we were about to write a new and less anguished chapter in our European Cup history. Though that hope was confounded, with the most bitter irony, in Belgrade by Partizan in the semi-final, now, as I prepared for another one in the World Cup, there did not seem to be compelling reasons for self-doubt.

Much as I respected the quality of men like Eusébio and Coluna, I also believed Alf when he said, 'Unlike the last one, this is a game in which you can look forward to expressing all of your ability.'

Yet, still, it was only one thing to emerge successfully from a Wembley which had been turned into a dark and potentially treacherous place and believe for some very good reasons that your return there would be bathed in a quite different light. It was quite another to reflect that there had been times that afternoon against Argentina when it had been hard not to question the very purpose of what we were doing. Those kind of musings, I found, could not be so easily dismissed.

Had Argentina progressed, if the streets of Buenos Aires and Córdoba had filled with joyful fans, what really would there have been to celebrate? A brave stride towards the peak of world football? The perfect expression of superior skills? No, it would have been a triumph for sleaze, a ticker-tape parade celebrating nothing so much as sharp practice.

I thought of that footballer I so admired, Alfredo Di Stéfano, and I knew what he would have thought of the performance of his former compatriots. He would have seen in it so much that he despised in the game to which he had brought great power and courage in his urge to compete.

Such thoughts had brought me to a rare but unshakeable edginess when our hotel filled up with English and Portuguese journalists and throngs of local people drawn to the growing drama of the great tournament. No doubt it would have been the last thing I would have admitted to Alf – our conversation in the Rio bar would always linger – but perhaps most deeply I craved a Sunday in the company of my wife Norma and daughters Suzanne and Andrea – a few hours that were not dominated so completely by the need to win still another football match.

Maybe we would have taken a walk in the Cheshire countryside around the village of Lymm where we had set up home and I once saw Bill Shankly, who was staying with Liverpool at a nearby hotel, peering over our garden hedge. I invited him in for a cup of tea and he had been charmed, this great football man who was alleged to have taken his wife Nessie to a reserve match by way of a wedding anniversary celebration, when Norma sought his opinion on the value of 4-3-3. It was only when the Liverpool team arrived at our gate that he got up to leave. But then even someone as passionately driven as Bill Shankly could invest only so much time and thought and obsession into a single objective before the weight of it threatened to become crippling. When I think about that now, I have to recall there were some who said that in the end that was indeed a tragically sad aspect to his wonderful career. When the game was over for him, and he came to agonise on lonely walks around the walls of Liverpool's training ground over the fact that it was by his own decision, many who knew him well had to conclude that something had gone from the core of his life.

Another who found that his existence became so much more complicated when he stepped back into the realities he left behind for a little while when he crossed the touchline, came to our house in Lymm. It was George Best, the joyful young conqueror of Lisbon's Estádio da Luz.

We had played in a Uefa representative match in Cardiff and on the homeward train journey I asked him what he would do when we parted at the station in Manchester. He said he didn't really know beyond the fact that he would find somewhere to have a drink and while away a few hours.

Norma was away with the girls and I remembered that she had told me she would leave some scampi in the fridge for me to cook for my supper. I invited George to share it with me and was rather amazed when he accepted the invitation.

Throughout the meal – the scampi, as I remember, wasn't so successful – he seemed eager to know about my experience of married life, the rhythm of it, the demands and the pleasures. He also made a fuss over our new pet, a chow, and soon after that he bought a dog of his own. He also had a house built and became engaged to a Danish girl he met when we played in Copenhagen.

It led me to speculate, rather too hopefully, that one of the most brilliant footballers I would ever know might just be finding a little secure contentment away from the great public stage that his life had become. Sadly, it never happened for any sustained period of time and the memory of that night we spent together came poignantly to mind when I travelled down to see him shortly before he died in a London clinic.

George never got the break from the pressure that built around the image that he created so early in his life, never got the release from it that I needed, in admittedly hugely different circumstances, so keenly that Sunday morning in the England team hotel.

Much to my relief, Ray Wilson said that not only did he understand my mood, he shared it. And though it wasn't practical to seek the solitude and peace of his beloved moorland, or make some foray into southern hills, he did agree to come with me to the nearby South Herts Golf Club where earlier Alf had allowed us to play a round on a rest day.

Then, we had been told by members that we should consider their pleasant surroundings a safe refuge if in the next few weeks we felt the need for one. Now was the time to take up their offer. For a little while we could retreat from the frenzy building in the hotel lobby and that increasing sense that we had become the property of much of an expectant nation.

We sat on the clubhouse terrace and, as was often the case when we retired to our room, we didn't say a lot. We didn't really have to because we knew each other well enough by now, how our minds worked and our emotions played.

As the golfers came in from their rounds, joking about winning and losing side bets, we surely had reason to reflect that if professional sport was such a hugely important part of our life, it wasn't quite all of it. Alf might have suggested otherwise at times down the years but not at this point. Sometimes, even he allowed, the pressure had to be lifted, and that was why he had relaxed his normal vigilance in the hotel bar when we arrived back from Wembley.

Ray and I agreed on the value of this, especially now when we were less than a week away from the end of the World Cup, and that in forty-eight hours we could, if we achieved everything we set ourselves, be just one step, one regathering of confidence and ambition, away from making it to the final which had been at the centre of our hopes and our work for more than three years.

Around us there was the growing clamour of the nation – we would have fresh evidence of this on a shopping trip to Selfridges after training the following day – and, of course, we had to separate ourselves as best we could from this swell of mounting hopes. We had to do our jobs; we had to be good pros.

But then, as the shoppers and the golfers and an increasing number of passers-by in the street reminded us all so strongly in those normally much less demonstrative days, it was also impossible to completely ignore the weight of support, even yearning, that had grown around our campaign.

When I considered this, sometimes back in the hotel room when I found it hard to sleep, I went back to the weeks I spent with Norma and the girls on a Majorcan beach before returning to the final push of Lilleshall and the sweep of those final games in Scandinavia and Poland. And, inevitably, I thought of Trevor Atkinson. He had come most strongly into my mind on that first night of anti-climax against Uruguay. I hoped he understood then that it was a disappointment that my colleagues and I would fight to overcome with everything we had to offer, and that of all the factors that had been created there had not been the faintest shadow of indifference.

Each day Trevor would appear at my side on that Spanish beach, a lean, fit figure with short-cropped hair and eager eyes. I might be napping in my deckchair, talking to Norma or helping the girls with their buckets and spades and sandcastles. He wanted to talk about every aspect of the World Cup and how important it was for so many people at home that England did well.

In other circumstances he might have been regarded as a bore, even a pest, but I never thought of him in that way and Norma, too, seemed to understand something of what he represented – and his good intentions. He was a footballer from my part of the country, having started with Spennymoor United and then moved on to Darlington. He accepted that he had gone as far as he would ever go in the game, but that didn't stop his imagining how it might have been playing for England in the World Cup.

That reality was endearing enough in itself. It was also

humbling, a reminder of one's own good luck to be involved and how so many might dream of exchanging places with somebody like me.

He always had a new question, a fresh exhortation, and long before the end of the holiday I accepted him as an extra presence, perhaps even a spokesman for the football nation I would so soon be representing. When he died many years later, I regretted that I hadn't sought him out and let him know how much he had become part of my thinking as we moved towards the end of the campaign.

He had, with his hopes, his enthusiasm, become almost a part of my professional conscience and so, in a way, he had taken his place beside all those extra companions of mine on the bus to the Roehampton training ground and to Wembley, all those who had helped me along my way, from Tanner and the footballing uncles, Jimmy Murphy, and, supremely still, Duncan Edwards.

That Sunday at the golf club is maybe a faded snippet of memory now, but in it does linger strongly an old sense of time and place and that need I felt, as I'm sure so many of my team-mates did, to step for a little while away from some of those horrors – for that is the word – of the Argentina game and any hard consideration of the new challenge which came with facing Portugal.

We did it in our different ways. Ray and I attempted to be flies on the clubhouse wall and, much less successfully, just faces in the crowd in Selfridges on Oxford Street.

Nobby made his daily pilgrimage to mass, a ritual which gave some wry amusement to a George Cohen of Jewish heritage but not practising faith. George, on the way to the breakfast room, encountered Nobby as he walked into the street. He looked at his watch and asked where he was going. 'I'm off to mass in Golders Green,' said Nobby. And George said, 'Good luck with that, Nob. It would be a little easier to find a synagogue.'

Bobby Moore and Jimmy Greaves were like-minded companions in the off-duty hours and, when Jimmy wasn't fretting about his dwindling chances of returning to the team, he was groaning about the ordeal of having to sit through still another John Wayne film.

Bally was reanimated again. His daily phone conferences with his father were no longer laden with fears that his great chance, which had shone so brilliantly in Madrid and gave him such confidence before the opening deadlock with Uruguay, had passed for at least another four years. When Bally put down the phone he reported to Nobby, 'Dad says I have a duty to enjoy every second from here on in. He says I have to make it something to remember for the rest of my life.'

That indeed was the conviction shared by all of us in our different ways, Banksy and Ray in their quiet but hard Yorkshire commitment, Martin and Geoff happy in the belief they had so quickly adjusted to their new challenge, and George and Roger utterly sure about who they were and what they had to do.

Above everything there was a sense that we had indeed moulded together at a most critical time and if this plainly worked against the hopes of Jimmy Greaves, survival against Argentina had the feel of a final statement of unity, of a settled force ready to take our final steps along the road that now wended all the way back to a wintry night in Paris.

That, at least, was my mood of restored calm on the eve of the Portugal game. By then we knew the reward of victory: a place in the final against West Germany. We were not unhappy with the outcome of the other semi-final at Goodison Park. Much as we admired the talent of the prodigious young Franz Beckenbauer, the midfield craft of Wolfgang Overath and the leadership and predatory instincts of the captain Uwe Seeler, who had scored the decisive goal against Spain in their final group game, we had also come to watch the development of the USSR team with some growing apprehension.

They had powered their way through the sensational turbulence of their group, winning all their games and putting down the North Koreans in their opening match with an authority which made the subsequent eruptions from that quarter all the more amazing. Italy and Chile also finished up firmly beneath the Soviet heel.

More impressively still, the threat of Hungary's brilliant forwards Ferenc Bene, Flórián Albert and János Farkas was dismissed with much power and, at times, a touch of brutality. Perhaps the Soviet football was not illuminated by the sweep of Beckenbauer's imagination or the sharp skill and intelligence of Overath, but we had been forced to acknowledge less spectacular but increasingly solid contributions of such as the captain Albert Shesternev, Igor Chislenko and Valeriy Porkujan. They seemed to be men who became more effective in direct proportion to the pressure applied to them.

It was thus – and this seems a little strange now in view of the tumultuous events that were still to stretch before us – something of a relief when Beckenbauer deceived Lev Yashin with a shot that gave the Germans the two-goal lead that survived a late strike by Porkujan. The most significant fact was that it had been a poor match, one hardly guaranteed to provoke the trepidation that had been created by the menace of Argentina – or, now, the possibility that men like Eusébio and Coluna would suddenly find new levels of inspiration.

In any event, I went to my bed confident that one small speck of concern, the last residue of my fleeting anxiety, would be gone by the morning. This was a stiffness in my neck, for which I had received some treatment after a brief consultation with the team doctor. There was no need for great concern, we both agreed. The problem, caused by a touch of fibrositis in my left shoulder, flared three or four times each season but it was always swiftly cured by physiotherapy. Still, I heaped up the pillows and offered up the prayer that a night of rest would leave me perfectly primed both physically and mentally.

To my horror, I discovered it had not. My neck was still stiff and the result was a morning of growing tension. I could hardly bear the thought that after all the years, all the times I had pulled on the England shirt, a random quirk of my body, which had always been so reliable, might just betray me at such a moment.

It didn't help that when at lunchtime Alf came to sit by my side I still had to hold my head at a certain angle.

As always, Alf went straight down to business. He asked me, 'How's your neck, Bobby? Are you fit to play?'

My life, all my ambitions, swept before my eyes when the question came in. I had a duty to be honest but I also found it impossible to believe that a problem I had been successfully negotiating for some time now had suddenly become insurmountable. I would be fine when the time came, I would be able to continue to fulfil the destiny to which I had elected myself for so long now. So I breathed deeply and said, 'I can feel it slightly, Alf, but I'll be fine.'

I will never know how I would have stood up to some deeper

probing from the manager who so often had put aside the call of sentiment while making his most taxing decisions. It is one of those mysteries which, however riveting at the time, get lost in the course of a lifetime. The pause in our conversation may have been exaggerated in my mind but it seemed like an age before Alf said, 'All right, we'll keep the same side.'

Of course, this did not signal the end of my ordeal. That afternoon seemed to touch eternity. What if Alf and I had performed too great an act of faith? What if my ambition had overreached itself and been abetted by the judgement of a man whose most basic belief had always been that no one player was bigger than the team? They were not the kind of questions to make for anything like a serene nap before they served the poached eggs on toast.

But then, on the bus ride to Wembley, and in the rituals I shared again with Ray, the pain in my neck eased, my movement was free.

The voice of Bally sounded less shrill; indeed, along with the now familiar eccentricity of George Cohen's preparation, and the amiable bickering of Jack and Nobby, it was soothing. My world was back on an even keel. I had a game to relish and a performance to put in that I hoped, as much as I had for anything in all my career, I would remember with pride.

15. Laughter and Tears

We were there, we could touch it now. Taking hold of the World Cup, which for so long had been a mirror of our imperfections as a football nation that lacked the humility to learn from either its own mistakes or the brilliant progress of others, was one step, one firm grasp away.

In Sweden, where I was a restive spectator, and in Chile, where some were inclined to celebrate our first appearance in a quarter-final, the prize had seemed as remote as it had ever done since England's first misadventure in Brazil in 1950.

In Gothenburg I watched the champions elect Brazil strolling in the park with the easy, confident gait of men who believed they were about to inherit the world. Four years later, on a Chilean mountain top, I could see clearly enough they still occupied another stratosphere.

Now, the years of waste, and muddled arrogance, might just be redeemed.

We would meet West Germany in the final in four days. The thirtieth of July 1966: a day to bring home the game we had once given the world, a day to make men and women come out into the street in national celebration. A day which those of us who had lasted on the long road, and the others who had elected themselves to the march, like Nobby and Jack and, most urgently, Bally and Geoff and Martin, had to make it so it would last for ever.

Our progress at the end had hardly been carefree, but this only served to lift us still higher when we looked up at the scoreboard and saw it in black and white: England 2 Portugal 1.

Sometimes, I suppose, you only come to value something most truly when you see how easily it might have been taken away. So we clutched ourselves and each other just to confirm that it had happened. Our dream, our work, had not been wrenched away.

There were many reasons to celebrate, but two were the most powerful and uplifting.

Firstly, no one had to tell us that for most of the match we played as well as we could have hoped. Everyone could say that they had played a valuable part in the most important challenge we had ever faced. And that when the pressure came down so heavily, when the heart of so much of the nation had missed a beat, our nerve held. Secondly, the man who had shaped our performance had his own cause for satisfaction. Alf, not for the first time or the last, had read it perfectly.

The Portuguese had indeed also come to play. They were making a death or glory investment in their rich skills, and this was evident in our first glance at their team-sheet. Missing were the names of João Morais and Vincente, the defensive enforcers who had besieged Pelé so unscrupulously.

They put on their very best face. It was exemplified by the strong, beautiful talent and leonine countenance of Eusébio, who for so many in football here and across the world seemed poised to assume the mantle of the departed Pelé.

Now, though, he was walking away, proud head down, shoulders slumped, eyes awash.

If we wanted to measure our elation, consider the height of it, we only had to look at the degree of pain that had come to one of the greatest players the game would ever see. In the last minutes of the game we had seen once more the scale of his ability and the passion he had brought to his task. At the moment of the final whistle, when we had survived a late eruption from him and his superb team-mate and captain Mário Coluna and the towering José Torres, he began to shed his tears.

My compassion for a great footballer, one I would always admire, was tempered, though, I still remember vividly, by a wave of relief which filled every corner of my body and my mind.

When Eusébio beat Gordon Banks from the penalty spot with eight minutes to go – after Jack had fended away with his hand a header by Torres – appalling questions had leaped into my mind. Could it really be, after all the work and the pain and the exhilaration, and with far from the least of it coming in this game in which I had scored two goals and put in, said the most demanding of critics, Brian Glanville of the *Sunday Times*, my best showing in an England shirt, that we might not win the World Cup? Could we have come so close to a final statement only to be sent away?

Such questions made the last minutes as torturous as any I would ever know out on the field. Suddenly, it seemed that our control might be ripped away. Eusébio, so deftly frustrated by the carefully measured attention of Nobby – and forced for a while to claim corner and free-kicks as his best chance of making a significant impact – was now aflame.

He surged along the left flank in the last moments to create, quite beautifully, a chance for Coluna. Banks made a brilliant save from under the bar. It was a catastrophe avoided and then suddenly it was over, we were in the final. When Gordon turned away Coluna's shot I looked immediately for Eusébio and saw his shoulders sag. I also saw the first hint of his tears.

You never want to see such despair in a great opponent but you also have to be honest: his pain was my joy and that was something I had to force myself into containing as I embraced him before he left the field. I told him that I could so easily have been in his shoes and he nodded his thanks and left. As I watched him go, I was reminded once more of how fine sometimes is the line between the fulfilling and the dashing of all of our hopes. A few hours earlier I had been made wretched by anxiety as I felt the pain in my neck. Now the world lay at my feet.

For Eusébio there would still be many years of acclaim before his career drew to a close in the lower reaches of the Portuguese game and on fleeting pioneering duty for the old North American Soccer League in football outposts like Toronto and Las Vegas.

He would win six more league titles with Benfica and when he died in 2014 and was buried in a Lisbon cemetery before being allocated a place in Portugal's pantheon of heroes, the national flag was placed in his grave. He had been voted into the top ten players of the twentieth century and Alfredo Di Stéfano, no less, declared that he had never seen a better, more powerful footballer.

He was Africa's first great player and his emergence from poverty in Mozambique was a major milestone in the growth of the world game, but despite all the ceremonials and the respect and love so tangible in the rainy streets of Lisbon I couldn't detach any of it from the image of his departure from Wembley.

Already he had a career of great distinction – as a twenty-year-old he had made his first impact on Di Stéfano when Benfica beat Real Madrid for the European title in Amsterdam in 1962 – and when he came into our semi-final so many believed that he was just two strides away from rivalling Pelé for the title of the world's best player. But then, when he disappeared down the tunnel – and we hugged ourselves in the knowledge that we were just ninety minutes away from the greatest prize of our football lives – he was, if he knew it or not, walking away from the peaks of football.

Two years later on the same field, and with Nobby again standing sentinel, only a brilliant save by United goalkeeper Alex Stepney prevented Eusébio from seizing another European title. Again, he had brought terror to English hearts but once more he found fulfilment elusive.

Still today I think of Eusébio when I come to consider my own good luck, the way that I was able to tick away my disappointments as a young player and, one by one, replace them with the warm and lasting glow of major achievement. It is one of the many affinities I have with Nobby that we share the distinction of being the only Englishmen to win both the European and World Cups and it is impossible to forget that he played such a huge role in both achievements.

Twice Nobby was handed the job of containing the force and the talent of a player who had seemed to be moving towards the zenith of his powers. Twice he had responded with endless application and a superb awareness of what was happening around him.

Of course, for me there was never going to be a victory which would ease the pain of Munich – but here was the satisfaction, and the gratitude, which comes when you have reason to believe you have managed to become strong at some broken places.

Eusébio's career was played out on a different trajectory. First it soared, then it drifted away from the highest possibilities. Maybe it is wrong to drape a fabulous career in such poignancy because of a couple of results but try as I might I can never banish the sight of Eusébio coming to terms with the greatest disappointment of his career. In Portugal they still call our semi-final 'the Game of Tears'.

For us – and not least Alf – it was a game of great vindication. His 4-3-3 system, whatever people would make of it later, and however many levelled the charge, emptily in my view, that it was ultimately a cause of decline in the quality and the imagination of English football, not only produced a winning performance of hard and functional effort. It was also touched by beauty and quite a lot of it was made in England.

At the same time it did indeed show the effects of an intelligent application of a team's collective strength. One of these was a series of outstanding individual performances. If it was true I had my best match for England, that I was able to produce all the strongest aspects of my game, a huge reason was that I felt perfectly attuned to all that was around me. Until Eusébio made his last roar of defiance, we had dominated what most agreed was the best game of the tournament.

Remarkably, given all that was at stake, it was also among the cleanest. The absence of Morais and Vicente was the first announcement that Portugal had put behind them the violence of their assault on Pelé. The second was an astounding amiability on and off the ball. The first foul took twenty-two minutes to arrive and then it was committed by Martin Peters, who obstructed Eusébio. By the end, and despite the huge rise of tension in those last few minutes, the French referee had blown for just ten transgressions.

No one was more restrained – or more effective – than Nobby. It was the supreme example of his ability to read the game. He shepherded Eusébio quite brilliantly, refusing to lunge in but always jockeying him out of easy space or opportunities to strike, and the more the great threat was subdued, the more confident we became.

Of course it was beyond the resources of Nobby, or perhaps any defender on earth, to entirely stifle one of the most potent talents football would ever know, and inevitably Gordon Banks was also involved in the task. But by then we had laid claim to the game – and all the spoils that went with it.

Our first goal after half an hour flowed from Alf's principles of teamwork and selfless running and the creators, appropriately enough, were Ray Wilson and Roger Hunt.

Ray brought the ball out of defence and fed it into the goal area to Roger who, sensing the unfolding possibilities, had made space for himself there before turning the ball inside and inducing panic in the Portuguese keeper José Pereira. His dive failed to prevent the ball reaching me fifteen yards out. I saw a clear gap – and two options. I could either attempt to blast in my shot – or try to stroke the ball home with the side of my foot. I took the latter course and the yells of the crowd echoed perfectly my own sensation, one that was not dissimilar to when I exploited another piece of Roger's foraging against Mexico. Yes, surely, we were on our way.

That feeling was redoubled with just ten minutes to go when

I got the second at the end of another move that might have been ordained by Alf on the training field. This time my co-authors were Alan Ball, George Cohen and, most crucially, Geoff Hurst. I find it a little haunting at this long distance to return to an earlier recall of mine of the moments which, all logic insisted, had carried us to the final. It reminds me yet again of an old truth in sport: the one that says the moment you believe the job is done you put yourself at risk.

'The Portuguese,' I said, 'clearly did not share my assessment, or the crowd's, that the job was essentially completed when I slotted in the first goal. Indeed, their entire attitude to this game reminded me of why I liked them so much. There was no hint of passivity from them. In the first half Pereira had been under considerable pressure but now the action was beginning to move steadily in the direction of Banks. The towering Torres was locked in battle with Jack and the wingers Augusto and Simões were stretching us wide, so much so that Cohen and Wilson and Moore were not slow to call back defensive recruits from midfield.

'Ball, who was now such an integral part of the team it seemed odd that he had been stood down for those two group games, Peters and I were repeatedly required to help out as Stiles battled on with all his great spirit (and nous) in the toughest contest of all, the decisive one with Eusébio. While Peters, particularly, was capable of tackling with the precision of a specialist defender and Ball was tigerish, my own contribution at this point was necessarily running, supporting and offering channels of relief when the ball was won from the clever touch of the Portuguese.

'My tackling had always been the despair of Jimmy Murphy but he acknowledged that I didn't shirk from any running on behalf of the defence. If I could run all day, and from time to time I could score, it mostly left the hardest taskmaster I would ever know content enough. My second goal of the game came with just ten minutes to go and again it was the fruit of Alf's insistence that players must work for each other and that if a team simply relied on flashes of virtuosity it was never going to win the big games – or be a consistent force.

'The flow of the move and the vital role of Geoff Hurst live in my mind for, I believe, one basic reason. All of it seemed to define the team Alf had made.

'The ball was moved out of defence to Alan Ball, then switched across the field to Cohen via Moore. We were operating on another law of Ramsey. You did not sit on a lead; you do not invite dangerous opponents into your parlour. As much as possible, and without any concession on the need to be strong always in defence, you prosecute the game as aggressively, and as honestly, as you can.

'Cohen sent a long ball down the right to Hurst, who was running so strongly he outstripped the defender, Alexandre Baptista, and though Geoff's angle was acute my inclination would have been to shoot. Instead, he did something that, who knows, may well have clinched finally any argument left in Alf's mind over Geoff's challenge to Jimmy Greaves.

'I'll never forget it for what it said about the ideal of being unselfish on the football field. He checked for a moment as Baptista resumed his attention and held up play long enough for me to run free beside him. He rolled the ball into my stride quite perfectly and the moment I hit it I knew that it was going in.'

That was the detail of the moments which made us believe we had reached the final, a conclusion which in the strangest, and as it turned out most illusory, way the Portuguese seemed be confirming when Augusto raced up to me before the restart and offered me his hand in congratulation. Slightly stunned, I accepted it.

When Eusébio scored his penalty almost immediately after, and the Portuguese made their last and threatening push, Augusto's gesture became a suddenly faded, even ancient memory. But in the next few days it came back to me so strongly, and said so much about the good feelings that can build between opponents who bring a certain mutual respect to the most demanding situations, that I sought out a jeweller's shop and bought some gold cufflinks. I planned to present them to José at a banquet to be attended by the players of the top four teams but in the last hours before the final I regrettably mislaid them. Later, I reflected that what we shared on the field would surely be as enduring as any small piece of gold.

Alf set a mood of quite measured celebration when we came back to the hotel after the semi-final victory. He said that we had reason to congratulate ourselves – but not too extravagantly. By then I had called home and got a strong sense of the enthusiasm – and the expectation – that was building around the country. This was confirmed for me by the fact that after Norma had said, 'Well done, Bobby, you couldn't have done better', my mother-in-law came to the phone and added a few words of praise. Norma said that there had been great excitement in front of the black and white television. I said how much I would have liked it if she had been in the stadium but, as she pointed out, she had our daughters to care for and a home to keep. She was already, she assured me, making her plans for the London weekend.

In the hotel bar Alf wore a broad smile and said that, most

certainly, we deserved a celebratory drink but at no cost to anyone's understanding that the hardest work, and pressure, was still to come. There would be no repeat, he insisted, of the 'tiring emotionalism' that developed in the bar after the Argentina game. Nobby remembered this command, and the way Alf dressed it, very precisely because he had assumed, glumly, that he would be sipping a fruit juice while his team-mates once again did a little serious drinking after such an important victory.

This was because, in that last desperate phase, Gordon Banks had attempted to punch away a Portuguese cross while only succeeding in landing his fist on Nobby's ear. When the team doctor examined the damage in the dressing room he decided that he needed to give Nobby an injection against the risk that he develop a cauliflower ear. 'This means,' said Alan Bass, 'you can't touch a drink for twenty-four hours. If you do, the injection will not work.'

Thus, Nobby's precise recall of Alf's announcement is, by his own admission, that of a man suddenly released from a sharp pang of envy for team-mates whom he expected to be allowed to do something he had been denied.

'Alf said,' reported Nobby, ' "Gentlemen, congratulations on a fine performance and on making the final. You have done well for yourselves, for me and, most important of all, for your country. But tonight I want you to have just two pints. After the Argentina game you were, well, how can I put it, rat-arsed. But not tonight, gentlemen, you have a World Cup to win on Saturday. When you do it, I will make sure you are then, and for quite some time, permanently pissed." '

It was maybe a speech unlikely to be encountered on the pages of Shakespeare; it was not Henry V before Agincourt, but the effect was impressive enough. Alf's words brought a rousing cheer in the bar.

The feeling of wellbeing was only strengthened by the reaction of a previously sceptical world press. Most agreed it was the showpiece game of the tournament, an exhibition of strong, flowing football played in a superb spirit.

The applause could even be heard on the other side of the Iron Curtain. The Russian news agency Tass was so lyrical it might have been discussing the latest policy statement by the Supreme Soviet. They declared, 'England gave their finest showing in the championship. The match came like a spring of clear water breaking through the wave of dirty football which has flooded recent games.'

Maybe the most heart-warming sentiments came from Lisbon and the newspaper *A Voz*, which asked the Portuguese team, 'Why tears, boys, unless they are out of emotion? You carried out your mission bravely, and we are proud of you in this defeat as we are proud of you in your triumphs.'

My own performance provoked a considerable response, some of it rather more fanciful than the message from a wine-importing company saying they were sending me a case of the best port. A Stockholm newspaper speculated that my goals might just earn me a place in the House of Lords, if not a statue to replace the one of Lord Nelson in Trafalgar Square. However, a Czech sports paper stayed much nearer the ground and, it is not falsely modest to say it, a little nearer to one of the most important reasons for a successful campaign. Commenting on the resistance of the defence to that late surge of Portuguese aggression it said, 'The English backs are almost indestructible.'

That was hardly an overstatement. When Eusébio drove home that briefly destabilising penalty it was the first goal we had conceded in the tournament and in our previous seven matches, which is still a record unlikely to be threatened at any time soon.

In Fleet Street, though, much more attention was being paid to the ever-intensifying speculation concerning the fate of Jimmy Greaves. Would he be brought back for the final, would his ghostly scoring touch be Alf's last tactical stroke, another, maybe surreal dimension to the work that had disposed of Argentina and Portugal? In truth, within the team, and certainly in my mind, it had become a phantom debate.

It meant that in the burst of cheering in the Hendon Hall bar Jimmy was, inevitably, one of the least voluble contributors. In truth he had moved deeply into the margins of the drama.

Clearly, it was now about the energy and force and constant relevance of Roger Hunt and Geoff Hurst up in the trenches. It was about the endless combativeness and sharpness of Alan Ball and the seamless versatility of Martin Peters. In my view, and more importantly in Alf's, they had become indispensable in our ambition.

Indeed, if there was a single element in those cheers it was the sound of conviction, of a belief that there was no sliver of doubt about the identity and the purpose of those men who in four days would stride out for the final of the World Cup.

If Hurst and Hunt and Peters and Ball had made unanswerable claims for themselves, so too had Gordon Banks, who was already being nominated as the natural successor to the world's best goalkeeper, Lev Yashin. George Cohen and Ray Wilson had grown ever stronger as the tournament wore on. Bobby Moore and my brother Jack had formed, in their sharply different ways, a superb fulcrum at the heart of defence. Nobby had justified, magnificently, Alf's willingness to go to the brink on his behalf.

Me? Well, I had scored some important goals and it was said I had just enjoyed my best performance in seventy-three appearances for England. Maybe I wouldn't be called to the Lords, or see my statue rising in place of Horatio Nelson's, but now I would have football's biggest stage to express all that I considered the best of my game.

Or so I thought.

16. A Date with Franz

As I went up the Wembley tunnel and heard the roar of the crowd and walked out beneath the racing clouds to meet the Queen and play the most important football match of my life, I had reason to see in a new light the leadership of Alf Ramsey.

I also had cause to re-examine the depth of my understanding and acceptance of his most fundamental principles. The starting point was that, while it was all very well admiring a man for the strength of his decisions, the fearless independence of his thinking, how much easier this is when you are not touched personally by the unexpected weight of them.

When a hard word is going into someone else's ear, when it is not you being pushed into a corner and told you have to do something quite specific and utterly vital and measurable in a way you had never been asked to contemplate before, or considered part of your nature, it is one matter. But then, when it is you having to stare at the biggest challenge you have ever faced, and with consequences that might well colour the rest of your life, it is, I had just discovered, quite another.

So, yes, though I had felt some compassion for the broken

hopes of team-mates and friends like Jimmy Armfield and Jimmy Greaves, it was also true I had come to accept implicitly the judgement of Alf. Brick by brick, he had built his team and even when criticism of his style and his most basic beliefs about the game was at its highest, both inside and out of the squad, I would say, perhaps to Ray Wilson in the privacy of our room, 'What on earth are these people talking about, can't they see that in so many ways he is doing a sensational job? He is making a team, a strong team. He knows what he has to do to make us more effective and he has the courage to do it.'

My luxury, I had grasped finally, was that none of it had touched me directly, none of it had been threatening to me, still less had it invited me quite harshly to reassess every aspect of my claim to a place in his plans.

Indeed, if I am honest I have to say that if the idea of my being left out of the side, of finding myself after so long on the outside looking in, had crossed my mind it was only as some vaguely considered and unaccountable disaster. My role, I didn't need to be told, was in many ways enviable. I played my game, I did that which I was best at. Nobby did my tackling, he minded me. Hunt and Hurst foraged for opportunities that I had been able to exploit at telling and much celebrated moments in this campaign.

This is not to say that I never heard a cross word, the occasional rebuke for something Alf thought smacked of a little self-indulgence. But nor had I been obliged to fret like young Bally about my chances of being involved in the climax to all that we were attempting to achieve. I didn't get the shock of Martin Peters when, to everyone's surprise except Alf's, a string of superb performances failed to win him a place in the opening game against Uruguay.

Alf was so many things to so many people in so many different places and situations. However much you admired him, or ultimately came to love him, you could never be sure about quite what was going on behind his inscrutable gaze. It might be the forming of a dry aside – or an announcement that would wreck the dreams of a Greaves or an Armfield and so many others on the way from a winter night in Paris to a summer afternoon in north-west London.

Yet if his mood and his deepest thoughts could sometimes be elusive I was always sure we were in the most dependable hands. He would, I came to believe, always get it right in the end. And as for me, well, I didn't have to twist or turn or question too deeply who I was, what I was doing or where I was going.

At least this was true until twenty-four hours or so before I was due to play in the World Cup final.

Alf would tell ten members of the team that their places were secure in the evening before they filed into the local cinema to watch his latest film selection, the First World War flying epic *The Blue Max*. But by then I knew my situation. It was one I had never faced before in all my appearances for England.

My assumption had been that I would play the game that had worked so well against Portugal, that while Hunt and Hurst ran at the defence, while Bally and Peters gave width and bite and ceaseless energy, I would use my running ability and attacking skills to a largely creative purpose. But this was before Alf sat down beside me and said that my job was to mark Franz Beckenbauer.

Without any kind of preamble, he told me, 'Bobby, I want you to do something for me. I want you to stick on Beckenbauer for every minute, every second of the match. This boy is the only German player who can beat us. They have some other very good players but I can plan for every one of them except Beckenbauer.

'I don't know what he's going to do from one minute to the next – and I don't think he does. So I can't lay plans for him. I don't know when he's suddenly going to try to get behind our defenders. It means that I have just one plan for him – and it is you. I want you to stay with him throughout the whole game, don't go anywhere else. He is your responsibility. I know he's young and he can run, but then you can run. You have a good engine. If you do your job he will not do any damage and I'm sure we will win the World Cup.'

I took a deep breath as a thousand thoughts swirled in my head but the most dominant one – and looking back I have to be thankful for this – was that it was no time to withdraw trust in a man who had been right so many times, one who had indeed convinced me of the value of the concept of the team always coming first. It was a principle which I recognised quickly enough had gone right to the heart of our brief conversation.

If I had not demurred when a striking talent as luminous as Jimmy Greaves had been cast aside, if I accepted that Alf had a case when he opted for the strong defence of George Cohen over the more rounded skills of the former skipper Armfield, how could I possibly challenge his decision about the best contribution I could make to the winning of the World Cup? This, of course, remained the whole point of what we had all been working on for more than three years.

So I said, after a few torturous seconds, 'Okay, Alf, I'll do that.' He nodded and walked away, another decision made and accepted. I sat for a while, still stunned by the scale of the role reversal he had just imposed upon me. I didn't do man-marking. Other people had always done that to me. But then Alf had, as usual, not shown much inclination to debate the point. He had reached a decision. Yes, maybe I had other assets, like passing and shooting, but the most relevant one now was that I could run fast and strongly and as long as was necessary.

Alf didn't say it in so many words but the implication was plain enough. I'd had my taste of glory, now I had to do a job for the team and if this meant I might not get the opportunity to do something spectacular, well, it was simply too bad.

This wasn't a hunt for personal glory. It was the pursuit of the most important prize in football. It was the final expression of a winning team. This was something I had to come to terms with. He had, after all, given me all of twenty-four hours.

There was also the huge responsibility. I certainly agreed with Alf that Beckenbauer was, at just twenty, the outstanding German player. He was quick and poised and had carried the precious quality of surprise. Of course Alf had most thoroughly assessed the strengths and the weaknesses of the Germans.

He had reason to respect the smooth and clever passing of Wolfgang Overath and the attacking menace of Sigge Held, Uwe Seeler and Helmut Haller. But Beckenbauer was the man with the imagination – and the killer touch. We had been very impressed by him in the 5-0 defeat of Switzerland in Germany's opening group. He had scored twice and his play had brimmed with the sharpest of authority. He also stood out in the quarter-final defeat of Uruguay, when he scored again and had been a constant worry to the South Americans even before they had two men sent off.

For Alf it was a simple enough equation. If I could neutralise

Beckenbauer with my running, if I could make myself his sole preoccupation, the calculation was that any negative effect on my own productivity would not be too significant. We had enough elsewhere in the team to get the job done. It was not what I had in mind and inevitably I had a sense that my wings had been clipped as I watched those aerial dogfights on the silver screen.

No doubt I would have been more philosophical had I known that around the time Alf was handing me my assignment an almost identical conversation was going on between Beckenbauer and the German coach Helmut Schoen.

Schoen had identified me as the greatest single threat to the German defence and, he said, it was Beckenbauer's job to be my shadow at every stage of the game.

Some years later Franz gave a gracious and, to me, extremely flattering account of the German thinking. He said, 'Before the match our manager Schoen and his assistant coaches decided that I should mark Bobby Charlton. They knew that if I did it would reduce my own strength for attacking but they were insistent. "It's very important," Schoen said, "because you're fast enough to stay with him, to control him."'

Down the years we have laughed about our irritation at being denied the positive roles to which we had been accustomed, but we have also agreed that there was compelling logic on both sides of the strategy.

That kind of understanding was not so readily available on the eve of the final, however, and there were, no doubt, other members of the cinema audience who were rather more exhilarated than me, and not least Martin and Geoff as they hoarded the confirmation that they would be playing in the final. Martin revealed later that when they returned to the room they shared they gave great cheers of celebration.

Along the corridor, Ray and I were rather more restrained. We had a cup of tea and we talked about what was in front of us, how well we would deal with the pressure and how we had come too far to let such an opportunity slip away. As we talked, I wondered how it was possible to sleep the night before such a challenge.

How did you put a brake on all the thoughts and the possibilities that teemed into your mind? In my case, I began to think through the challenge presented by Franz Beckenbauer. I remembered what torture he had inflicted on the Swiss player who had been given the job I faced in the final. But then Ray, as always, was calm and reassuring. He pointed out that I had the pace and the experience of big occasions that the Swiss player had lacked. 'You'll be all right, you'll see that the moment you go out on the field. We'll all be all right. We can get this job done.'

Whereupon, we got into our beds and slept like babies.

There had been occasions, perhaps provoked by the enduring memory of Munich, when I had wondered whether I might be in danger of placing too much importance on the outcome of a single football match, but when I woke from the good night's rest I knew immediately that this day would not be one of them. I was extremely pleased that before it was out I would again be in the company of Norma, I looked forward very much too to seeing my daughters, but first I had to help in the winning of the World Cup. It brought the familiar edge that comes to any competitor whose ambitions and talent and character are about to be tested more intensely than ever before.

Over a hearty breakfast I told Ray that I planned to fill some of the dead time by going to Golders Green to replace a shirt I had bought earlier in the week and buy José Augusto his ill-fated present and he said that he also needed to do a little shopping before the arrival of his wife. So we went down there together and though we received plenty of attention it was less oppressive than in the hotel. We were offered discounts in some of the shops and, like a good Yorkshireman, Ray took advantage of one of them and bought a new pair of shoes to wear at the evening banquet.

Alf was as calm as I had ever seen him when we returned to the hotel in time for an early lunch and a brisk briefing. He said we all knew what we had to do, we had done the work and now we just had to execute it one last time.

The lunch menu, as always, was designed for comfortable digestion – a choice of poached eggs, chicken or beans on toast – but for once it was difficult to find an appetite. The morning excursion had heightened our awareness of an expectant nation and now only the first sound of the referee's whistle would lift some of the weight from our shoulders.

We left for Wembley at 1.15, past the saluting firemen and all the people in the street and those leaning out of their windows waving flags – a new phenomenon – and each mile brought a little edge to the tension.

The sensation of a normally reserved nation willing itself to believe in a great triumph grew so strong I said to Ray that London was surely creating the greatest din since VE Day. The bells of the fire engines rang. Factory hooters blared. It was, I would say many years later, as if all of London was moving in for the kill. But still mostly we spent time in our own thoughts. We had said to each other all that we had needed to say, we had after all had plenty of time, and the man who sat by my side – inevitably it was Ray Wilson – shared my understanding of this.

In between acknowledging the waves and the cheers rising up from the streets, I thought of the usual people, Duncan and the others lost in Munich, and Jimmy Murphy, Matt Busby and all those who had helped shape my career, and when I looked across to my brother Jack and exchanged determined nods, it brought to mind one of the visitors to our hotel after the victory over Portugal.

It was Fritz Walter, the captain of West Germany when they beat Hungary so sensationally in the 1954 World Cup final in Berne. He talked about what it meant to play in the final, the pressure and the challenge and, in the end, the liberation it brought when you finally got to play the game that would settle all the questions about a team and the individuals who formed it.

In one sense at least I would be walking in his footsteps and sharing some of the emotion he still remembered so vividly twelve years later. He had played against Hungary in the company of his brother Ottmar. Jack and I could only hope we enjoyed the same result.

We arrived at Wembley at 1.45. I saw Norma and my mother Cissie and father Robert. They all wished me well, my mother with her usual passion and confidence, my father more quietly but I could see how intensely he was hoping for our success and he said that he knew that both Jack and I would do our best, which in the end was all we could do. Norma squeezed my hand and kissed my cheek and said she was confident we could achieve all that was set before us.

Some of the lads went out to the pitch to taste the atmosphere and also test for the right length on their studs. Ray and I sat together in the dressing room. I read through mail and telegrams, moved by all the different postmarks which retraced my travels across the world and lingering a little longer on those from the North East where it had all begun, before joining Ray in our now automatic pre-match rituals.

Much to our surprise, though, it was not the usual dressing room. It was filled with television crews, reporters, well-wishers and, as someone noted, the man who made the tea but on this occasion was proffering only an autograph book to be signed. Geoff Hurst was especially aghast, saying, 'This just isn't the Ramsey way.' Bobby Moore was also irritated by the break in tradition but he did say, 'Perhaps Alf thought it would give us something to occupy our minds, help the minutes slip by.'

Everyone, though, was determined to prepare as we always had. George pounded away at his unique preparation. Banksy was, yet again, claiming his own space, inhabiting once more his world of confidence and constant vigilance and hair-trigger reflexes. Bobby Moore, despite his displeasure, was as cool as ever, sprinkling the passing time with his jaunty enquiry, 'All right, Bobby?' and his usual exhortation, 'No worries, mate.'

We all had our massages, Jack, as usual, insisting on going last. Bally had something to say to everyone. Geoff Hurst and Martin Peters seemed to be weighing how far they had come so quickly. Roger and Ray, as always, were quiet and composed. And Nobby was, of course, Nobby, ready for battle.

There was a final word from Alf as he mingled among us, patting our backs and saying that he was absolutely sure not one of us had been given a task beyond our ability. We simply had to remember all that we had achieved so far and how hard we had worked.

Alf shook hands with each of us as we walked out of the dressing room in the bright red shirts of our changed strip. Alf was clad in his official blue tracksuit and preferred black brogues. In the tunnel there was a brief delay to allow, we were told, the Queen and the Duke of Edinburgh to take their seats.

I found myself standing next to the German goalkeeper Hans Tilkowski and I looked into his eyes for any sign of nerves. It was not a rewarding exercise. It left me speculating on whether he was one of the most fearless opponents I had ever encountered – or one deserving of an Oscar nomination.

Then we were moving forward, locked again in the awareness that the decisive moment had come. If anyone had forgotten there was a deafening reminder from the 93,000 crowd. Some would say later that we had been handed a great advantage by playing all our games at Wembley, a charge which Fifa countered with claims that the guaranteed extra income from ticket sales was for the benefit of all the game. My own, maybe prejudiced, view was that there was no finer playing surface in the world and, at least in those gentler days, a less intimidating crowd and that any team of skill and character would have welcomed the chance to play there.

Certainly there was much pressure on us as the pre-match ceremonials slowly unwound. They took all of fifteen minutes from the time the Queen first set foot on the red carpet and each one of them brought another notch of tension.

I glanced at the man I was charged to stop, young Franz Beckenbauer, and he held my gaze. One of us was heading for the highest ground we might ever know. That, or an abyss. Both of us had been told that we had the power to shape that difference.

It was a call, no, a demand, that would carry us to the very edge of our limits.

17. The Leaves that Never Fade

I knew from the moment Alf gave me my battle orders it couldn't be as I might have imagined and if there was the slightest doubt about this it disappeared at the kick-off. This was when Franz Beckenbauer, like a young guardsman reporting for sentry duty, came to stand beside me.

Yet there is not one small eddy of regret as I walk once more among the trees and go back fifty years to play again the World Cup final. It is early spring now and there are the first green buds to replace those fallen brown leaves of autumn that were under my feet when I started this final accounting. But then I too am young again – or, at the age of twenty-eight, at least relatively so – as I return to 30 July 1966. It is to come back to the well that I know will never go dry.

Here is where in my mind's eye Alan Ball will never stop running, where Nobby is still indeed Nobby in all his battling will and Bobby Moore is immortal and never more demonstrably born to lead.

I see them all on our football day of days. I see the nerve of Gordon Banks holding despite the late assault on our belief that we had done all that we had been asked to do. I see George

Cohen, so indomitable when it mattered most, and Ray Wilson gathering himself brilliantly after a rare mistake which might so easily have broken the most accomplished and experienced of players.

I see Martin Peters, acute in his reading of the game and utterly sure of himself at a moment on which everything seemed to hinge and which my brother Jack would never forget for what it said about his ability to be perfectly still in his mind and so fast to execute and, yes of course, I see Jack, making his maybe unlikely but miraculously effective partnership with Moore.

I see the hat-trick hero Geoff Hurst and his relentless workmate Roger Hunt hammering at the German defence and I wonder all over again how it was that Alf was able to measure so finely the potential of all the men in whom he would place his final trust.

And what do I see of myself? I do not see so many of the spectacular flourishes which helped make my reputation but I do remember, with a touch of lingering pain, one missed chance to settle everything. However, I see mostly someone, inevitably and almost completely inseparably, in the company of the man Alf deemed the greatest threat to our chances. And yes, more than anything I feel pride and great relief and satisfaction that I was able to play my part, even if it was one I would not have selected for myself. It is, after all, the most essential requirement of any member of a side which has any serious ambition to become a team of champions.

Most fundamentally of all, and in the face of any of the questions that are still raised fervently in Germany about the legitimacy of our third and Geoff's second goal in extra-time, I have never questioned our right to carry that title. In this I am very happy to be buttressed by the opinion of the man who over the years has become one of my closest friends in the game.

Thirty years after the drama – and with the perspective that came with the huge personal success which included winning the World Cup as both a player and manager – Franz Beckenbauer declared, 'The World Cup final of 1966 remains in Germany one of the great talking points. Was it, or wasn't it, the third goal for England? People still argue. I think that's a shame because it reduces some of England's glory. To be truthful, England were the better team, over ninety minutes and then in extra-time. There's no argument. They deserved the trophy.

'That tournament enabled me to become well known, a star as they say, so I was grateful that we should have such a memorable final against the host nation. Before the game our coach Helmut Schoen had given me the job of marking Bobby Charlton, who was the best player in the world at the time. I never remember being so exhausted as I was at the finish that afternoon.'

Whatever the merit of his generous assessment of my ranking in the world at that time, I prize Beckenbauer's statement most for its concession that the better team won. And, I will always believe, it was a great game to win. It was not a classic example of flowing, beautiful football in the way of our semi-final victory over Portugal, and it may have lacked some of the grandeur of our collision with Brazil in Guadalajara four years later, but for me it was always filled with the lifeblood of the game. It had a fine competitive edge and it was, as Beckenbauer said, inhabited by so many players who were ready to go to the very edge of their ambition and physical endurance.

That intention, and the intensity of it, was established beyond any doubt within five minutes. In that time both Banks and Tilkowski had been seriously engaged – and required to make excellent saves, Banks flicking away a twenty-five-yard drive from the powerful Seeler and Tilkowski scrambling to stifle a header from Hurst which came in low and threateningly at the foot of the post.

The tempo was set and it would rarely fall below the thunderous. Given the nature of both sides, that was hardly a surprise. It was a statement of will which never flagged and it was announced in every corner of the field, most stunningly by Bally. Before the game he boasted to Nobby that he was going to put the celebrated full-back Karl-Heinz Schnellinger on the rack, one that would be tightened another notch with every passing minute.

It was a promise he fulfilled right up to the last and conclusive passage of play and, as I look back, I cannot recall a single moment when it was necessary to question his commitment. It was indeed almost as though he became both our legs and our conscience. He did to Schnellinger, a lauded figure with AC Milan who in Italy enjoyed the special aura that to this day still surrounds the master defenders, precisely what he said he would and this was a huge factor in our early momentum. The Germans had produced moments of danger but without the biting, creative edge that Beckenbauer might have provided, without the responsibilities he shared with me.

It meant that when the Germans went ahead after thirteen minutes to leave us trailing for the first time in the tournament – and bringing additional alarm to those who knew that a World Cup winning team had never been behind in the final – it had the effect of a surprise slap in the face. More shocking, still, was that it was Ray Wilson, of all people, who made the critical mistake.

The details are still etched clearly in the memory and many years later Ray and Gordon Banks were still recalling them, as survivors of what might have been a disaster to haunt all their football lives.

It was a routine build-up by Germany with Helmet Haller, Seeler and Schnellinger moving the ball out to Sigi Held on the left. There it seemed that the danger had evaporated when Held sent over a poorly directed cross which, conservatively speaking, Ray would ninety-nine times out of a hundred treat as the smallest disturbance of an afternoon nap. For a little while, though, the consequences threatened full-scale nightmare.

Banks remembered the breakdown with the precision of a man for whom the measuring of danger, of time and space, had become fundamental to all his success – and our defensive security. He said, 'It was going beyond Ray and I shouted, "Leave it." But Ray wasn't too sure about Haller and decided he'd better not take a chance in case he tried to come round the back of him, so he headed it but the ball dropped straight at Haller's feet. He only half hit the shot but Jack had come in to cover and was standing about three feet away. The ball was travelling between us and Jack went as though he was going to try to stop it. I couldn't move until it came past him in case of a deflection, and by the time I went down it was on top of me and I was too late and it skidded into the corner of the net. Jack and I looked at each other as much as to say, come on, let's get back into it.'

I've always believed Ray defined himself as a great professional in his reaction to that potentially catastrophic misjudgement. He played on with such easy composure and anticipation that five minutes after the incident you might not have guessed it had happened. Despite all that followed, however, the wound would never fully heal. Twenty years later he was recalling it with the same raw horror that came in the moment of breakdown.

He said, 'It was an awful mistake, no doubt about that, it was a Third Division ball. I had a lot of time and I doubted if Haller would come in to challenge me for it but I had an awful feeling that Seller might be lurking somewhere behind me. With the indecision, I was rocking on my heels and I finished up with this marshmallow header.

'It just dropped down for the lad and bingo . . . he just had to knock it in. It was the only time I was grateful to be thirty-one. If I had been younger it could have destroyed my game. I looked at Jack. It wasn't just unlike me, it was unlike anyone in the defence over the last few years. Afterwards Alf said to me, "That's the first mistake you've made for me in four years." I sit back sometimes and think about it, the sort of mistakes like that which cost matches.'

That it didn't prove so decisive in our case was due to several factors – and each of them recreates an old but still-powerful surge of pride. Pride in my immediate sense that I was surrounded by team-mates who were able to treat Ray's mishap as less a disaster and more an impertinence. That radiated from every England player and I still remember clearly my own thoughts as we lined up for the restart. This was a passing inconvenience, I told myself.

We had come too far, and we were too good, to be denied now. Hurst and Hunt were too persistent, Bally and Peters were too sharp and combative and inventive in midfield, and for myself it was easy to see the point, even at this early stage, of Alf's strategy regarding Beckenbauer. Most pervasive of all was the sublime leadership of Bobby Moore. His response to the setback was hardly frenzied. That was never part of his make-up and one cheaply conceded goal wasn't going to change that for a second. However, he had never been more commanding, or more urgent, and it was through him that we were level again in six minutes.

Moore both shaped and willed the equaliser. The job of containing the greatest German threat still had to be paramount in my mind and nor was this any time for our captain to be distracted from his defensive vigilance but when I flicked the ball away from Beckenbauer and into Moore's path the consequences could not have been more galvanising.

His vision, and instinctive understanding with his West Ham team-mate Hurst, had never been more refined. When he was brought down by Overath I ran to his left to give him the option of a short free-kick but he had seen a weakness in the German cover. It was square and after dummying to pass to me he put perfect flight and weight on his ball into an unprotected place in the German penalty area. As the ball arched in, Hurst filled the space and his header went into the left-hand corner of Tilkowski's net. Once again it was our game to win, our World Cup to collect.

The Germans had a tough defence, personified by the uncompromising Willie Schulz at the back and stiffened by the tackling of Wolfgang Weber and Horst Hottges, and just before half-time they reminded us of their threat when Seeler produced a sudden, explosive shot which stretched Banks to his limits in making another fine save.

At the break, Alf spent some time urging Hunt to stay forward at every opportunity to put pressure on Schulz, saying that it was more important than his coming back in pursuit of the ball, but overall he was happy. Beckenbauer was as quiet as he was ever likely to be, the Germans had already felt the menace of Hurst and, Alf believed, the more the game wore on, the more they would be stretched by the mobility and desire of Ball and the subtle running of Peters.

Alf displayed his usual calm. He moved among us, spreading his belief that we had already established that we were the stronger, better side. England's hopes, he had seen, were in good hands.

The decisive moment would surely come. It did, at least out on the field we assumed it had and there seemed to be a similar conclusion on the terraces, filled with great passion and, at moments of pause, the beat of a single drummer, with just twelve minutes to go. As the rain showers ceased and the clouds dispersed, and we felt the sun on our faces, it was Bally who had again recharged our attacking tempo.

Schnellinger was a beaten man now as his tormentor won a corner and raced to take it with the urgency he had displayed right from the kick-off. His corner was headed out, but only to Hurst to the left of the goal. He went one way, then another, before his shot struck Hottges and looped into the air. Advancing on the ball were two Englishmen, Peters and Jack. Peters, to everyone's relief, and not least Jack's, won the race and placed his shot unerringly into the empty space on the goal-line left by Tilkowski and the worn-down Schnellinger.

After the game Jack was asked if he felt as though he had been denied a moment of glory. His expression said that the question might as well have come from outer space. 'No, I didn't feel cheated,' he said. 'I'm glad the bugger didn't come to me because I would have hit it over the bar.'

At the same time Peters was reluctant to paint himself as a

master of the most precise finishing but his account of the goal still gives an insight into the workings of a fine football brain. He said, 'Geoff probably shouldn't have shot because the angle was too tight. Hottges stuck out a leg and the ball went up in front of me and I only thought of keeping it down, I didn't really try to place it and the goalkeeper went one way and Schnellinger the other – and the ball went straight down the middle.'

I had never seen a more beautiful sight on a football field and my own reaction was the purest exhilaration. I raced into the arms of Nobby, shouting, 'Nobby, we've won, we've won, they can't beat us now.' That euphoric conclusion might well have been confirmed by me with just four minutes to go and when I say that I have no regrets about the events of that historic day I speak in a general way. There is always somewhere in the corner of your mind where you dwell on the fact that you might have done something better and certainly that was the case when I lost Beckenbauer for a moment and found myself with Hunt outnumbering a suddenly stranded Schulz in front of the German goal. Again it was a result of Bally's incessant desire but when Roger passed to me it came a little too square and I hit it too early.

It was the chance of a matador's sword stroke but there was no great cry of olé, just a huge sigh, and three minutes later, with just one minute left on the clock, it was not German blood on the sand.

Jack will always believe that the late convulsion was a result of an error by the Swiss referee Gottfried Dienst. The referee decided that Jack had fouled Held when he went up to head clear a ball lofted into the right-hand edge of the penalty area. Jack contended, and it was a view supported by a panel of international referees four years later, that the free-kick should have gone the other way, Held making no attempt to get to the ball but simply presented his back to the man in the air.

For Banks and Nobby the imperative was not outrage but a frantic attempt to defend against the free-kick which, everyone on the field sensed, was Germany's last chance to extend the battle into extra-time. Banks recalled his sickening fear that everything was about to unravel. He said, 'Well, I had to set up the wall. The kick was from just outside the penalty area. We set it up, Nobby dragging five players in and there was probably only one of our men on the half-way line.

'Germany knew it was their last chance to get back and they shoved everyone in the area. Emmerich had a crack, the ball hit the wall and ricocheted out to the left and Schnellinger, pushing forward like everyone else, ran in for the sake of running in, and we thought the ball hit him on the arm. Had it not hit him, it was right out for a throw-in, it wasn't even good for a goal-kick, Emmerich mishit it that badly.

'Schnellinger's arm took the pace out of it and it just went slowly across as Weber closed in. The ball was on the floor and I thought he might keep it down there until I saw Ray Wilson with his leg stretched out, so I dived that little bit higher over Ray's leg in case the ball came off it but Weber was stretching and he lifted it, and it went over my arm.'

It was for me the confirmation of the dread that had come with the missed opportunity. I thought of the wonderful release, the great rush of finality, a successful strike would have brought and the yearning for that was only increased by the last, desperate force of the Germans. Held and Seeler were now the chief threats, along with their most creative midfield allies Beckenbauer and Overath. With Bally and Peters I did all I could to help the defence while maintaining my Beckenbauer vigil.

And then it was breakdown, a spectator's role for me in the wall formed by Nobby, the referee blowing full-time just after I restarted the game in the centre circle and Seeler walking up to me and saying, 'Bobby, that's football.'

Forty years later I reflected on that moment and a decade on there is not a word I would change. Certainly it returns me to some of my deepest feelings about the game and, though it may not be written on a tablet of stone, I believe it has weathered in the years well enough. I recalled, 'I could only nod my agreement with Uwe Seeler. It was indeed football. It was dreams made and snatched away. It was a referee's decision going the wrong way. It was that fine line which had been so vivid when I ran out of the tunnel a little more than ninety minutes earlier.

'So what do you do? You play on, of course, you fight for what you still believe belongs to you and if anyone had forgotten, Alf was moving among us now with the reminder. He asked Bobby Moore, who was lying down on the pitch, to get back on his feet because it was imperative that the Germans did not get the idea that we were exhausted. At the final whistle Jack had also gone down. I will never forget the sight of my brother sitting there, after having spent so much of himself, with his head in his hands.

'Alf made a short but extremely effective speech, one which two years later would be echoed by Sir Matt Busby on this same pitch after a second goal by Benfica had forced Manchester United into extra-time in the European Cup final. Alf said that we had won the game once but it had been taken away from us. Now we had to go out and win it again. We had to make sense of all the work and all the sacrifice. We had to do something that would make us proud for the rest of our lives.

'Bobby Moore was not a man easily impressed by words intended to be inspirational but he would always insist that this was among Alf's finest moments. He touched all the players. He reminded us of all that had been achieved, how far we had come and, most of all, how it would be absolutely intolerable if the prize was allowed to slip away.'

It was indeed the perfect speech, and demeanour, from Alf. It embodied all the good things that I had come to value in him so much, and beside which any of those oddities of speech or manner that his critics were so eager to mock – and sometimes made his players chuckle – disappeared like wisps of morning mist. There it was in the now bright afternoon sunshine, the meaning of Alf and all he had come to represent – professionalism, nerve, team unity – carrying our tired limbs and bruised spirits into the last thirty minutes of a three-year campaign.

Everyone who follows English football and has glanced back at the barest outline of its history will know the details of what followed. Now as I recall it all once more the most abiding conclusion on why it happened as it did was that Alf had concentrated our minds – and hearts – on the most important truth. It was the one Franz Beckenbauer so generously conceded so many years later. We were indeed stronger than the Germans and it was as if Bally was determined to re-establish this reality at the first opportunity. In a minute he had forced Tilkowski into a fine save after still another run down the right so determined that he might have been appearing on the field for the first time that afternoon.

He left a marker which said that we could not and would not be beaten. I quickly attempted a postscript when I put in a shot which the German goalkeeper could only turn against the post.

When the breakthrough came, 100 minutes into the battle, it would, of course, launch a controversy that is still not settled in some German hearts but then our greatest blessing would come in the last kick of the match when Geoff Hurst scored again. Both goals, including the first one which, down the years and after close inspection of film evidence, I have come to accept was maybe not legitimate, undoubtedly shared the same glorious trademark. It captured the essence of Alf's last rallying cry. The goals were about superb individual contributions to a bone-deep team ethos.

The first one may have become something of a pantomime of confusion but that was in the attempted measuring of millimetres around the goal-line. But then about the execution there had been a roaring conviction – and the participation of three players on whom Alf had done nothing less than stake his reputation.

In the case of Nobby he had risked everything, his job and all our hopes, and it was my great friend who sent the ball down the right to the scampering feet of his room-mate Bally. Schnellinger now had glazed eyes as he contemplated the final stages of his ordeal and he could do nothing to prevent Ball sending a pass to Hurst. So there it was, a devastating, ultimately game-breaking strike fashioned by Stiles, who the FA and Fifa wanted to eject from the tournament, Ball, who had done so much to persuade Alf that he should abandon one of football's greatest and most crowd-pleasing traditions, the winger, and Hurst, who had claimed the place of the much loved national hero, Jimmy Greaves.

Hurst, who had already justified Alf's decision with that superbly timed equaliser, swivelled and smashed the ball against the underside of the bar and as it came down the nearest English player, Hunt, threw up his arms in celebration. I too was convinced it was over the line and whether or not I willed it to be so was a question that only gathered strength down the years.

In the end, though, I have to admit I was obliged to share the opinion of Franz Beckenbauer both on the sweep of the game and the legality of a goal which, satisfactorily from my perspective, did not in fact prove to be the difference between the teams.

When it happened I was as ecstatic as when Peters had given us the lead so close to the end of regular time. I embraced anyone near me who I believed was wearing the shirt of the new world champions. Then, in the corner of my eye, I saw the referee running over to the mustachioed linesman from Azerbaijan, Tofik Bakhramov. There is a fine statue to Tofik, the man who brushed against football history, in his home town of Baku, and I have to say I was turned to stone before the referee pointed to the centre circle and confirmed my best hopes. No one knew how the officials settled on their verdict without a word of each other's language but that was something that could await historic analysis.

When it came it was not so easy to dispute the German argument. The evidence of Beckenbauer is certainly impressive, and especially in the light of his generous verdict that we had deserved to carry the day. He said, 'We had been lucky with our second goal to draw level moments from the end of normal time, first with the free-kick given against Jack Charlton and then the deflection and a scrambled goal-mouth shot. At the time of England's third goal I was in the penalty area with quite a good view. I was convinced the ball touched the goalline – but was not completely over – when Geoff Hurst's shot bounced down from the crossbar and therefore it was not a goal. What language did the Swiss referee and the Azerbaijani linesman use when they discussed the incident? Who said what? We'll never know.'

One of the ironies was that it was Bally who ushered the referee towards the linesman – and later he said, 'I was in a better position than him [the linesman] and I couldn't really tell myself. It had been a good move leading up to it. Nobby knocked the ball inside the full-back and I've got almost to the by-line and clipped it back and Hurst had made a near-post run. Because I was worried about being offside I made to step off the pitch but as Geoff shot, I came back, and as it hit the bar I was right in line with the linesman ten or fifteen yards behind me. As Weber headed over the bar I've turned and said, "Goal?" and there was a lot of shemozzle and the referee and linesman hardly said a word to each other because they couldn't understand each other and the linesman just pointed to the circle and off he went, but in all honesty, hand on heart, I couldn't say whether it was or not.'

When I was last asked to go on the record with my own verdict I found myself very close to Bally's position. I said, 'The film probably shows more that the ball wasn't over the line. My inclination at the time was that it was a goal, because I'd moved forward in case Geoff turned it square to the left, so I felt I was in a reasonable position to see.'

I was probably influenced strongly by the reaction of Roger who was closest in and immediately threw up his arms to claim the goal. But then later Roger also implied that there had to be doubts, saying, 'Normally in that situation I would have gone in and, looking back, I still don't know why I didn't. I don't think, in fact, I'd have got the ball. It bounced down and high up to my left and Weber headed it away. I have thought many times since, "Why didn't I go in?" The linesman definitely couldn't have seen. When I looked across moments later he was still moving back towards the corner flag, he was still so far away and hadn't got his flag up.'

Such doubts might well have festered somewhat down the years if Geoff Hurst hadn't scored the goal that brought us home even as some fans began to encroach on the field in anticipation of the final whistle. But in that triumphant moment – when Kenneth Wolstenholme famously shouted into his microphone, 'They think it's all over. It is now . . .' – history could not have been shaped more appropriately. Not only was it the climactic moment of the long campaign, it was another perfect expression of so much which had made it a success.

As Bobby Moore ignored the urgent advice of Jack to send the ball flying somewhere close to the North Circular Road, and Bally made still another searing run along the right, our captain produced the last perfect brush stroke to what would be an undying image of his leadership. He picked out Geoff again with a ball that could not have been more finely tailored in Savile Row. And Geoff made one last run, his final claim on a place in football history. His shot flew into the top corner of the net and then you knew, everyone knew, it was over.

There was nothing left for me to do after a last run in the company of Franz Beckenbauer except to seek out my brother so that we could share our wonder at being together on such a day and with such a result. Along with the others we tried to persuade Alf to enjoy, at last, a little of the limelight but he pushed us away, saying, 'This now is for you players, you won it' and when he said that I felt the first unashamed tears welling in my eyes.

As I said at the time, I never believed in crying in defeat but victory, well, that was an entirely different matter. It spoke of all the emotions that you had carried to the moment for which you had worked so hard. It was a mixture of relief and an intensely personal benediction, a prayer of thanks for the blessings I had received.

Certainly I knew, as I wiped my eyes before going up the steps to receive my medal from the Queen, a part of me would now always reside in the football heavens.

Epilogue

So there it was and how it will still so powerfully linger as I join my comrades for our golden anniversary reunion. The landmark will no doubt create a special fervour when we raise our glasses to the departed who did so much to make the glory that we will always keep so close to us.

The cares of the day, so far removed from the sunlit release that came to us so overwhelmingly in the late afternoon of Wembley, and then in the joyful streets of the West End of London, will again be put to one side.

Old debts will be acknowledged and tributes paid and inevitably so many of them will go once more to the men to whom we had to say farewell: Alf, who so unflinchingly reached all the hard decisions that made it happen; Bobby, who steadied us so profoundly with the aura of his greatness; and young Bally, who never stopped believing in himself and the men he came amid to prove so quickly that he was not some mere noisy apprentice but the most natural-born competitor any of us had ever seen.

We will do, those of us who have survived and are fit enough to attend, what we have been doing for half a century now. We will rekindle those happiest hours of our football lives which unfolded when we drove away from Wembley in possession of the World Cup.

Of course we will pick out the personal memories that endure most strongly. George Cohen will laugh and wince again when he recalls the kiss Nobby, minus his dentures, planted on his lips. For me, perhaps inevitably, it is of the easy weight of Jack's arm on my shoulder as we jogged around the pitch. Few brothers, however more consistently devoted they had been, had surely ever felt quite so close at a certain imperishable moment in their lives.

'You know, Jack,' I remember saying, 'I don't suppose our lives will ever be the same again.'

Most wonderful for me was to see Norma again and feel her pride in what had been achieved, and that of my mother and father, and this was after travelling through the streets of a city which was plainly preparing for a night of spectacular celebration. None of it would be more vigorous than that of Jack, whose wife Pat was pregnant and close to labour and had stayed home in the North East. In her absence, Jack went on the town with his close journalist pal Jimmy Mossop of the *Sunday Express*, who later reported they had woken up, chilled and a little mystified, in a back garden deep in the suburbs.

It was, as Jack's hangover confirmed, a night of rare and pleasurable tumult – a night when nobody around us seemed to want it to end.

It was on the balcony of the Royal Garden Hotel in Kensington, to where we had been moved from Hendon Hall with our wives, that I first saw that Alf was at last relaxing in the knowledge that he had achieved all that he had desired. As we showed the great trophy to the crowd, and the cheers swept up from the street, his face was covered in a wide and most uncomplicated smile. The stern face of the commander was replaced by that a young boy standing beneath a Christmas tree.

The mood of the night was as perfect as it could possibly have been in those days which in one extraordinary detail will doubtless seem quite bizarre to the generation of today. This was the fact that our wives, from whom we had been separated for so long, were not invited to the official reception and dinner. They were entertained in a room away from the great banqueting hall, a place entitled the Bulldog Bar. When all the FA committee men and Fifa officials, some of whom had been so keen to banish Nobby, had been catered for, there was simply no room for the most important people in the lives of the men who had achieved the victory.

As it happened, my mother – perhaps on the strength of the fact that she had provided not one but two members of the winning team – made it into the great banquet. I was pleased for her, naturally, but it didn't lessen the irritation I shared with my team-mates that our wives had not been recognised. George Cohen was so indignant he threatened to boycott the official celebrations and go into the London night with his family and friends.

Alf, predictably, argued against such a rebellion. He had shaped the triumph on his own terms and it was one which all those of us involved would have for ever. He could have pointed out that there was no place on the high table for his own wife Vicky but instead he said we should honour those who had given us so much support in our own ways – and for the rest of our lives.

Later he wrote letters to each of us saying how proud he was of our achievement and what we had done for our country. Deep down, I think he feared that there might be any kind of blemish on the greatest day – and night – of our careers.

Of course it was outrageous that our wives were snubbed but then, I suppose, we have to remember they were different days with different values and it was not as though we did not have time to rescue a night that not one of us was likely to forget – and for much more uplifting reasons. This was because at almost every moment of an often chaotic night – Norma was alarmed especially when the overloaded lift in the Royal Garden jammed and seemed to take an age before spilling us back into the noisy crowd – somebody had something to say about an aspect of the game, an emotion that had carried us to the stars or, briefly, cast us back to earth.

None of us could quite believe that London, of all places, could so quickly and so completely shed its inhibitions. From the moment Nobby had performed his joyful jig out on the field, it was though a great and long-established national restraint just melted away.

And no one was more touched than Alf. When we arrived at Hendon Hall, where we changed for our night of celebration, he produced a jeroboam of champagne a well-wisher had thrust into his hands as he left Wembley. Alf recalled, 'It was really terrific. We had a lot of laughter and fun before we piled into the coach.' And then as thousands flooded into Trafalgar Square and around our hotel in Kensington, Alf became the most enchanted observer of the homage being paid to his team and, he didn't need to say it, his work.

He gave a most vivid report on our halting progress into the West End, saying, 'Everywhere there were people lining the pavements and waving and shouting. There were more and more and more as we neared the centre of London. One man stood in the middle of the road with his arms in the air and then ran towards us until we had to stop. Then he climbed up, put his head through a window and all he could say was, "I love you all, I love you all."

'It was fifteen minutes before we could move on. He was quite a chap. Further along our way was barred by a car parked slap across the road like a barricade and a young girl in a bright red mini-skirt danced on top of it. And there was a public house with about forty customers outside, every one of them holding up a pint of beer in a toast. I felt the excitement then and there is nothing quite like it.'

Running through all the night and into the early hours of Sunday morning was this purest of elation. It shaped utterly our mood as we made our different ways from the Royal Garden, where the prime minister Harold Wilson had appeared to join in the euphoria – and perhaps make a little political capital.

One large party including Nobby, Bally and Geoff Hurst and their wives headed for Danny La Rue's nightclub.

Bobby Moore had been invited to the Playboy Club in Park Lane and Norma and I, the Easthams and the Wilsons joined him. The Playboy Club was maybe not my natural habitat but I enjoyed it well enough even while following my habit, formed after excessive celebrations as one of Manchester United's youngest first-teamers, of merely sipping an exotic World Cup cocktail. I suppose I didn't want to blur the edges of my contentment.

That certainly held as Norma and I returned to our hotel room at the first streak of dawn and I tried to explain the depth of my happiness but she said, 'Bobby, I know. You will always remember these hours – and rightly so.'

In that, as in so many other aspects of our life together, she was right. Over fifty years the glitter has never faded. Whatever has happened to me, good or bad, it has been maybe my safest harbour and I know that it is also true of all my team-mates, including those less fortunate ones like George Cohen and Gordon Banks, who have had to fight serious illness, and Nobby and Ray who have had to deal with the fading of the brightest light of memory.

My greatest wish now is the one that has accompanied the years since we learned all of how it felt to be champions of the world. It is that another generation of English footballers get to know the same feeling. If it should happen, certainly no one will be able to say that the important lesson of how it might do so had not been waiting, decade upon decade, for some serious perusal.

It has all been there, from the moment Bobby Moore walked up to receive the trophy from the Queen. It has lain in the vision and the strength of Alf Ramsey, who was so shabbily treated by the men for whom he so brilliantly accomplished the greatest task they set him.

Today, when the administration of world football has to remake itself from under the shadow of corruption, when the deepest values of the most popular game are under siege, he remains the great hero of the story I have been proud to tell.

He is still the diamond shining in the leaves.

Acknowledgements

Of all the privileges of a football career that I will always see more than anything as a huge and sometimes unfathomable gift, none was greater than being part of the team of '66. My strongest wish is that this gratitude is expressed fully in these pages.

I cannot separate one from another any of my dear team-mates. Each one of them was a champion I was proud to play alongside.

Away from the field I have always been wonderfully supported and sustained by the love of my wife Norma, my daughters Suzanne and Andrea and my grandsons Robert and William and granddaughter Emma.

In the producing of this book I join my friend and collaborator James Lawton in appreciation of the skill and encouragement of editors Frances Jessop and Matt Phillips.

James Lawton would also like to thank his agent David Luxton for his unflagging help and advice and, as always, the long-tested patience of his wife Linda.

List of Illustrations

team play golf during a break from training (Central Press/ Getty Images)

8. Team visit to Pinewood Studios (Rex); The England team playing cards (Mirrorpix)

9. Sir Alf Ramsey speaking to the press (Mirrorpix); The England team at Roehampton on the eve of the World Cup final (Mirrorpix); The England team travel to Wembley Stadium (Mirrorpix)

10. England fans, England v West Germany (Art Rickerby/ Getty Images); England and West Germany line up before the final (TopFoto); Bobby Charlton with the ball (Fox Photos/Getty Images)

11. Martin Peters scores (Press Association); Martin Peters, Geoff Hurst, Roger Hunt celebrating (Gerry Cranham/ Offside)

12. Bobby Charlton and Franz Beckenbauer (Popperfoto/ Getty Images); Bobby Charlton after a missed opportunity (Gerry Cranham/Offside); Wolfgang Weber's equaliser (Press Association)

13. Alf Ramsey and his management team with players during break before extra time (Mirrorpix); Geoff Hurst's controversial third goal (Gerry Cranham/Offside); England celebrates Geoff Hurst's third goal (Art Rickerby/Getty Images)

14. Parading the trophy (TopFoto); Queen Elizabeth II presents the World Cup to Bobby Moore (Mirrorpix); The final score (Mirrorpix)

15. Bobby Moore kisses the World Cup trophy (Popperfoto/ Getty Images); The victorious England team (Popperfoto/ Getty Images); Wives of the England squad during a celebration banquet (Mirrorpix)

16. Bobby and Jack Charlton set off on a triumphal tour of Ashington (TopFoto)

Index

Note: 'BC' denotes Bobby Charlton. All references are to BC's England career unless otherwise stated. References to countries, cities and towns are to teams unless otherwise indicated.